IT USED TO BE WITCHES

RYAN GILBEY

IT USED TO BE TO BE WITCHES

UNDER THE SPELL OF QUEER CINEMA

faber

First published in 2025
by Faber & Faber Limited
The Bindery, 51 Hatton Garden
London EC1N 8HN

Typeset by Faber & Faber
Printed and bound by CPI Group (UK) Ltd, Croydon, CR0 4YY

A CIP record for this book
is available from the British Library

ISBN 978–0–571–38152–4

MIX
Paper | Supporting
responsible forestry
FSC® C013604

Printed and bound in the UK on FSC® certified paper in line with our continuing
commitment to ethical business practices, sustainability and the environment.
For further information see faber.co.uk/environmental-policy

Our authorised representative in the EU for product safety is
Easy Access System Europe, Mustamäe tee 50, 10621 Tallinn, Estonia
gpsr.requests@easproject.com

2 4 6 8 10 9 7 5 3 1

For my husband and my children

AUNT IDA: Queers are just better. I'd be so proud if you was a fag, and had a nice beautician boyfriend . . . I worry that you'll work in an office, have children, celebrate wedding anniversaries. The world of the heterosexual is a sick and boring life.

John Waters, *Female Trouble*, 1974

1

DEATH IN VENICE

Each winter, he travels to Venice to deliver a handful of lectures about cinema to gap-year students on an art history course. In the past, he has sometimes come here on the sleeper from Paris, chugging through the Alps in the snow-blue darkness, feeling like a spy or a fugitive when the train is halted for a middle-of-the-night passport check, then dozing off again until the carriage is flooded with sunlight between Milan and Verona. These days, he tends to arrive late in the evening on a budget airline before taking a bus and then a *vaporetto* into the clenched, canal-veined heart of the city. The hotel staff insist on calling him *professore*, which used to make him laugh and blush – it always sounds so grand! – whereas now it simply ages him. With every passing year, he feels increasingly like the Gustave von Aschenbach of easyJet.

As a creature of habit, it should bring him contentment to be here in Venice again. The landing tonight was so gentle that the wheels seemed almost to be kissing the tarmac. The engines exhaled in relief as the plane inched closer to the terminal building, and his fellow passengers began rattling their seat belts as if in some ancient celebratory rite. From the pill-shaped window, he gazed out at the void beyond the runway, the dabs of distant colour hinting at unknowable roads and buildings. It was like a dot-to-dot puzzle awaiting the pencil lines that would finally make sense of it all.

But a vague concern which entered his mind earlier tonight sharpens now as he treads gingerly down the steps from the aircraft and shuffles towards passport control, a shabby sports holdall slung over one shoulder. It started an hour ago, when the plane hit a pocket of turbulence. He did what he always does in that situation: he made a list to distract himself. In this case, he scrolled mentally through all the film clips that he intends to use in his lectures this week. Some he has been showing since he first came here fifteen years ago, such as the police station identification scene from Pier Paolo Pasolini's 1961 debut *Accattone*: the director pans silently across angular, pock-marked male faces in close-up, the camera moving at the unhurried pace of a tourist at Sant'Ignazio. Or the moment from Rainer Werner Fassbinder's 1971 western *Whity* where Günther Kaufmann freezes in the act of proffering a wad of notes to a sex worker played by Hanna Schygulla, while the camera prowls from one side of the bed to the other. It must have inspired the waxwork-style sex scenes in Gus Van Sant's *My Own Private Idaho*, but it also pre-empts those show-downs in *The Matrix*, directed by the Wachowski sisters, which leave a combatant suspended in mid-air while the audience is treated to a 180-degree view of the action.

To illustrate the friction that can occur between sound and image, he will show the students a scene from *Nénette et Boni*, made in 1996, in which what is heard – the voice of a priapic young pizza seller fanta-sising about what he plans to do to a female baker with his 'big French stick' – is subverted by what is seen. While we listen to this snarl-ing sexual reverie, the camera surveys the pizza seller's bare torso, the sculptural slopes of his shoulders, the unstable tiger-stripes of shadow and light rippling on his mahogany skin and finally his sleep-smeared face as he is woken by the burbling of his bedside coffee maker. The poor dope thinks he's in charge of his own erotic fantasy. He doesn't realise he is being watched: by the director Claire Denis, the cine-matographer Agnès Godard and the innumerable eyes of the unseen audience. The desirer has become the desired.

There will be snippets, too, from Shirley Clarke's 1967 *Portrait of Jason*, in which the camera never averts its gaze from the raconteur, entertainer and hustler Jason Holliday, and Cheryl Dunye's *The Watermelon Woman*, from 1996, the first full-length movie by an out Black lesbian director to receive distribution. One lecture will feature Ron Peck's 1978 *Nighthawks*, generally considered the first British narrative feature about contemporary gay life. But that would be to overlook *A Bigger Splash*, Jack Hazan's 1973 study of the artist David Hockney and his coterie. Hazan's slippery quasi-documentary, inspired by what he called Andy Warhol's 'two-people-sitting-on-a-sofa' films, is as staged as anything scripted. Hazan even added a scene to the movie after realising that viewers of an early cut had no idea that the people on-screen were gay: they thought they were merely tactile and affectionate. A splash of sex cleared up the confusion.

The week's lectures will kick off, though, with François Ozon's *A Summer Dress*, the ideal gateway drug for students unfamiliar with world cinema. That 1996 short, which begins with an extreme close-up of the bulge in a teenage boy's black Speedos, contains a pair of sex scenes which gratifyingly reverse the audience's expectations. The straight fuck occurs between strangers in the wild, the supposedly taboo gay one in the tame domestic setting of a kitchen. On top of a washing machine, no less.

Only now does he begin to see what he's done. For the first time since he started teaching in Venice, the queer clips in his selection outnumber everything else. Even the straight ones aren't entirely straight. *All About Eve* features Bette Davis as an acting legend refusing to be put out to pasture when a young fan encroaches on her terrain; for all its gay overtones, the film could still technically be described on the witness stand as a heterosexual story if the need arose. *Raging Bull* has flashes of homoeroticism, not least when the boxer Jake La Motta (Robert De Niro) listens to an adoring account of his upcoming opponent and laments that he now doesn't know whether to fight him or fuck him, but the film isn't *gay*-gay. At least the array of work he will be showing by Jafar Panahi and Samira Makhmalbaf will put him in the clear, sexuality-wise. Thank goodness for Iran, he thinks. Not a thought that many queer people have had cause to entertain.

That won't count for much once he screens for his students Joseph Losey's 1963 film *The Servant*. Its star, the infinitely insinuating Dirk Bogarde, had surrendered his former status as a matinee idol a few years earlier in favour of pursuing more ambiguous roles. Though these sometimes came in varying if discreet shades of pink, they were hardly bolts from the blue. Bogarde's pained work in earlier films such as *The Spanish Gardener*, where he is a young handyman conducting a forbidden friendship with his employer's son, and *The Blue Lamp*, in which he brings real relish, as well as a transgressive crackle, to his scenes as a cop killer, had already hinted that, as Matthew Sweet put it, 'there was something dreadful burning under his skin'. The new phase simply represented a more pronounced coming-out – even if Bogarde himself never went that far.

In 1961, he was impressively grave as Melville Farr, a closeted barrister targeted by blackmailers, in *Victim*, the first British film to deal explicitly with gay themes. The picture looks polite today, but there is no dulling the force of the graffiti that Farr's wife sees daubed across the front of their garage: 'FARR IS QUEER'. (Other actors, said Bogarde, had 'backed away like rearing horses in terror at the subject'.) With the Wolfenden report into public attitudes towards homosexuality having heralded a move towards greater tolerance four years earlier, *Victim* did its bit to nudge open a door that was already ajar. Six years after its release, sex between consenting men aged twenty-one or over was partially decriminalised in England and Wales under the Sexual Offences Act 1967. 'That *Victim* helped, even in a small way, to ease [the act's] turbulent trajectory is beyond any doubt,' wrote John Coldstream.

The picture's embrace was far from universal. *Time* magazine found its 'implicit approval of homosexuality as a practice' to be 'offensive'; the US censors refused it a certificate for being 'thematically objectionable'. Terence Davies, who expressed in films such as *The Long Day Closes* and *Benediction* his own thwarted sexuality in exaltedly lyrical terms, saw *Victim* when it was first released in the UK, and recalled the shock of hearing the word 'homosexual' spoken aloud. 'You could have heard a feather drop in the cinema – the atmosphere was electric. That word was never used in England. Never!' He singled out 'the exquisiteness of Bogarde's performance. Not only in the way he delivers the lines but also his gestures. Partly because [Bogarde] was gay himself, although he couldn't say so, he could play with all those little nuances of guilt and terror that a straight actor wouldn't know about.'

Still a decade away was Luchino Visconti's 1971 adaptation of *Death in Venice*, in which Bogarde glowed radioactively in his bone-white suit as Aschenbach, an ailing composer who is briefly revived on a Venetian sojourn by the sight of an angelic teenage boy named Tadzio. Losey had long hoped to make the film, though the actor griped to him that 'you never asked <u>me</u> to do it . . . or offered me the chance, or remotely thought that I even could!' No matter: he and Losey already had one queer masterpiece to their name, and it had given Bogarde the most enigmatic role of his life. In *The Servant*, he is Barrett, the 'gentleman's gentleman' who infiltrates and contaminates the life of Tony (James Fox), a clueless young toff so pale he could be his own photographic negative.

Barrett's arrival in Tony's puzzle-like home, with its concealed doors, warping mirrors and steep, incarcerating shadows, is casual – this is no home invasion – but it heralds a slow-motion collapse of convention. The two men drift into see-sawing power games, mutual humiliations and even a mock-marital pantomime in which they squabble over cleaning duties and the household budget. Bogarde's lifelong partner and manager Tony Forwood was uneasy about the actor doing 'two in a row' after *Victim*, worrying that audiences might find him a shade too convincing in these roles: no smoke without a flaming queen. Bogarde kept mum on such matters, likening himself to a hermit crab. 'I'm certainly in the shell,' he told Russell Harty in a 1986 television interview. 'And you haven't cracked it yet, honey.' Perhaps it was Forwood who pressed Bogarde to ask Losey and the screenwriter, Harold Pinter, whether *The Servant* was a gay project. Either way, he didn't receive an answer, though the director had already insisted the film shouldn't be 'simply a study of a little homosexual affair'. Losey got his wish: it's altogether murkier than that.

Disembarking the shuttle bus now, and galumphing across Piazzale Roma in the dark to meet the *vaporetto* bobbing on the inky water, he thinks back to the first time he heard about *The Servant*. It was Levi, a video artist he met in his twenties at Vaseline, a queercore club night in north London, who raved to him about Losey's movie. He can still see his nose-ring, the sweat beading on his dark scalp, the skin razored so closely that it had lost any memory of hair.

'You call yourself a critic and you haven't seen *that*?' Levi said, disdain flashing in his eyes.

Obsession was too weak a word for how he felt about the film. He said it had shaped his entire sensibility, ignited his interest in S&M and formed the basis of his postgraduate degree: a Master's in *The Servant*.

When they left at around 3 a.m., Levi gave him his first-ever pillion ride, the Essex Road whooshing past in a jaundiced sodium smudge, his face hot and damp inside the foam vice of the crash helmet. Clutching onto this stranger's waist, he imagined himself an outlaw, though they can't have been doing more than 20 mph, what with all the speed-bumps Levi had to swerve around, as though negotiating an obstacle course.

They pulled up next to the canal, where the street lights couldn't pick them out. Levi killed the engine, then helped him over the railings by turning his hands into a platform to step on. Their bodies dropped into the undergrowth one after the other, landing with a muffled thud. They were like parachutists making it across enemy lines.

'Should we be in here?' he whispered, eyes darting.

'No,' Levi said.

———————

'Experiencing myself as a fictional character has been a mode of survival for me,' Jenni Olson says in her film *The Royal Road*. It's an occupational hazard for anyone obsessed with cinema. But there's something else, too, which he associates with being gay: as soon as you become cognisant as a child of the deleterious effect your presence has on other people, and the words they use to excuse or diminish you, it becomes impossible not to watch yourself being watched, and to differentiate between who you really are and who you need to be to survive. Building a persona, or observing yourself as a character, creates space for play and performance, but it also means that the bad things aren't really happening to you – they're happening to the fictional you, the counterfeit one. The realisation now that he has tipped the scales towards queerness in his choice of film clips is enough to make him step outside himself once again, as he has spent his whole life doing, and anticipate the ways in which he will be judged and found to be Too Gay.

He knows these thoughts would sound delusional if anyone else could hear them, especially now that queerness is ubiquitous: public figures with no specific LGBTQ+ affinities appointing themselves 'allies', rainbow flags a boon for any business. And queer visibility in cinema has never been greater. A sizeable chunk of the movies competing at the Oscars in the first half of the 2020s had some gay or queer component: the Best Picture-winner *Everything Everywhere All at Once*, which ends with its multiverse-straddling hero learning to admit without embarrassment that her daughter has a girlfriend; *Tár*, with its domineering lesbian conductor behaving in as beastly a manner as any of her straight male antecedents; *Aftersun*, told from the perspective of a queer woman trying to make sense of her father; *Glass Onion: A Knives Out Mystery*, starring Daniel Craig as a dapper gay detective, with Hugh Grant as his husband; the animated allegory *Nimona*, which was dumped by Disney when the studio got the jitters about its LGBTQ+ content; *Anatomy of a Fall*, with Sandra Hüller as a bisexual novelist suspected of killing her husband; the musical *Emilia Pérez*, which made history when its star, Karla Sofía Gascón, became the first out trans performer to be nominated for an acting Oscar; Netflix biopics of a bisexual composer (*Maestro*), a lesbian swimmer (*Nyad*) and a gay civil rights leader (*Rustin*). Even viewers who like their queers to be holy suffering martyrs, as they were in the bad old days, could whoop it up at the kitsch, masochistic pity-party of *The Whale*.

Around a quarter of the 2022 intake of titles inducted into the National Film Registry, which is administered annually by the US Library of Congress, contained LGBTQ+ characters, themes or content. These included Kenneth Anger's fetishistic phantasmagoria *Scorpio Rising* (1963); *Pariah* (2011), a zesty lesbian coming-of-age story written and directed by Dee Rees; the heartfelt 1977 documentary *Word Is Out: Stories of Some of Our Lives*, tender enough to disarm the most sceptical viewer; and *Tongues Untied*, Marlon Riggs's rousing, poetic 1989 video essay on Black queerness, which makes no concessions to anyone. The end of 2022 also ushered into the multiplexes the slick romantic comedy *Bros*, co-written by a gay man (Billy

Eichner, also its star) and marketed as the first gay rom-com from a Hollywood studio. There was an LGBTQ+ presence in everything, everywhere, all at once.

When Vito Russo published the first edition of *The Celluloid Closet*, his exhaustive 1981 critique of queer representation in mainstream cinema, audiences may have been starved of this range of images, but they were scarcely famished overall. Queer viewers quickly learn how to rustle up a hearty banquet from crumbs: you take what you can get, and you're always on the lookout. Provocative renegades were not thin on the ground: Warhol, Anger, Fassbinder, Pasolini and Jean Cocteau (*The Blood of a Poet*), as well as John Waters (*Pink Flamingos*) and Jack Smith (*Flaming Creatures*), Barbara Hammer (*Dyketactics*) and Rosa von Praunheim (*It Is Not the Homosexual Who Is Perverse, But the Society in Which He Lives*). Access to those films was an obstacle – the raggedy gay western *Lonesome Cowboys* was never going to get block bookings in the Midwest, even before Warhol, its director, withdrew most of his work from circulation in the 1970s and 1980s. But there were always queer-coded bulletins being made within the Hollywood system by the likes of Dorothy Arzner (*Dance, Girl, Dance*), George Cukor (*Sylvia Scarlett*), Nicholas Ray (*Johnny Guitar*) and Douglas Sirk, whose masterpiece, *All That Heaven Allows*, inspired Fassbinder's *Fear Eats the Soul* and Todd Haynes's *Far from Heaven*.

Eventually, there were marvels, too, in gay porn, thanks to early-1970s pioneers like Arthur Bressan Jr (*Forbidden Letters*), Wakefield Poole (*Boys in the Sand*) and Jack Deveau (*Drive*). Fred Halsted went within the space of a year from being Vincent Price's gardener to making *LA Plays Itself*, a fragmented hardcore triptych which throbs with menace and sadism, much of it emanating from the brutish director–star himself.

What queer audiences manifestly did not have when Russo wrote *The Celluloid Closet* was the reasonable expectation that they wouldn't be used by Hollywood and its emissaries as punchline or punch-bag. That situation is never coming back, not in the movies anyway. Undisguised homophobia is so rare on screen today that when it does surface, it looks retrograde, even quaint. Near the end of Steve McQueen's 2011 drama *Shame*, a straight sex addict played by Michael Fassbender, having reached his lowest ebb after being beaten up and spat upon, submits himself to the most degrading act the film can imagine: receiving oral sex in a gay club drenched in hellish red light. Homophobic the scene may be, but its earnestly censorious tone pushes it out the other side and into camp.

When the palaeontologist played by Cary Grant in the 1938 screwball gem *Bringing Up Baby* was caught wearing Katharine Hepburn's marabou-trimmed nightie, the actor's inspired ad-lib – 'I just went gay all of a sudden!' – somehow sneaked past the censors of the Hays Code era, even though references to homosexuality were forbidden; today, Grant's line can be applied to much of popular culture. As can Joe Dallesandro's speech to his fellow hustlers thirty years later in *Flesh*: 'You straight? Nobody's straight. What's straight?' Todd Haynes's wish 'to turn every gay person straight and every straight person gay' with his glam-rock odyssey *Velvet Goldmine*, made thirty years after *Flesh*, has seemingly come true. And in 2023, Stephen Winter, who directed *Chocolate Babies* in 1996, noted how the queer vernacular had permeated popular conversation. 'Listen to white straight millennial news pundits and they're all talking about "throwing shade", he said. 'They probably don't even know why they're saying it, but everyone understands what they mean because Black-drag-queen-trans-woman lingo is now American lingo.'

This hasn't prevented homophobia and transphobia from flaring up in virulent legislation across the world. It may be tempting to focus on extreme situations such as the one in Uganda, which has only worsened since the events highlighted in the 2012 documentary *Call Me Kuchu*, directed by Katherine Fairfax Wright and Malika Zouhali-Worrall, which revealed the role of the country's media in encouraging vigilantism: the daily newspaper running squalid attacks on citizens suspected of homosexuality in its 'Homos Exposed!' unmasking campaign, the attempts to blame terrorism by al-Qaeda on 'Homo Generals'. *Call Me Kuchu* ends with the murder of one prominent LGBTQ+ rights activist, David Kato, and chilling threats being made against others. In 2023, Ugandan politicians were nearly unanimous in voting into law a bill that proposed punishments for LGBTQ+ people, ranging from severe custodial sentences to the death penalty.

But it would be misleading, not to mention implicitly racist, to suggest that bad things only happen *over there*, wherever that might be, or that the necessary battles have all been won at home. On the contrary, the treatment of trans and gender non-conforming people in the UK and US has degraded sharply at every level: social, civic, political, medical, legal. The right of the trans body to take up space, whether in schools, competitive sports or public bathrooms, is constantly imperilled; lives that should be prized and protected are instead being used as wedge issues to widen division and foment hostility. By the end of 2023, hate crimes against trans people in the UK had increased by 11 per cent over the past year, and by 186 per cent over the preceding five years, while hate crimes on the basis of sexual orientation had risen 112 per cent since 2018. And those are merely the ones which were reported.

In that context, his trepidation about the films he has chosen to show his students in Venice seems trivial to say the least. He just wishes he had noticed the abundance of queer material sooner so he might have corrected it. Of course, it's no mystery why he got carried away and let his sexuality colour his film choices in this of all years. He must have felt emboldened by the two significant events which had occurred in his life in the past few months. First, he had married his boyfriend after nine years together. Then he had signed a contract to write a book about queer cinema. Marriage and a book: it doesn't get much more demonstrative than that.

———————

The courtyard gate is locked when he arrives shortly before midnight. In the absence of any other sound, his echoing footsteps cling to the air for a second or two once he has come to a halt, transforming reality briefly into a poorly dubbed Italian film. Eventually, the buzzer screeches, the gate unfastens itself with a scraping clang, and he crosses the flagstones into the golden, glowing lobby. In his room upstairs, a single lamp has been left on to provide some half-hearted resistance against the gloom. With one foot, he nudges his holdall under the escritoire, then stands by the window overlooking the ghostly deserted piazza. From here, he can see the same strip of Dorsoduro where Katharine Hepburn toppled backwards into the canal in David Lean's 1955 *Summertime* – such a perfectly executed pratfall, with the little Venetian urchin snatching the camera from her as she flails past him.

Why didn't he pick Lean's film to show his students instead? Then again, perhaps one of them would have pointed out that this straight love story, like Lean's *Brief Encounter*, which was written by Noël Coward, is gay at source. It originated as *The Time of the Cuckoo* by the gay writer Arthur Laurents, which was also the basis for the 1965 Broadway musical *Do I Hear a Waltz?*: lyrics by Stephen Sondheim, choreography by Wakefield Poole, who within six or seven years became the leading innovator in US gay porn. The film has other queer connections: in *The Royal Road*, Jenni Olson declares an affinity with *Summertime*'s story of impossible love; and the gay actor

Michael Jeter in *The Fisher King* plays a distraught homeless man who, when asked where he wants to be, sobs: 'Venice! Like Katharine Hepburn in *Summertime*. Why can't I be Katharine Hepburn?'

Arthur Laurents also co-scripted *Rope*, the queerest of Hitchcock's movies, which both Cary Grant and Montgomery Clift turned down for fear that they might be tarnished. When the screenplay was returned by the censor, Laurents said, it had 'HOMOSEXUAL DIALOGUE' scribbled all over it in 'furious blue pencil'.

Sprawled on the bed now, he goes over tomorrow's lecture in his head. Keep this in perspective, he tells himself. It's not as if he will be trying this week to win over a phalanx of retired army colonels or a hive of alt-right trolls: his audience will consist of young, open-minded students, many of whom are more at ease with their sexuality than he will ever be. But then the problem isn't them; it's him. He knows rationally that the world is different today to how it was when he was growing up in Essex in the 1970s and 1980s. Home was a notch on the green belt, a two-pub tumbleweed village located three miles beyond the dangling red nerve-ending that was the easternmost point of the Central line. Traces of the fear and shame from those years still linger inside him, stubbornly resistant to the detergent properties of words like 'inclusion', 'tolerance' and 'diversity'.

He reads so often about films and directors who are 'unapologetically queer', has probably even used the phrase himself in fact, that he sometimes wonders what 'apologetically queer' might look like. Then the penny drops: it looks like him.

Cinema and sexuality have always been as closely intertwined for him as the stripes on a barbershop pole. For much of his life, though, his queerness has existed in theory rather than in practice. The title of a 1991 short film, directed by Jane Dowie and starring Jane Horrocks as a shy lesbian, describes almost perfectly the circuitous route his life has taken: *Came Out, It Rained, Went Back in Again*.

As a child, he felt fizzy thinking about other boys, long before he acquired the language to express that – or the wisdom not to. At fourteen, he couldn't hold on to his wretched and brilliant secret any longer: it was like a gobstopper obstructing his airway. He confessed to two friends in the back row of biology class; once the words were out of his mouth, he found he could breathe again. That he wasn't bullied once his sexuality became common knowledge was a minor miracle. But his negligible same-sex experiences over the next few years failed to extinguish his sense of isolation, or the suspicion that life would be like this forever.

It was the mid-1980s: homophobia was too routine to be remarked upon; AIDS had given the world an even broader licence to demonise; the hostility peaked with Section 28, the Conservative government's legislation banning local authorities from 'promoting' homosexuality. There was verbal abuse when he was out at night. Eventually, there was violence, too. Adults had always told him he had a lively imagination, but the one thing he could never envisage was a future in which he would be happy as well as gay.

Shortly before his eighteenth birthday, he tumbled into a relationship with his closest female friend. Lying next to her, he stared up at his bedroom ceiling, which was papered with posters of River Phoenix torn from *Just Seventeen* and *Jackie*, and felt like what he was: a gay boy with a girlfriend. Nobody expected this to happen, least of all him. He was going against the gay! He was Dylan gone electric!

He was a father of two before he was twenty-three.

After he and his girlfriend broke up, he drifted back into dating men, only to fall in love with another female friend. The posters were different now – it was the forlorn, bony-faced Guillaume Depardieu of *Les Apprentis* gazing down from his wall – but the sensation was the same. There was nothing fake about either of those straight relationships. Even after his third child was born, though, he knew that gayness was still the foundation on which the rest of him was built. When he eventually came out for the second time at forty-one, he found to his surprise that he was no longer young. Craigslist personal ads and Grindr profiles contained the warning: 'Don't be over forty.' He had skipped the part where he was on the inside. How did that happen?

There was a new word now to explain who he was ('fluidity'), but he had always experienced sexuality more as an identity crisis, and that wasn't about to end simply because he had chosen to live honestly at last and the world had decided to let him. Here he is today, married to a man, benefiting from freedoms new-found and hard-won (even if none of them were hard won by him), yet he squints with disbelief at same-sex couples holding hands in the street, glows with grand-motherly delight whenever he hears of someone he knows asserting their gender identity, blushes obligingly when one of his children corrects him for muddling up a friend's pronouns. All this came to pass without him. Now he is as gauche and dowdy as a time-traveller from Thatcher's Britain, still partying like it's 1989.

One constant, whether he has been in or out of the closet, is cinema. Film served as a helping hand, even a turbo-booster, in comprehending his own desires when he was younger. If movies didn't make him gay in the first place, he is happy to give them the credit, at least until he can dredge up an origin story which pre-dates the one he already has: three years old, kneeling in his seat in the Granada cinema in Walthamstow, mesmerised by *The Jungle Book* and by Mowgli's perky bottom twitching in his snazzy orange pants. He could measure out his childhood and adolescence in the underwear he has coveted: Mowgli's orange number; Johnny Weissmuller's overstuffed loincloth in the black-and-white *Tarzan* films which filled the TV schedule in the never-ending summer holidays; John Travolta's skimpy black briefs in *Saturday Night Fever*; Michael J. Fox's faded purple Calvins, the exact shade of Parma Violets, in *Back to the Future*; and the pants worn by boys at school, which he glimpsed in the PE changing rooms and committed to memory. Each pair was like a new word in the exotic language he was learning.

Film depends for much of its potency on the pleasure of sitting in the dark, staring secretly at strangers' bodies on-screen, so no wonder the act of cinema-going itself feels to him like a queer pursuit with its connotations of transgression, concealment, voyeurism; the suspicion that there is something dirty down there in the dark.

What he experienced in the cinema when he was a boy taught him how 'gay' felt, long before he heard the word or knew it applied to him. During his Rip Van Winkle years of adulthood, film provided a kind of IV line for his queerness, feeding him the necessary nutrients to keep that part of him from dying off even while it was outwardly dormant. But it was also a kind of torture seeing the discrepancy between what happened on-screen and his own life. He recognised in *Brokeback Mountain* the sort of constricted existence he had engineered for himself. He saw in the lovers in *Weekend* the self-acceptance that had always been out of reach for him. Perhaps his best-case scenario would be to end up like the father played by Christopher Plummer in *Beginners*: come out in his seventies, take a younger lover, sport an array of coloured neckerchiefs, then die.

The week's lectures go smoothly enough. The students are bright, buzzy, appreciative. He scours their faces for disapproval but none of them seems the least bit perturbed by the queer bias in his clips. Afterwards, he lounges in the sun outside a café in Campo Santa Margherita, letting his Americano cool as he studies the youths romping past in fours and fives, rowdy with their cryptic, jousting banter.

Those shrewd faces know everything about the internet. Confidence trails behind them like a superhero's cape.

He wonders how Aschenbach from *Death in Venice* would have coped with the abundance of queerness and beauty on the streets, the avalanche of images in the digital age. It might have diluted his passion, killed off his quest, if there were blemishless Tadzios on every corner, each with their own Instagram and OnlyFans accounts.

The prospect of Aschenbach adrift in the vulgar modern world is treated with tenderness and humour in Richard Kwietniowski's 1997 film *Love and Death on Long Island*, a bittersweet spin on Thomas Mann's novella adapted by Gilbert Adair (who wrote *The Real Tadzio*) from his own novel. The Aschenbach surrogate here is a reclusive widowed novelist (John Hurt), who sets out to see the latest period drama at his local cinema only to stumble into the wrong screen, where he is greeted by the image of a teen idol (Jason Priestley). Having found his Tadzio, mercifully older than Mann's fourteen-year-old original, he flies to the US, tracks him down and befriends him in a calculated seduction.

It felt natural that John Hurt should arrive at this role in the autumn of a career so closely associated with queerness: from playing Quentin Crisp, resplendent beneath a laurel of copper curls in *The Naked Civil Servant*, to The Countess, the vulture-like mogul of feminine hygiene products in Gus Van Sant's *Even Cowgirls Get the Blues*. Hurt seems to carry Crisp's queerness with him into space in *Alien*, where he is doubly distinct from the rest of the crew. First, he is one of just two Brits on the spacecraft. More importantly, he is the only male to be penetrated by the alien. It enters him orally – this is the deepest of deep-throats – before erupting from his chest, ghoulishly sexual: a slicked, sticky phallus with glinting metallic teeth like an outré piercing. By the time Hurt starred as an effete gay cop flung together with a homophobic colleague (Ryan O'Neal) in the cheerless comedy

Partners, he looked so miserable that another chest-bursting parasite could only have been a blessed relief.

Love and Death on Long Island, then, represented a culmination for Hurt, and a triumph all round. When it comes to taste, nuance and wit, the film knocks *Death in Venice* into a cocked Panama hat. Visconti's movie plays as if it were directed by Aschenbach himself, the camera desperate to appear decorous even as it practically quakes at the sight of young Tadzio prancing in the striped clingy skin of his bathing suit. There is the sense on the page that he was spoiled forever once he noticed the older voyeur's erotic interest. No such subtlety on-screen. Visconti's Tadzio, as played by the fifteen-year-old Björn Andrésen, is an incorrigible tease who co-opts the city as his catwalk.

'As Visconti portrays the boy, he is seductive from beginning to end, "cruising" Aschenbach so often you wonder why the old man doesn't sneak into an alley with him,' wrote one reader to the *New York Times* in 1971. Of course, the reason Aschenbach stops short of jumping his bones is that he knows age has rendered him invisible and irrelevant. 'Don't be over forty,' the hook-up apps would tell him.

Film language does its best to play Cupid. When Aschenbach spots Tadzio, the boy looks bored, posed like a doll, resting his face on one limp hand as he waits with his family in the hotel salon to be assigned a table for dinner. He is dressed in a sailor suit, making him well placed to navigate a sinking waterlogged city, whereas Aschenbach is out of his depth from the moment he arrives and blunders into a contretemps with a gondolier.

From that initial shot of Tadzio, the film cuts back to Aschenbach, who raises his newspaper to his face as if to protect himself from the glare of the boy's beauty. Then he lowers the paper again. He strokes his chin, creating in his pose a direct mirror-image of Tadzio. Each figure has a hand touching the side of his own face, Aschenbach raising his to his left cheek, Tadzio to his right. Later in the same scene, the camera moves away from the boy, panning around the restaurant and eventually coming to rest on Aschenbach. The unbroken tracking shot unites the observed and the observer in the same take, the same held breath. The film is languid, but Bogarde plays Aschenbach as a man who is all eggshells and tenterhooks. Perched at his little writing table on the beach, he is beside himself with glee at having bagged a front-row seat to watch Tadzio capering in the sand. The candy-striped canvas tent behind Aschenbach ripples and flaps in the wind: it could be his diaphragm quivering as he struggles to breathe.

Visconti protested that 'the love in my film is *not* homosexual. It is love without eroticism, without sexuality . . .' Bogarde didn't get that memo; he described his character as 'a fifty-two-year-old Jewish Genius with a "hang up" . . . on kids. Male.' The film got off to a rocky start. The actor complained of 'the agonies' beginning with 'paying off Jose Ferrer 100,000 dollars to clear off (he had half the rights we discovered the day we were to start shooting!)'. Visconti ordered a prosthetic nose for Bogarde but it filled with sweat and kept falling off. Instead, he wore a moustache and a pair of 'Granny glasses' that Forwood had found in a box of junk jewellery. Bogarde feared the get-up might turn him into a cross between John Lennon, Lloyd George and Peter O'Toole in *Goodbye Mr Chips*.

He predicted before shooting began that his young co-star would be out partying 'until seven every morning doing the "Frug" or something frightful with the kids on the Lido . . .' Once the shoot was over, though, he pronounced Andrésen 'absolutely extraordinary' and 'the perfect Tadzio'. He had one final perceptive observation: 'The last thing that Björn ever wanted, I am certain, was to be in movies.'

It is common knowledge now that Andrésen's life was blighted by his involvement in the film, and by Visconti's callous objectification of him, which began with an audition where the boy, clearly uncomfortable, was made to pose first clothed and then in trunks, and ended at the press conference for the movie's Cannes premiere, where the director joked about the teenager losing his looks. 'Luchino was the sort of cultural predator who would sacrifice anything or anyone for the work,' Andrésen later said. An entire documentary on the subject, *The Most Beautiful Boy in the World*, was made in 2020 with the co-operation of the former Tadzio, who was by that point in his early sixties. Watched now, *Death in Venice* seems to absorb retroactively the misery that it engendered for that young actor. Asked in 2021 what he would say to Visconti if the director were alive, Andrésen didn't need any time to consider his response. 'Fuck off,' he said.

But for all that the film is as spoiled as those cholera-corrupted strawberries which spell doom for Aschenbach, it captures one thing with mortifying accuracy: the alienating force of queerness in a world hostile to difference.

———————

Pinning a few euros under the saucer to pay for his Americano, he troops back across the little bridge to his hotel. As he walks, he does a quick spot of mental arithmetic, and works out that he is now, at fifty-one, a full two years older than Bogarde was when he made *Death in Venice*. He expects to feel a jolting stab at this fact, signalling some impending mortal crisis, but it doesn't come. Age, he realises, is incidental to his alienation: he was already in Aschenbach's shoes when he was seven or eight years old, a good decade before he opened the pages of Mann's novella or first clapped eyes on Visconti's film. He was set apart irretrievably from other boys by his desire for them. It turned him into a snoop, a sneak, a double agent. Carrying a secret not only put him at one remove, it aged him internally. His gayness was like a curse rendering him elderly before he had so much as touched puberty. If he is Aschenbach today, then that is only because he always has been.

After he came out in his forties, an acquaintance reassured him that she would never have guessed he was gay. He received that as the highest of compliments, the mark of a job well done; his camouflage had been complete. It made a change from when he was out and about in his teens, seemingly unable to set foot in a pub or on a Tube train without strangers remarking on his effeminacy; it was as if his sexuality were visible from space. Over time, he ironed out most of the giveaway quirks and kinks and cringed at anyone who hadn't. Aside from that breed of closeted politician who vehemently opposes gay rights, internalised homophobia never had a greater success story than his.

It has produced in him a curious sort of tension. Standing in front of his students earlier this week in Venice, he policed his voice and his mannerisms, taming the ghost of his childhood lisp, and tried not to come across as too gay. Sitting at home today in London to begin writing his book, he doesn't feel nearly gay enough.

The trick, he feels, will be to build an account of queer cinema that conceals his own compromised position. His use of the word 'queer', though, is dishonest; it was a term of abuse in his youth, one he never quite got around to reclaiming in the way that good modern gays are meant to do. For the next generation down, it has a different sort of connotation. As the twenty-something Harry, played by Paul Mescal, puts it in *All of Us Strangers*, 'queer' sounds polite: 'It's like all the dick-sucking's been taken out.' Monika Treut, the pioneering director of *Virgin Machine* and *My Father Is Coming*, approaches the word from the opposite angle: she has expressed nostalgia for 'the time when queer people were outcasts', as well as a distaste for the casualness with which 'queer' is bandied around today: 'It used to be associated with activism: not agreeing with family values, having a different view of society. Now "queer" is more like a fashionable way of going with the flow. I'd say 80 per cent of the students I teach would call themselves "queer" without having had any real fights.'

Even in the no-risk realm of the superhero blockbuster, queerness is part of the brand, albeit one which can be easily jettisoned without endangering the integrity of the whole – such as the gay kiss in the Marvel adventure *Eternals*, which was expunged in markets hostile to LGBTQ+ rights. When *X-Men 2* was released in 2003, it seemed adventurous of the film-makers to include a coming-out scene for one of the young heroes, who owns up to having mutant powers; 'Have you tried not being a mutant?' asks his mother. More than two decades on, subtext is now text – and greater visibility can feel like a diminished presence.

Venom: Let There Be Carnage (2021) is a case in point. The CGI monster Venom spends most of his time living the dream of many gay men: being inside Tom Hardy, that is. He offers sartorial tips to Hardy's character, Eddie, makes references to Barry Manilow and even gets a coming-out party at a masquerade ball, where he declares himself to be '*out* of the Eddie closet'. The sight of all this Day-Glo corporate queerness, jazz-handing at the multiplex, calls to mind the life cycle of punk: from the Sex Pistols at the 100 Club to shredded jeans at H&M.

Queerness in film started to become a commercial possibility in the 1980s with the rise of independent cinema, which provided a dedicated platform for stories of marginalised lives, as well as the flourishing of queer auteurs like Pedro Almodóvar and Gus Van Sant. The market exploded like a glitter cannon in the 1990s, sending sparkling product raining down in every direction. AIDS activism provided a defined focus for anger. Trans lives hit the mainstream (*Orlando, Boys Don't Cry*) alongside dynamic renderings of the Black queer experience (*The Watermelon Woman, Young Soul Rebels,*

Chocolate Babies), jubilant celebrations of drag (*Paris Is Burning, The Adventures of Priscilla, Queen of the Desert*), provocations from the New Queer Cinema (*Poison, Swoon, Edward II*), auteurist masterpieces (*Beau Travail, Happy Together*) and after-school coming-out stories (*Beautiful Thing, Show Me Love*). The Wachowski sisters, Lisa Cholodenko, François Ozon and Bruce LaBruce all made their debuts in that decade; Almodóvar and Van Sant went stratospheric.

If the movement feels diffuse now, that is an inevitable consequence of proliferation. It is still possible to single out genuine renegades, like Yann Gonzalez (*Knife+Heart*), João Pedro Rodrigues (*O Fantasma*), Sebastián Silva (*Rotting in the Sun*) and Gustavo Vinagre (*Three Tidy Tigers Tied a Tie Tighter*). There are adrenalised celebrations of the queer female libido in films like Emma Seligman's fight-club comedy *Bottoms*, Ethan Coen and Tricia Cooke's crime caper *Drive-Away Dolls* and Rose Glass's torrid, swaggering thriller *Love Lies Bleeding*.

The most convincing groundswell of innovation today, equal to the revolution of the 1990s, belongs to transgender film-makers: Jessica Dunn Rovinelli, who made *So Pretty*, an elliptical portrait of a fictional queer commune; Isabel Sandoval, whose films include the fine-grained immigrant drama *Lingua Franca*; Lyle Kash, director of *Death and Bowling*, which frustrates the notion that trans-ness can be distilled and defined; Alice Maio Mackay, whose first splatter movies, including *T-Blockers* and *Satranic Panic*, were made while she was still in her teens; Paul B. Preciado, whose malleable documentary *Orlando, My Political Biography* riffs magically on the Virginia Woolf novel previously filmed by Ulrike Ottinger in 1981 (as *Freak Orlando*) and a decade later by Sally Potter; and Jane Schoenbrun, described by Paul Schrader in 2024 as 'hands down the most original voice in film in the last decade', whose chronically unsettling horror movies *We're All Going to the World's Fair* and *I Saw the TV Glow* find mind-bending new metaphors for trans identity struggles. Meanwhile, Vera Drew, in her subversive trans coming-of-age comedy *The People's Joker*, co-opts DC Comics iconography and characters (including Batman, the Joker and the Penguin) with all the last-chance, do-or-die derangement of an airplane hijacker.

What he intends to do in his book is to use films such as these to illuminate queer cinema's past and to indicate what its future might hold. He wants to explore how movies have shaped and intersected with queer identity, and to ask how queer film can retain its element of the coded and the contraband even though it is no longer strictly underground. To be queer is to be outside, oppositional, different, wrong, freakish, even criminal. As Jean Genet wrote: 'The greater my guilt in your eyes, something I entirely embrace, the greater my free-dom and the more perfect my solitude and singularity.'

The answer to how that outlaw spirit can survive in the age of assimi-lation must lie in the distance between the early 1980s, when Russo in *The Celluloid Closet* argued in part for the equitable treatment of queer characters on-screen, and today. Not only does representation alone no longer cut the mustard, but it has morphed into one of the tentacles of capitalism. 'When people start seeing representation as the end-all, be-all,' said Julio Torres, the writer–director–star of the queer art-world comedy *Problemista*, 'what it allows is for a company to be, like: "OK, we re-cast it, now buy it." And we're tricked into thinking that consuming is an act of activism.'

———————

Sitting at a table in the corner of the British Film Institute library, in the same building in which the critic and theorist Robin Wood delivered his lecture 'Responsibilities of a Gay Film Critic' in 1977, he starts work on what he intends to be his introduction.

This is a book about queer cinema, he writes. But what exactly is queer cinema? Though the narratives of queerness and gayness overlap, there is a difference between how those modes manifest themselves on-screen. Todd Haynes's 1995 masterpiece *Safe*, starring Julianne Moore as a timid San Fernando Valley 'homemaker' who is seemingly allergic to her surroundings, features no major gay characters, yet in its form – which depends on a denial of specific pleasures and consolations, and a rejection of convention – it is fastidiously queer. The romantic comedy *Bros*, on the other hand, has a *dramatis personae* that is almost exclusively LGBTQ+ (as is most of its cast and crew), yet nothing about its form feels queer. It perpetuates a narrative orthodoxy deployed since the beginning of cinema to erase, thwart and invalidate queer or non-conformist desire.

What exists today in so much LGBTQ+-themed cinema is plenitude without depth, abundance devoid of analysis, queer characters manufactured from straight moulds. Writing in the 1980s, the film-maker Barbara Hammer argued that the apparent glut of lesbian representation at the time, in pictures such as *Desert Hearts* and *She Must Be Seeing Things*, served to 'posit the lesbian inside the heterosexual discourse . . . The lesbians act out heterosexual gender roles and positions rather than claiming any difference: even the sexual practice is situated in heterosexuality . . . The romance, the on-screen gaze, the plot, the character development are all situated within a heterosexual lifestyle or a Hollywood imagination.'

There is another way. Reflecting on the New Queer Cinema, Todd Haynes, who went on to make *Carol* and *May December*, said:

> The thing I dug . . . was being associated with films that were challenging narrative form and style as much as content. It wasn't enough to replace the boy-meets-girl-loses-girl-then-gets-girl with a boy-meets-boy version. The target was the affirmative form itself, which rewards an audience's expectations by telling us things work out in the end . . . Queerness was, by definition, a critique of mainstream culture. It wasn't just a plea for a place at the table. It called into question the table itself.

Queerness is a mechanism for disruption; it can reinvent structure and language as it goes along. In this way, it mirrors the experience of being queer in an intolerant world. One of the reasons Hammer gravitated towards experimental film, she explained, was that 'being a lesbian *is* experimental. We're creating a new life for ourselves. Why not create a new media form as well?' Queerness in cinema is an innovating force and a catalytic power. It is the future. *And the future always wins.*

He squints at that line as it floats in the white electric sea of his laptop screen. He thinks it strikes roughly the right valedictory note and helps to disguise some of the timidity he feels about himself and his book. The 'future always wins' idea he stole from Zackary Drucker, co-director of *The Stroll*, a documentary about trans sex workers of colour in the 1990s in New York's Meatpacking District. 'The future always wins,' said Drucker in response to a question she was asked about anti-trans legislation. The audience at the BFI Flare festival applauded her, and no wonder: the line has an inspirational feel, a kind of 'We shall overcome' flavour.

But when he repeats those words to one of his friends, she insists they are gibberish.

'What does Drucker mean, "The future always wins"?' she scoffs. 'Is the future winning for queer people in Uganda or Turkey or Russia? Is it winning for trans kids *anywhere*?'

He thinks about that now. He opens his laptop and deletes the line. Later, though, he is back at the keyboard, typing it out once more, even italicising it this time. He's going to keep it in, he decides. It is precisely the sort of rallying sentiment with which the opening chapter of a book on queer cinema ought to end, whether he believes in it or not.

2

FEMME

It might be considered a setback when writing such a book to be told that 'queer' as a term is over. 'In the US, we're totally past that,' says Jessica Dunn Rovinelli in her seen-it-all tones, pushing aside the long platinum hair from her cool-kid-sister face. 'I think it was helpful for a lot of my generation. For trans and non-binary people, it was this space in which you could play. But as brands started to market and sell the idea of queerness, it became this sort of homogenising impulse.'

We are talking over video call on a wet spring Monday, and the director of *So Pretty* and *Empathy* is doing a rotten job of breaking it to me gently that 'queer' is passé. 'On the one hand, the bleeding edge of politics is done with the word "queer", but at the same time it's still useful to articulate to a certain group of people what that term might mean,' she says, belatedly trying to cushion the blow. 'Don't forget, you're also talking to *me*. A lot of other people would tell you it's really important and that I'm a homophobe or a transphobe for not liking it.'

What's coming next if that word has expired? What is my book about if not queer cinema? 'Ugh, I dunno,' she groans, her expression making it clear that this is a me-problem. 'I am trying to care less about terminology. As I get older, I become more invested in asking: what are the material freedoms that we can afford for all genders?' The word itself has no negative connotations for her. 'I always found that hilarious: "We're reclaiming it!" No one's *ever* called me "queer". They called me "faggot".'

Rovinelli made her feature debut in 2016 with *Empathy*, a non-fiction film – though one, like Lizzie Borden's *Born in Flames* or

Juliet Bashore's *Kamikaze Hearts*, that is not exactly a documentary either. The crowdfunding campaign for *Empathy* did deploy the D-word, however, pitching the film as 'a performative documentary on sexual-social work'. Donors who contributed $100 received a signed postcard, a thank you in the credits and 'a video of the director kissing any object you desire'.

The picture follows Em Cominotti, a sex worker weaning herself off heroin; she gets a 'story by' co-credit, which is an early sign that any documentary component will be conditional. The camera is rarely acknowledged in *Empathy*, but artifice is sewn into the film's fabric. In a nocturnal exterior shot outside a Taco Bell, an off-screen voice says: 'Shot two, take one.' Em waits for 'Action!', followed by the snap of the clapperboard's jaws, before biting into her burrito and beginning the scene. So much for *vérité*.

While going cold turkey, she deals with quotidian issues: dates with clients, healthcare bureaucracy, a possible move from New York to Pittsburgh. Rovinelli prioritises largely static takes that create or dwell on contemplative spaces in Em's life. An extended scene in a bare white room where Em is meeting a client shows the couple in bed together, the john reading Shakespeare's sonnet 57 to her: 'Being your slave, what should I do but tend/ Upon the hours and times of your desire?' The 'slave' in this case holds all the cards and is being billed according to the hours and times of *his* desire. The scene also pings us back to another queer film about a hotel room assignation: *The Hours and Times*, which imagined what Brian Epstein and John Lennon got up to on holiday in Barcelona.

During an unshifting six-minute shot, the camera hangs back as it observes Em and her client shedding their clothes and slipping into foreplay. Rovinelli keeps the doorframe always in view on the right of the shot, so we never forget that this is an observed moment, perhaps even a staged one. She emphasises this through sound, too, blasting out Magic Fades' euphoric, throbbing 'Ecco' at the beginning of the scene but not replacing the song with anything else on the soundtrack once it ends. Save for the occasional moan or whimper, the remaining two or three minutes of sex play out in a stilted, yawning silence. The whole of *Empathy* hangs in a series of limbo states: between addiction and sobriety, travelling and arriving, waiting and happening. Near the end of the film, we hear the voice on Em's meditation tape telling her: 'In any circumstance, you can start afresh. You have the power and control to start a new moment at any time.' Quite the queer concept.

The tensions in *Empathy* between life and its cinematic facsimile are amplified in Rovinelli's 2019 follow-up, *So Pretty*, adapted from Ronald M. Schernikau's novel *So Schön*. The film's form keeps shifting, just as the relationships – between a group of queer friends and lovers in a Brooklyn commune – morph within it. There are moments in which the characters read from Schernikau, seeming to will into existence the adaptation we are watching, while commenting on their own relationship to the text or their resemblance to the book's characters.

Interludes show them standing at a microphone in a field, reading from what appears to be a script. 'This film tells of four young people attempting to organise their love,' announces Erika (Rachika Samarth). Theatricality is foregrounded, only for documentary realism to intrude repeatedly in the shape of footage of real New York City demonstrations and protests, or intimate scenes of conversation or sex, or the creeping spectre of an inevitable break-up. The naturalism in the performances collides with casual acknowledgements of artifice: 'This is a flashback,' says one actor; 'This is a flash-forward,' says another. In this way, *So Pretty* is not merely a film that knows it's a film, but a text making the transition to the screen, writhing and wriggling in front of our eyes. Rovinelli captures a state of flux that is political, social, sexual and artistic. The process of the movie discovering what it is becomes the movie itself.

I won't be the last person to describe *So Pretty* as Brechtian. What Rovinelli has tired of hearing, though, is the word 'gaze', which has become the Japanese knotweed of film theory. 'I don't want to talk about the "gaze" ever again in my life,' she says. 'It's like: "O-*kay*, the female gaze!" These floppy generic terms don't help us make better cinema or understand women or men or trans people.' Isn't *So Pretty* a film of many gazes? 'Yes. One of which hopefully belongs to the audience.'

Her own responses to films as a younger viewer were initially visceral. 'Crying is what attracted me to the movies as a child. I would go see them largely with male friends – most of the little teenage cinephile circles I was in were young boys – and it was very beautiful that we would chase this act of sobbing together.'

Consequently, she pays close attention to how her own teenage fans online respond to *So Pretty*. But in an age of fluidity, she resists the idea of the film as a manifesto. 'I have a certain frustration with *So Pretty* because it does represent, I think, a milieu of utopian queerness – and I do worry that it can participate in the same universalising nothingness that I spoke about earlier. But the film has a lot of young fans, and most of them seem able to recognise the fantasy elements. The film says, "We live like this. You can live like this!" And *nobody* lives like this. In reality, the quote–unquote "trans community" is filled with incredible cruelty, as any minority group that is isolated from larger spaces is going to be. Any woman who has existed as a trans woman will discover: "My God, these people do *not* have my back." So this is how it could be, but it's not how it is.'

It's an awareness that only occurred to her subsequently. 'I started making *So Pretty* as a man. It was aspirational. I knew it was fantasy. It was an attempt to make a film that's set in a world I might want to live in, which is what Schernikau was doing in the original text.' Where is her head at now? 'The phase I'm in is anti-representational. I want to continue working with a diverse group of people in front of and behind the camera as a labour issue, because I think these labour politics are incredibly important, but the idea that representation can save us is, I hope, dying. Representation is *not* fucking working. And I don't want to make films to present us as good subjects. I'd rather present us as vile subjects. Because if we can only exist as the best version of ourselves, we will die.'

If representational politics has a political thrust in the real world, she says, it is one of provoking actual violence against the very people it's supposed to help. 'It creates the image of some who are deserving of participation, of inclusion, of material benefits, and some who are not. The response to the accusation that trans people are groomers and rapists should not be to say: "No, we're not." You cannot engage in a discourse with your oppressor. You cannot just pick the opposite pole.'

As Rovinelli insists, queer people need the freedom to be anything on-screen, even deplorable or irredeemable. Advocates of that idea may be gaining in number. In April 2023, the British film-maker Campbell X (*Stud Life*) put out an invitation on social media to 'please share with me your most controversial take on LGBTQI films'. Among those who responded was Francis Lee, the director of *God's Own Country* and *Ammonite*. 'Make your gay characters complex,' Lee said. 'Problematic. Nasty fuckers who do bad things. Unapologetic. Evil. Manipulative. Unlikeable. Three-dimensional. Villainous. Not just the "cute" teens holding hands.'

It's an admirable goal. And yet that manner of portrayal invariably encounters opposition from funding bodies, festival selection panels and distributors before it can even reach critics and audiences. One of the most egregious examples of a radically queer film being stymied on its way to the marketplace is Sam H. Freeman and Ng Choon Ping's 2023 thriller *Femme*. Nathan Stewart-Jarrett plays Jules, a statuesque drag queen whose confidence is shattered after he is the victim of a homophobic attack. Months later, he spots his closeted assailant, Preston (George MacKay), in a gay sauna. Preston doesn't recognise him out of drag, which gives Jules the chance to contrive a sexual relationship with him as revenge. He is playing the long game, not knowing where or how it might end.

Raising the budget was a challenge even off the back of a BAFTA-nominated short of the same name. A leading UK body turned the film down at the funding stage. One company pledged a chunk of the movie's budget, only to withdraw it six weeks before shooting was due to begin. Privately, its executives expressed doubts about the commercial viability of Black queer content, as though the casting of Stewart-Jarrett as Jules might limit the film's appeal. It was always Ng's preference that one of the leads should be played by a person of colour. 'Our desires are shaped by what we see,' he says. 'So I was keen to tell a story that was outside the usual two white guys. But it wasn't a deal-breaker.' None of the characters were written as a specific race; it just so happened that Stewart-Jarrett was the best actor who auditioned to play Jules. 'No one we saw held a candle to him,' says Freeman.

In its tension between physical presence and emotional fragility, its splinters of vengeance and victimhood knitting together under the skin, Stewart-Jarrett's performance is comparable to Sigourney Weaver's in *Death and the Maiden*. Like her, he leaves many of his character's beat-by-beat emotions and motivations daringly opaque, even to himself. As the film proceeds, Jules's mission becomes adulterated by desire and even affection for his attacker. Those emotions, never verbalised, feed into the film's suspenseful overarching enigma. The secrets that Stewart-Jarrett carries in his eyes still haven't been spilt by the final shot.

Femme had its world premiere at the Berlin International Film Festival, or Berlinale, in February 2023. 'People gasped in the right places,' says Ng. 'There are many ways Jules's story could have gone: it might have addressed healing and reconciliation, or it could've been an exploitation traumapalooza. But we wanted to make a thriller, which is not traditionally a space for queerness, and that's how it went across in the room that night.'

The film received a standing ovation. 'I was crying,' says Stewart-Jarrett. 'But I was wearing this silk shirt, so I couldn't use it to wipe my tears. I said to George, "I don't know what to do!" And he was like, "Wipe them on my back." Here I am on stage wiping my face on the back of George's shirt. It was emotional. We all believed in the film, and here we were in this moment of joy.'

What happened next was unfortunate. 'There were 800 people, it was the first time we had shown the film publicly, and we were exhausted from a full day of press interviews,' says Freeman. 'It's 11 p.m., we're all up on stage – Ping, Nathan, George and myself – and the moderator asks a few things. It's going well. Then they go to the audience for questions, and this guy stands up. He has something written down, and he starts reading from it: "In a world where violence against trans people is at an all-time high, why would you choose to make a film where . . ."' He sighs. 'I can't remember the rest. Ping and I looked at each other and panicked. It's not like we hadn't thought about the question before, but we were in such a nervous place. We just went blank.'

'It was yelled at us,' says Stewart-Jarrett. 'The words were screamed.' He stepped in with a rejoinder along the lines of: when it stops happening on the streets, we won't need to show it on-screen. 'I wanted to close it down without being rude.'

'Nathan handled it so well,' says Freeman. Who was the disgruntled speaker? 'I heard he was a film-maker. He had this campy, queer sci-fi film on the festival circuit around the same time as us. I'm trying to remember his name. Rabbit something. *Harvey* Rabbit maybe?'

'Before we proceed, I would like it to go on the record that the story-telling and everything about the film-making was great. I do not want to insult these folks. I'm choosing my words carefully, and I need that to be very clear.'

Harvey Rabbit is speaking from his apartment in Berlin. He has black-framed glasses and thick mutton chops and is wearing bright blue dungarees over a striped long-sleeved T-shirt. He is the director of *Captain Faggotron Saves the Universe*, a comic fantasy about a swishy superhero, his intergalactic alien non-binary ex-lover and a horny gay Christ. The film is decked out in calorific colours, includes faux-naïf animated inserts and climaxes with a literal climax: Captain Faggotron's copious ejaculation on a church altar, which enables queer satyrs, nymphs and demons to emerge from a quivering pink sphincter known as the Anus of Hell.

After the Berlin screening of *Femme*, Rabbit was the first to take the mic. 'Someone has to, right?' he says. 'It's usually me. And I'm a good talker, I guess. I knew this was their world premiere. I didn't want to ruin their moment but I was just so mad.'

His displeasure began before the movie did. 'The directors came on stage to introduce the film. They've got this huge audience and they've both chosen to represent themselves in a masculine fashion in terms of clothing. And that's fine. I know there's a lot of discrimination against cis gay men, and that they face violence and threats, too. I get that. Especially as I appear to be a cis gay man, and I can tell when some dude is not OK with who I am. Even if they have no idea I'm trans, I somehow threaten their masculinity. But to go to a movie called *Femme* and then to see these cis men on stage who don't have any gender-fuck going on, no make-up, no display of queerness – that's a little bit of an alarm bell for me.'

The film started. Jules performs his late-night drag act; still in his stage costume, he then visits a nearby convenience store where he is mocked by Preston's friends; in response, he taunts Preston for eyeing him up in the street earlier that evening. In the attack that follows outside, Jules is slammed against a wall and thrown to the ground. His clothes are torn from him. It is as if he is being stripped of his queerness.

'Right away, I started making notes,' says Rabbit. 'I have an agenda. I will not be shy about saying that. My agenda is: more trans joy. More queer joy. We need joy. Did you see the TV show *Pose*? That was great. It changed the world for trans women, and maybe trans people. But it seems like we always have to be punished for going outside the gender lines, and I'm sick of it.' His voice rises indignantly.

When the microphone reached him that night, he let rip. 'I was at the peak of my agenda. I was attempting to make my point and be diplomatic, but I wanted an answer to my question.' Which was? 'Just: "*Why?*" Why show that people who challenge the gender binary are going to face violence, even if you're saying it shouldn't happen? Why show it at all? But especially in the time we're in right now, with so much violence against femmes and trans women of colour.'

Did he receive the answer he wanted? 'They didn't really address my global concern. Not everyone is as political as I am, and that's OK. I'm only speaking from my super-campy perspective.' What about Stewart-Jarrett's response? 'I don't disagree with him. But there were a lot of bourgeois heterosexual people in the audience who have no contact with the queer world. And even more than the film-makers needing to hear my voice – sorry, film-makers! – I felt the audience needed to hear what I had to say. To hear from a queer person that we can be represented in other ways.'

He didn't stay for the rest of the Q&A. 'I was mad. I waited outside for my friends to come out of the Kino. Most people didn't make eye contact with me. Fine. But one person, who was femme-looking, came up and thanked me.'

A month after the premiere, Rabbit posted a one-star, one-paragraph note about *Femme* on Letterboxd. It concluded: 'Why are we all so addicted to queer tragedy and pain? Can we please flip the script?' Among the thirty-two users who hit 'like' on his post was bruceclarklois, who left an even harsher score – half a star – and the following comment: 'haven't seen (and will not bother to watch!) but I trust all the negative reviews I've seen on this one so I'm trying to do my part to bring down the average rating.' Then a saluting emoji.

I read that aloud to Rabbit, and he laughs. 'That's funny. But having people not watch the film was not my M.O. I just want to see more femmes and trans characters having a good time on camera. With the protagonist here, I don't even know if getting revenge made him feel better.'

It's been more than a year since he saw the film, so I remind him how the story plays out: Jules fosters with Preston a sexual and emotional closeness over several months, leaving his assailant vulnerable, invested and (as the final scene shows) capable of tenderness. Jules's revenge is anything but sweet. It's ugly and complicated, and it's intended to leave the viewer conflicted.

'I do think there's room for that kind of story,' Rabbit says. 'But another way *Femme* could have gone is the protagonist might have gotten attacked and then – OK, this is a different movie – but he could have formed a gang and gone after guys like his attacker. Or he could have become a killing machine. My issue was he didn't get to experience any joy. None. He's just miserable. I want to see femmes win! I want to see trans people win!'

———————

In the months that followed the premiere, Freeman and Ng received multiple knock-backs. They heard that people in the industry were wary of supporting a film that had a Black protagonist but no Black director – a judgement call which paradoxically robbed Stewart-Jarrett of any agency.

'There is a lack of directors who are not white,' the actor points out. 'We know that. So am I only meant to work with Black ones? If so, I'm not going to work very often.'

Concerns over the subject matter proved even more pressing, and soon a pattern began to emerge. First, there would be initial enthusiasm from prospective distributors, even the promise of a bid. Then the heat would cool after other employees on those teams voiced objections to the brief scenes of violence which bookend the film, or to the idea of queer trauma.

'There was a good amount of interest from relatively big names,' recalls Freeman. 'But generally, you'd hear that younger members of the team weren't happy.' In such situations, it becomes possible for a well-meaning liberal aversion to the dramatisation of trauma to coincide, albeit inadvertently, with a right-wing tendency to police or nullify challenging queer material. 'There's this weird point where they kind of meet, even though they might hate each other.'

It happened on a larger scale in 1980, when opposing political flanks savaged another thriller spiked with queerness: William Friedkin's *Cruising*, starring Al Pacino as a cop going undercover in New York's BDSM scene to search for a serial killer who is butchering gay men. On one side was the MPAA, which demanded extensive cuts to escape what the board's chairman, Richard Heffner, predicted would be a rating of '5 billion Xs'. Some exhibitors refused to play the film or posted warning notices to customers: '*Cruising* is a picture we sincerely wish we did not have to show,' said the Mid-America Theatres chain, cornered by its contractual obligation. On the other side were the gay activists who had successfully disrupted the shoot. Arthur Bell in the *Village Voice*, who in 1979 called the then-unfilmed script 'the worst possible nightmare of the most uptight straight', encouraged gay New Yorkers and business owners to 'give Friedkin and his production crew a terrible time if you spot them in your neighborhoods', which they duly did. Protestors redoubled their efforts once the movie was in cinemas by picketing screenings, handing out leaflets which promised that 'gay people will die because of this film'. Between them, right and left gave *Cruising* quite the bruising.

One of the most significant snubs to *Femme* came from the BFI London Film Festival, which declined to programme the movie. 'There was pushback,' says the film's executive producer, Harriet Harper-Jones. 'We did fight. We wrote to the LFF. It felt particularly important given how the film was made. It was the most diverse crew I've ever seen, both racially and gender-wise. There were several trans and non-binary crew members, which is unheard of. It was extraordinary. So that was really hurtful.'

When Stewart-Jarrett heard that *Femme* had been rejected by the LFF, he met with the festival's director, Kristy Matheson. 'I did this kind of pilgrimage, just to ask "why?" I was sweating beforehand: I had a fantasy that I was going to get us in. That didn't happen.'

I ask Harvey Rabbit whether he thinks his Berlin tirade might have harmed the film's chances at the LFF. 'That's highly unlikely,' he says. 'Films get rejected by festivals all the time. And I doubt my opinion holds that much weight with festival curators.'

Freeman isn't so sure. 'Who knows?' he says. 'There were people from everywhere in the room that night. Who knows how much damage he did? He really threw a grenade at us.'

Femme did find a UK distributor, which marketed the film bafflingly as a straightforward thriller, putting it predominantly into outer-London multiplexes when it should have been playing arthouses. Indeed, one of the sticking-points seemed to be that *Femme* doesn't behave like a gay film; sexuality isn't its subject. Instead, it trespasses on the heterosexual terrain of the genre movie, looking and acting like a thriller. The movie's characters are all in a kind of drag: Preston in his leisurewear, his tattoos, the bright lemon hoodie that he wears during the assault; Jules in his on-stage garb, and, later, the 'straight' wardrobe (including that hoodie) which he adopts as his undercover disguise. *Femme* is also in drag: too gay for some of those who saw it as a thriller, too genre-based for anyone hoping for 'gay'. How much queerer could a film get?

'It sat between two stools,' says Harper-Jones. 'The straight audience felt discomfort because it's a gay film that is not issue-based. And there was discontent within the privileged, mainly white gay community, where the reaction has been: "How dare you? It's a Black gay character suffering violence and you're trying to make it commercial." If Preston was vilified, and if Jules was a good gay Black man who was attacked but then sought redemption and became this happy drag performer, everyone would have loved that: poor Black guy gets beaten up and then becomes stronger for it! But Jules is both the victim of a violent act and a perpetrator. It's the whole fucking manifesto of the film: it's about the cycle of violence.'

The movie's profile was so low that by the time awards season rolled around, many voters simply hadn't seen it. While other British debuts, such as *Scrapper*, *Rye Lane* and *How to Have Sex*, were splashed on the sides of buses, *Femme* remained a grubby little secret. It did scoop the Best Feature Film prize at the LGBTQ+ Iris Festival in Cardiff, where *Captain Faggotron Saves the Universe* was also competing. (Harvey Rabbit's film took home the Best Performance Beyond the Binary award for its star, Bishop Black.) And *Femme* triumphed at the BIFAs (British Independent Film Awards), where voting is weighted differently from other awards bodies: a film earns nominations based on how highly it scores with those who see it, rather than the number of people who vote for it. In that instance, it received eleven nominations and won three prizes, including Best Joint Lead Performance.

At the BAFTAs, however, it failed even to make the long-list for Outstanding British Debut. 'Had we not been nominated at the BIFAs, it might have been different,' says Freeman. 'But to not make it to the long-list for BAFTA . . . well, that felt loud.' Harper-Jones puts it more bluntly: 'To me, that is a scandal.'

The movie was picked up by Utopia in the US, where it went down a storm. Ryan O'Connell, star and creator of the queer Netflix series *Special*, called it 'a fucking breath of fresh air, a movie that is challenging and complicated'. Megan Ellison, the producer who rode to the rescue of the queer animation *Nimona* after Disney dropped it, tweeted about *Femme*: 'I absolutely love this film . . . Content warning: it's very gay.' John Waters, Bret Easton Ellis and Bruce LaBruce are also fans.

'You always hope a film will live on,' says Stewart-Jarrett. 'And *Femme* does appear to be quietly snowballing. Making it was hugely positive and full of joy, even though it wasn't a joyous subject. But what came afterwards was hard to deal with. It's been this complex experience of rejection.'

Today, Freeman confesses to being exhausted by the picture's turbulent journey. 'We'd put so much of ourselves into making something we thought was honest and nuanced and complex. And so this response from certain parts of the industry that it was in some way dirty or offensive, or that it was a story we shouldn't be telling . . . that was tough. There were points, when I was caught up in it all, where I questioned whether I'd want to make something a little safer next time.'

'If we did the film again, I would make all the same choices,' says Ng. 'A year on from the premiere, I feel less emotional. Harvey Rabbit is not going to give me a job. He's not going to fund my work. He isn't in that position. When organisations and funding bodies have the same attitude, the same set of rules – that's when it becomes substantive. One should never expect 100 per cent support. That's unrealistic. But *where* the lack of support comes from can surprise you. There's this idea that you can only have one type of freedom, because only that type is real and valid. We even deal with it in the film, when Jules's flatmate tells him he shouldn't go around carrying all this self-loathing. It's queers policing queers.'

To have the freedom to be shown as flawed, complicated and at times reprehensible, as the characters in *Femme* are, must be a priority. 'That's why we keep going back to Fassbinder, right?' says Jessica Dunn Rovinelli. 'One of the best portrayals of a transgender woman in cinema is *In a Year of 13 Moons*. I can understand why certain transgender activists at the time found it abhorrent, but now it's great. Elvira is a full cinematic subject: she exists in Fassbinder's cynical anarchist realm, and she's allowed to become a woman solely for the sake of another. That feels freeing. That doesn't make her not a woman. She just does it so her boyfriend will fuck her, and I think it's fascinating; it's within the realm of capital and these sorts of brutal exchanges that characterise how Fassbinder constructs a film world. That's exciting.'

In a Year of 13 Moons opens with the Adagietto from Mahler's Fifth Symphony, which also dominates *Death in Venice*. (Fassbinder had recently directed that film's star, Dirk Bogarde, in the moribund *Despair*.) The picture spans the last five days in the life of a trans woman and ex-butcher, Elvira (Volker Spengler). Before the film begins, she has undergone gender affirmation surgery in response to her boyfriend indicating that he might consider having sex with her if she were a woman. Based upon that flimsy hypothesis, she has reshaped her entire body and existence. Now she must reckon with who she has become, and whether she can find love in an emotionally barren world.

Directly inspired by the suicide three months earlier of Fassbinder's lover, Armin Meier, the film was one of three made in 1978 by the prolific director. He was in the final four years of his life, yet he seemed indestructible: swaggering and burly, like an alley cat with baby fat, the threat of confrontation daubed on his torn slab of a face.

In a Year of 13 Moons apparently signalled a new level of immersion for Fassbinder. He was credited in all elements of production: directing, writing, cinematography, art direction and editing (with his co-editor, Juliane Lorenz, to whom he was married at the time of his death).

The critic Nigel Andrews, who was present on set in Frankfurt for two days, tells a different story. 'Fassbinder, heavily into abusable substances at this time, failed to turn up one morning, vanished one afternoon, and even when present for filming tended to hand the camera to one of his actors to rehearse and shoot,' he reported.

> Between sessions of waiting-for-Rainer, I and another critic buzzed off to an ice-cream parlour with main actor Volker Spengler. Since Spengler was dressed in drag, these trips tended to disrupt traffic and attract even more chaos around the production . . . When the bleary director finally rolled into view, he looked as if he needed eight black coffees. He encountered instead his mother. She stood on the pavement reading the riot act. Fassbinder sheepishly took it in.

Gay, queer and trans subject matter was not enough to guarantee Fassbinder defenders among those communities during his lifetime. The hankering even then for uniformly positive representations led to him being docked points whenever he strayed into negativity – which was always. Today, his 1975 drama *Fox and His Friends*, about an uncouth working-class lug (played by Fassbinder) who is exploited by well-off, carnivorous gays after he wins the lottery, is a cornerstone of gay cinema. This was far from the case in the mid-1970s. In *Gay Left*, Andrew Britton accused the film of presenting 'a version of homosexuality that degrades us all' and decided it 'should be roundly denounced'. He went on: 'Insofar as *Fox* portrays "the homosexual predicament" and reinforces deep-rooted preconceptions about it, the film allows the spectator to sit back and think, "God! What awful lives they lead!"' Britton's friend and colleague Robin Wood accused the film of 'sour determinism, with its incidental reinforcing of gay stereotypes for the bourgeois audience . . .'

There's no question that *Fox and His Friends* is unrelentingly grim. But audience expectations, like the times, have changed. We may be depressed by its crabbed, abysmal vision, and the fatalistic view set in place by the wheel of fortune at the fairground where Fox works, but there would likely be zero concern today about whether a cis-het audience took Fassbinder's film to be a microcosm of the LGBTQ+ universe rather than what it is: a distillation of life under capitalism. Britton's idea of 'the spectator' who must be convinced of the beauty of gay life gestures towards the pressures that have historically been heaped on the comparatively small number of queer films in circulation – and the romantic idea that there might be one perfect movie out there which will convince the haters to hang up their pitchforks. Cinema may on occasion correct homophobic misconceptions or assuage a viewer's self-loathing, but those can't be its primary functions, only incidental bonuses. Blaming Fassbinder for the hypothetical response of bigots is indicative of a problem that persists today: wanting every queer film to speak for each queer person, and to tell all their stories at once.

Fassbinder was unrepentant about the poisonous view of gay relationships presented in his films. 'Homosexuals have always been very self-pitying,' he said, 'and most of them are dominated by a sense of shame.' His view was no rosier when the queers in question were female, as he had already proved with *The Bitter Tears of Petra Von Kant*: 'All in all, I find that women behave just as despicably as men do.' In 2021, François Ozon repurposed that material in the gender-switched *Peter Von Kant*, which turned the tyrannical title character, played by Denis Ménochet, into a Fassbinder surrogate. It wasn't Ozon's first time in Fassbinder drag: while still in the foothills of his career in 2000, he adapted one of the director's early plays as *Water Drops on Burning Rocks*, grafting onto it the character of Véra, a trans woman modelled on Elvira from *In a Year of 13 Moons*. Petra Von Kant rose once more from the dead, or from the shagpile carpet where Fassbinder had left her, in Vahid Hakimzadeh's 2022 version, *The Bitter Tears of Zahra Zand*, which made the central character an Iranian fashion designer fleeing to London during the Islamic Revolution.

The trans press were no more impressed by *In a Year of 13 Moons* than Britton and Wood had been by *Fox and His Friends*. *The Gateway* discerned in the film's protracted slaughterhouse scene 'a recurring theme of "things getting cut off"' and complained that Fassbinder 'seemed to be saying: if you're contemplating a sex change, you'd better be sure you're an independent and self-sufficient person!' (A fascination with butchers runs through much of Fassbinder's work, stretching back to plays he wrote in the late 1960s. His first sexual experience was with a butcher's apprentice; Meier also worked in a slaughterhouse.) The trans magazine *Les Girls* lamented that the film 'will do little for the predicament of the transsexual . . . [A]s a transsexual film, it does not live up to the necessary qualifications of a work that will alter the general public's perception of this growing and exceptionally complex phenomenon.'

Today that's the last thing a film about trans issues would be expected to do. Later, I see that Rovinelli has tweeted on that very subject, imploring film-makers to move beyond the futile educational thrust of 'Trans Representation Validity Marginalisation' narratives and to make movies 'where we are form and not just content or deconstruction'.

As she and I are winding down our conversation, she has a light-bulb moment.

'Hey, do you know Liz Purchell?' she asks, straightening up suddenly from her slouching position.

I confess that I don't.

'She made *Ask Any Buddy*, this film that's cut together from lots of gay male porn. She transitioned recently and what she's discovering is a whole alternative history of the cinematic image of trans women which exists in pornography. She would be interesting for you to talk to.'

3

ASK ANY BUDDY

Elizabeth Purchell is wearing an olive-coloured baseball cap with the word 'DYKE' on it and a vest with spaghetti-string straps. On her upper arm is a tattoo taken from the press-book of the 1970 exploitation horror *Bloodthirsty Butchers*: it shows a cleaver with blood dripping from the blade to form the words 'In Gory Color'. She is sitting in her narrow, high-ceilinged office at the American Genre Film Archive in Austin, Texas, listening patiently as I explain where she fits into my book.

'At the end of the section about Jessica Dunn Rovinelli, she asks me: "Do you know Liz Purchell?" and I say that I don't, and she says: "She would be interesting for you to talk to." And then I'll go straight into this conversation that we're having now.'

'Oh cool,' she says.

'And then I'll have you saying "Oh cool" in response to what I just said.'

She gives a little nod. 'Right.'

I tell her that I'm taking inspiration in my book from the structure of some of the films that she included in *Ask Any Buddy*, which stitches together an entirely new narrative from 126 gay porn films made in the 1970s and 1980s. The ones I'm most intrigued by are those that contain a film-within-a-film, like *Hollywood Cowboy* or Arthur Bressan Jr's *Daddy Dearest*. Bressan was a sucker for that approach: his 1974 film *Passing Strangers* starts with shots of a movie playing on-screen in a porn cinema, while *Forbidden Letters*, shot in 1975 but not released until 1979, shows one of its characters imagining himself entering the porn movie that he's watching. For the clientele of porn cinemas, which were the only venues for these films, it must have felt like wandering through a hall of mirrors.

Most complex is Wakefield Poole's *Take One*, which, in a fish-eating-its-own-tail kind of way, is all about the events leading up to the premiere of Wakefield Poole's *Take One*. In the final scene at the Nob Hill Theatre in San Francisco, the cast members who have assembled for the screening start getting it on with one another in the stalls, which must mean that the same thing is happening at the end of the film *they're* watching – and at the end of the film which the characters in *that* film are watching, and so on.

Purchell has her own theories about why self-reflexiveness is so common in gay porn of that period. 'Partly I think it's because these film-makers were, like, crazy cinephiles,' she says. 'They all wanted to do their own version of Truffaut's *Day for Night*.' Even the relatively modest sample of 1970s gay porn that I've seen bears this out. The range of references is not only impressive but wittily incorporated; the film-makers were evidently hiding copies of *Cahiers du Cinéma* inside the latest *Blueboy* or *Mandate*.

Consider *Drive*, a 1974 hardcore science-fiction fantasy directed by Jack Deveau. Two years earlier, Deveau had co-founded the East Coast-based porn production company Hand in Hand Films at the urging of Sal Mineo, the Bambi-eyed actor who played James Dean's adoring, closeted buddy in *Rebel Without a Cause*. *Drive* concerns Arachne (Christopher Rage), a trans master-villain who tries to isolate and eliminate the male sex drive to free men from the bonds of their libido – a plot point later partly recycled by Todd Haynes in *Poison*. During a nightclub performance early in *Drive*, Arachne appears in costume as a gorilla, in homage to Marlene Dietrich in Josef von Sternberg's *Blonde Venus*; the episode climaxes, as the scene in *Blonde Venus* does, with the gorilla mask being removed. The difference being that von Sternberg didn't cross-cut his nightclub sequence, as Deveau does, with hardcore footage of two mossy-chested hunks going at it hammer and tongs.

Forbidden Letters also wears its cinephilia proudly: the closing credits are narrated by its director – 'My name is Arthur Bressan Jr and I made this motion picture' – in the manner of Orson Welles in *The Magnificent Ambersons*. Homages to Welles's work also form parentheses of sorts around the New Queer Cinema, with *My Own Private Idaho* (partly inspired by *Chimes at Midnight*) at the start of the 1990s and *Velvet Goldmine* (a glittery *Citizen Kane*) near the end.

Bressan, it's worth noting, was a friend and correspondent of Frank Capra during the 1970s, and was said to carry a signed copy of the *Meet John Doe* script wherever he went. (That film is referenced prominently in *The Joy of Life*, written and directed by Jenni Olson, founder of the Bressan Project, which is dedicated to restoring his films.) Another young gay director who befriended Capra was Richard Glatzer, whose academic writing helped revive critical interest in the film-maker. Glatzer made *Grief*, a 1993 queer comedy set behind the scenes of a daytime TV show, and later co-directed the Oscar-winning *Still Alice* with his husband Wash Westmoreland, who got his own start in the mid-1990s in the gay porn sector – an experience which forms the basis of his and Glatzer's film *The Fluffer*. The cinephile hero of *The Fluffer* is drawn into the porn industry after a mix-up at the video store: intending to rent Welles's masterpiece, he mistakenly returns home with *Citizen Cum* instead.

'I was interested in gay porn from the 1970s, when it was a very vital medium,' says Westmoreland. 'It was this amazing, pre-AIDS explosion of sex and liberation for gay men, which preceded the New Queer Cinema in providing access to narratives about our lives.'

Mainstream movies set in the porn industry often have an alarmist or patronising idea of that sector's motives. But the gay porn directors of this era were true experimenters and innovators. Their ambitions were gargantuan even when their means were meagre. (Films were often shot over the weekend, to take advantage of the free rental day while camera stores were closed on Sundays.) This was also the sole area of cinema in which gay film-makers were regularly putting out product for an identifiable and guaranteed gay audience.

'The obvious value for the gay porn scene in the 1970s was that it was a place to have sex with other people, where you're fairly well protected,' says Purchell. 'A lot of these film-makers knew that what they were making was the accompaniment to whatever was happening in the theatres. But there was always a power that people recognised in seeing gay lives on-screen, even if they were fantasy. And this was a period when there were gay movie theatres in the US, and you could see a gay movie any day of the week, any week of the year, twenty-four hours a day in some cases. Some of these film-makers were incorporating community events into their films. Wakefield Poole paired his Pride film, *Freedom Day Parade*, with some of his features – you'd go to see a porno movie and you'd get this ten-minute documentary about San Francisco Gay Pride beforehand.'

As well as *Day for Night*-inspired cinephilia, Purchell identifies another element to the self-reflexive tendency in gay male porn of that era. 'It's what I call the queer archival impulse, which is when queer people go out of their way to document their lives or community, and the times that they lived in,' she says. '*Take One* in particular is about a specific community: the people who were living in San Francisco and frequenting the Nob Hill cinema.'

It is this impulse which also partly drives Barbara Hammer's first full-length feature: *Nitrate Kisses*, from 1992, draws on out-takes from the 1933 queer short *Lot in Sodom* and ends with Joan Nestle, co-founder of the Lesbian Herstory Archives, imploring lesbians to save their scraps of paper, their shopping lists and letters, their snapshots, any piece of ephemera, in order to build a lesbian archive.

The example with the fastest turnaround must be Bressan's documentary *Gay USA*, released in squeamish parts of the country as *Glorious USA*. Bressan was in San Francisco in spring 1977 with the German film-maker Rosa von Praunheim, on what became known as Orange Tuesday. 'That was when the Dade County anti-discrimination bill was overturned by Anita Bryant and her whole campaign,' explains Purchell. 'Right there and then, Bressan said: "We need to do something. We need to make a film." Pride weekend was coming up, so he organised different camera crews in other cities, and they all filmed their parades. That was at the end of June. The movie premiered at the Castro in San Francisco at the beginning of September. No one else was documenting their lives, so they did it for themselves.'

There is also Pride march footage at the end of *Passing Strangers*, made three years earlier. 'One of the things I love about Bressan is he's a low-budget film-maker who constantly reuses his own footage.' Her interest in directors recycling material comes, she says, from 'that idea of making something new out of something old. It's not just a low-budget-film-maker thing. Probably the classiest version is François Truffaut's *Love on the Run*, where he's taking all the Antoine Doinel films and building a new framework around these long flashbacks to movies he'd made over the previous twenty years. On a deeper level, though, I think there's a trans element to that – taking old material and reframing it or turning it into something new.'

It's what Purchell did with *Ask Any Buddy*. 'Right. And my relationship to that movie has changed over the years since I made it. I think it's a very trans film because it is literally about taking pieces of movies that are fantasies and trying to turn them into a new reality.'

Ask Any Buddy began as a commission for the 2019 Contact Film Festival in Austin, where it was intended to be shown as a one-night-only installation in a room dedicated to gay porn. 'I wanted something that would catch people's attention so they wouldn't just walk in and say, "Oh gay porn, that's funny," and walk out,' Purchell says. 'I had a few different ideas. One was an East Coast to West Coast road-trip kind of thing, or an hour-long dream sequence. Then the whole day-in-the-life thing emerged. I made a list of every film I could think of that fitted one of those locations or ideas – the pier, the club – then took all the pieces and found a way to fit them together.'

In its structural audacity, *Ask Any Buddy* most strongly recalls Christian Marclay's twenty-four-hour installation *The Clock*, from 2010, which builds an entire day, minute-by-minute, from pre-existing film and television footage pertaining to time. From the excerpts she assembles, Purchell also creates her own day, albeit radically compressed, beginning with a dream sequence and progressing through shots of people waking up, going out, cruising on the pier and in public toilets, clubbing and so on. The footage is sexually explicit in places, but the principle is the same: think of Purchell's film as *The Cock*.

The appeal of *Ask Any Buddy* would quickly fade, though, if the film solely comprised sex scenes from wall to glory-holed wall. Its pleasures lie in the cuts and transitions. In one of the early scenes, a couple waking up together lean over to kiss one another; Purchell then cuts to a different kissing couple at the precise moment their lips make contact, so that the men ending the kiss are not the same ones who started it. Then one of the men walks to the bathroom for his morning ablutions – and Purchell jumps to a different man in a different film standing in front of *his* sink. Many of the cuts have that fleet-footed liberty to them, foregrounding the freedom to change location and identity in one nimble snip.

51

The bricolage format is in the spirit of Barbara Hammer's work, especially *Nitrate Kisses* and *History Lessons*, the latter of which presents an alternative lesbian history of the US, beginning with doctored footage of Eleanor Roosevelt. 'Thank you, my dears, for showing up for this wonderful lesbian conference,' says the former First Lady, the L-word brazenly dubbed over in another voice. The rest of Hammer's film puts a lesbian slant on archive material of women from the beginnings of cinema in 1896 to 1969, the year of the Stonewall uprising. 'I searched for lesbian images before Stonewall and was so dismayed in not finding them that I decided to take the multitude of images made by men and turn them on their head.' She converted that dismay 'into raucous humour. I wish you could have seen me at the editing table as I laughed my way through making this reinvention of lesbian history.'

Purchell's collage also follows in the tradition of William E. Jones, the artist and film-maker whose former day job editing US porn compilations gave him a comprehensive overview of the fashions, quirks and clichés of the form, and what they say about changes in queer life. The job required little creativity, Jones has said, aside from dreaming up punning new titles for the four-hour, $10 discs he put on the market: *The Filth and the Furry*, say, or *A Rimmer Runs Through It*. The job also made possible some of his own art, such as *The Fall of Communism As Seen in Gay Pornography*, a 22-minute video sewn together in 1998 from snippets of porn tapes made in Budapest, Prague and Moscow, and *All Male Mash Up*, which creates a teasing new porn narrative that fades to black each time sex is in the offing.

Purchell didn't feel an especially strong connection to porn when she was growing up. 'Even now, the stuff I watch is all older stuff. And it's not for the turn-on value so much as the cinematic kind. Transitioning helped answer the question of why I was never turned on by any of the gay porn I watched.' It was film, rather than porn specifically, that was crucial to her as a teenager. 'Joe Dallesandro was a big deal for me. He was androgynous-looking; the hair, the way he was in *Heat*. I was very tangled up when I was a teen and that carried into adulthood. I never had the words to say, "I want these things for myself and that means I'm a woman."'

Ask Any Buddy looks very different to her now that she has transitioned. 'It's like, "Wow, there's a lot of trans people and drag queens in this. I wonder why!" At the time I made it, I'd been living as a gay man for seven or eight years, and I knew how to perform in that role, but I'd never really felt part of the community. I think one of the things that drew me to these movies is the fact that there is a weirdly educational aspect to them. You can learn how to do this or be like this or be this person. In making this movie, which is a day in the life reflected through all these other movies, maybe this is what I want life to be like.'

One of the catalysts for Purchell's epiphany about herself was Fred Halsted's hour-long 1975 movie *Sextool*. (The poster contained an approving quote from Divine: 'I Would Eat This Film!!' Given what he ate at the end of *Pink Flamingos*, that's either a back-handed compliment or an acknowledgement of how repellent some viewers would find Halsted's gruelling vision.) While working on a restoration of *Sextool*, Purchell was drawn to the presence of two trans women in what is otherwise a male-dominated film: Andrea Nicole, who appears in one shot, and Charmaine Lee Anderson, who plays the mistress of ceremonies, initiating others into a world of sexual hedonism. 'She knows where the real studs are,' says one partygoer.

'It was a very stressful period for me,' Purchell recalls. 'I'd had these thoughts in the back of my head for a long time but I could never really put words to them. Researching Charmaine and that community helped unlock a door and make sense of everything. Andrea Nicole, too; she was a former Miss Continental and had won a whole bunch of titles in drag pageant world. Reading interviews with these people, I started thinking: "My experience is like that . . . Oh *I* feel that way too." Fred Halsted also said that he wrote Charmaine's character in *Sextool* as a cipher for himself. Which is why I maintain that Fred Halsted is a trans icon: he wrote himself *into* a trans character!'

As Jessica Dunn Rovinelli indicated to me, Purchell's interest in vintage porn has shifted to trans characters. 'They're more common than you'd think, especially in straight porn,' she says. 'Most people don't know these films exist or else they write them off: "Oh trans porn from the 1980s, it's gotta be problematic." But I find a lot of strength in those films. They're some of the only places you can see trans women in the 1980s being loved and desired.'

If there is trans material out there, Purchell has most likely seen it or is in the process of restoring it. One film she holds dear is *A Passage Thru Pamela*, which she describes as the trans version of *Carrie*. 'She doesn't have telekinetic powers but she gets hit by a car and wakes up with surgery, so it's a happy ending for her.'

The plot device of a trans person undergoing gender-affirming surgery after suffering an injury crops up worryingly often, as though fulfilment could only be hoped for (or justified) after a medical emergency. Several British movies take this route. There is the otherwise insightful *I Want What I Want*, from 1972, co-scripted by Gavin Lambert (the critic and screenwriter who was also romantically involved with Nicholas Ray) and featuring a bold performance from Anne Heywood as a trans woman in the process of coming out. In the 1985 oddity *Shadey*, Antony Sher plays a trans woman whose ability to project mental images directly onto film makes her an asset to the British security services, headed by a butch, cigar-smoking Billie Whitelaw. (The movie ends with Sher being knifed in the balls.) The Belgian director Lukas Dhont opted for the surgery-via-injury

54

route in his 2018 drama *Girl*, about a trans teenage ballerina. The 1977 *Cambio de Sexo* stars Victoria Abril, a future Almodóvar regular, as a trans woman who takes a knife to herself, goes on hormones and becomes a showgirl. And there is a grisly example involving a chisel and hammer in *Let Me Die a Woman*, Doris Wishman's 1978 contribution to the 'sex hygiene' subgenre of exploitation films masquerading as educational content.

Purchell has an insatiable curiosity and hunger belied by her easy-going manner and amused lilt. She is frustrated, though, with seeing the same old titles on the circuit. 'Queer film programming is in a dire state. There are very few queer and trans programmers in general; most are straight or cis. It's always the same things that get booked year after year: *Call Me by Your Name*, *The Watermelon Woman*, *Paris Is Burning*, maybe *Desert Hearts*. Those films should still be played, but it shouldn't be limited to Pride or one queer night a month. *The Watermelon Woman* and *Paris Is Burning* should be playing year-round; then your monthly slot could be deeper cuts or rarities. There's so much more out there. Once these films get restored and people start seeing them, they do become part of the canon.'

A movie that has flowered thanks to the persistence of queer programmers is *Funeral Parade of Roses*, Toshio Matsumoto's fragmentary, multi-textured 1969 melodrama set around a Shinjuku drag bar named Genet. The film mixes documentary interviews, Greek tragedy (the plot is swiped from *Oedipus Rex*) and visual coups, such as the close-up of a photograph being burnt from behind by a lit cigarette, so that the coiling ash seems to emerge from the subject's face – a violation of the screen every bit as jarring as the celluloid burning up in Bergman's *Persona*. '*Funeral Parade* went from being very obscure to becoming *the* trans movie that people know from the 1960s,' Purchell says. Seemingly wary of resting on her laurels, she adds: 'There are a lot of other great ones, though.'

What she desires from trans films today is simple. 'I want more movies about trans communities, and more diverse actors. I don't think I've ever actually seen myself in a movie. Not to go too deep, but as a trans person who is fat, I often feel like an outcast. Whenever you see a trans person in a movie or TV show or on Instagram, they're always very skinny. They're former twinks who are now girls. It kinda hurts to see people like that all the time. I also want more bad trans characters too. I *love* trans villains.'

She namechecks Emily, raised as a boy called Warren to protect her from her father's wrath, in William Castle's 1961 *Homicidal*, and the victimised and vengeful Angela, born male but raised female, in the grungy 1983 horror *Sleepaway Camp* and its sequels.

'I'd also like there to be fewer movies about transition necessarily,' says Purchell. 'I get the appeal of transition movies from the past. I find them fascinating. It was so different back then. Now it's like: "Well, I'm trans. I've made an appointment at the gender clinic. OK, I've got my hormones. OK, now I'm doing electrolysis."' She offers an apologetic shrug. 'It's not very dramatic, right?'

The crisis in early-twenty-first-century trans healthcare is not merely ubiquitous but catastrophic, with legislation in the UK and the US closing down many available pathways to medical affirmation, especially for young trans people. Fantasy offers no respite in *The People's Joker*, where a trans stand-up comic (Vera Drew) must fling herself into a giant barrel of oestrogen to facilitate her transition. 'Why'd the gay clown dive into a vat of feminising hormones in a chemical storage plant?' she asks before taking the plunge. 'Because gender health isn't accessible even in comic-book movies.'

Purchell is a rare and happy exception. 'The most dramatic thing about my transition story was having to drive an hour and a half to the gender clinic because it was the only appointment I could get.'

4

CALL ME BY YOUR NAME

Liz Purchell is correct to include Luca Guadagnino's *Call Me by Your Name* in her tally of LGBTQ+ films that dominate programmers' choices. Even *Moonlight*, which beat it at the box office *and* won the Oscar for Best Picture, hasn't left behind a comparable cultural footprint. Perhaps that film was disadvantaged in the long run by its focus on a Black gay boy in straitened economic circumstances rather than a wealthy white twink on holiday.

It isn't so much the financial success of *Call Me by Your Name* that marks it out, though it did well. Its worldwide gross of $43 million is comparatively small beer, but LGBTQ+-themed features don't generally set the tills jangling. That is, unless neutered biopics of gay figures, such as *Bohemian Rhapsody* ($910m), *The Imitation Game* ($233m) or *Rocketman* ($195m), are taken into consideration. Fictional stories that have exceeded the $100-million mark include *Philadelphia* ($206m), the *Cage aux Folles* remake *The Birdcage* ($185m), *Brokeback Mountain* ($178m), *Brüno* ($138m) and *The Talented Mr Ripley* ($128m), which all happen to have been directed by straight men.

'I wish he was gay,' said the director Don Roos about Ang Lee, who made *Brokeback Mountain* and the 1993 gay rom-com *The Wedding Banquet*. 'I would love to claim Ang Lee for our team, but he's not. That is one of the reasons it's safe. In order to put a gay thing over in this country, it helps if it's shepherded through by a straight person.' The shepherding can be done within the film itself by a fictional character, as demonstrated by Roos's spiky comedy *The Opposite of*

Sex, which is narrated by Dedee Truitt (Christina Ricci), a gleefully amoral trash-teen whose homophobia colours her fourth-wall-breaking commentary. During a scene showing two men kissing, her voiceover warns any female audience members that if their boyfriend is currently squirming and groaning in his cinema seat, then he may well be protesting too much. For Roos, she was the film's Trojan horse: 'One of the ideas I had for *The Opposite of Sex* was, "I have to make this lead character a buxom, beautiful, blonde straight girl who hates gays, or has the normal contempt for gays that most Americans have, and she will shepherd the gay themes and characters through this film and people will trust her."'

Brokeback Mountain, based on the story by E. Annie Proulx, had its share of gay handlers before finding its way to a straight shepherd. Pedro Almodóvar turned the project down, having failed to see the original story's 'animalistic' eroticism in the script by Larry McMurtry and Diana Ossana. He also confessed to feeling insecure about making an English-language feature, a leap he didn't take until 2024 with *The Room Next Door*, starring Julianne Moore and Tilda Swinton. That came after first testing the water with two shorts in English: *Strange Way of Life*, starring Ethan Hawke and Pedro Pascal as gay cowboys, and *The Human Voice*, with Swinton in a version of the Jean Cocteau monologue which had bewitched Almodóvar for decades. A performance of Cocteau's text crops up in his 1987 melodrama *The Law of Desire* as a play-within-a-film. Having failed to write his own adaptation, Almodóvar used it instead as the fuel for the screwball plot of his 1988 breakthrough hit *Women on the Verge of a Nervous Breakdown*. It was that picture which provided Swinton with her introduction to the director's overripe Pop-art dreamscape.

'I think the shot that truly did it for me was Julieta Serrano on the back of the motorbike in the chase sequence in the tunnel, with her wig blown backwards into a candy floss profile,' she said. 'The combination of *Johnny Guitar*, Ray Cooney, Jean Cocteau and the *Beano* blew my mind right there. I almost certainly saw it at the great Lumiere cinema on St Martin's Lane. It was 1988, I think: the year we were planning to shoot Derek Jarman's *War Requiem*. During the 1980s and 1990s, Pedro felt like a Spanish cousin to Derek and those of us working in underground and queer cinema in London.'

Gus Van Sant, too, was in the running to direct *Brokeback Mountain*. 'For some reason, we never got around to casting it,' he said. 'I wanted to cast very big actors, the Leo DiCaprios and so on, or else unknowns. That was my dilemma.' He approached DiCaprio, Matt Damon, Brad Pitt and Ryan Phillippe, who all turned it down. 'And then I dropped the ball, and it kinda languished.' It may have improved the film's commercial chances that neither Almodóvar nor Van Sant directed it, and that the lead roles of Ennis del Mar and Jack Twist, the mutually smitten sheepherders, went to two apparently straight actors, Heath Ledger and Jake Gyllenhaal. 'I'd like to be wrong but I think many audiences subconsciously prefer their gay roles played by straight people,' says Andrew Haigh. 'It's more comfortable for them. It's sad but I doubt that *Brokeback Mountain* would have been as successful if it had cast two "out" gay men, or, for that matter, been made by an LGBT director.'

Stage versions of *Brokeback Mountain* have put the text at last into the hands of gay directors. A 2014 opera based on Proulx's story was directed by Ivo van Hove at the Teatro Real in Madrid. Jonathan Butterell then staged the story in London in 2023 as a play with music, starring Lucas Hedges and Mike Faist as, respectively, Ennis and Jack; Butterell and his composer, Tom Gillespie Sells, had previously partnered on the stage and film versions of the happy-clappy drag musical *Everybody's Talking About Jamie*.

Neither was in a rush to brand *Brokeback Mountain* as a gay story. The film version may have been discreet, but Ossana did at least describe it as the tale of 'two obviously gay people too afraid to actually commit to their love, so they run off and marry women and live a life unfulfilled out of fear'. Butterell wouldn't even go that far. 'I have no gay agenda,' he said. 'It's not my job to assert anyone's identity. Ennis could be a straight man going through a complex negotiation of his sexuality.' Sells agreed: 'Of course, it's about two men who fall in love and have sex. But there's also nuance. That's why we're reluctant to go, "Oh, it's a queer story."'

That approach is consistent with the playbook of marketing LGBTQ+ product in the mainstream, where the subject of sexuality has traditionally been downgraded to a Brokeback Molehill. You can see it on the poster for the AIDS drama *Longtime Companion* ('A motion picture for everyone') and in the trailer for the film of Harvey Fierstein's stage hit *Torch Song Trilogy* ('It's not just about *some* people – it's about everyone'). Promoting *The Fruit Machine*, in which all the main characters, including Robbie Coltrane as a drag queen named Annabelle, are either gay or bisexual, and even the villain is a personification of AIDS, the director Philip Saville said he 'never saw this as a gay film at all'. His lead actor, Tony Forsyth, who plays a rent boy and dances in his underwear in a gay club during the movie's sexiest scene, said: 'It's not a film about being gay or anything.'

'*Cruising* is not about homosexuality,' claimed William Friedkin. Then again, he had said the same thing a decade earlier about his movie version of Mart Crowley's play *The Boys in the Band*. Even Frank Ripploh, creator and star of the sexually explicit, groundbreaking *Taxi Zum Klo*, toed the party line. 'There's no such thing as a "gay film,"' he told *Gay News*. '*Taxi* ... is a love story which, by chance, is between two men.'

The (gay) fashion-designer-turned-film-maker Tom Ford sang from the same hymn sheet on the press tour for *A Single Man*, his

2008 adaptation of (gay) Christopher Isherwood's 1964 novel about a (gay) college professor. 'It's not a gay story,' he said.

From the box-office summit of Ang Lee's movie, it's a sheer drop to *Love, Simon* ($66m), the first gay teen picture from a major studio, which opens with a note of reassurance from its hero, played by Nick Robinson. 'I'm just like you,' he says chirpily, setting the tone for a relentlessly upbeat rom-com that makes *Beautiful Thing* look like *Bent*. Just behind *Love, Simon* are *Moonlight* ($65m), *Milk* and *Dallas Buyers Club* (around $55m a pop), each of these three augmented by Oscar approval and a comforting dose of tragedy.

The same can be said of *The Hours* ($108m), though that film is an anomaly in another way: it is the one lesbian-themed movie to have cracked the $40-million glass ceiling that abbreviated the ascent of *The Handmaiden* ($38m), *The Kids Are All Right* ($34m), *Tár* ($29m) and *Blue Is the Warmest Colour* ($19m). There may be a sex scene between Natalie Portman and Mila Kunis in *Black Swan*, which grossed $330 million, but it would be a stretch to describe the film itself as queer.

One surprise is that many of the titles that have dominated queer seasons, film societies and discourse alike have barely registered among the public. Céline Sciamma's *Portrait of a Lady on Fire* caught light impressively, its $10-million gross surely assisted (as *The Handmaiden*'s haul was) by the costume-drama trimmings. Films as highly regarded as *Weekend*, *Stranger by the Lake* and *Happy Together* took only a fraction over $1 million apiece, the glorious *Tangerine* (which was shot on three iPhones for $100,000) slightly less.

That *Call Me by Your Name* shows every sign of enduring in popular culture, even as it has faced a backlash among some queer viewers, is attributable to a number of factors – only one of which is that it isn't too gay to scare the horses. Chief among its attractions is the old-fashioned pin-up power represented by its star, Timothée Chalamet. He plays Elio, the seventeen-year-old musical prodigy who falls for his father's twenty-four-year-old research assistant, Oliver (Armie Hammer), while vacationing with his family in Lombardy in the early 1980s. Their friendship passes through stages sceptical, fraternal, flirtatious and hostile before arriving at the erotic.

Chalamet is the one dazzling element of the film; his performance combines petulance, balletic grace and a startling goofball naturalism. He was also part of the reason it was made. The rights to André Aciman's 2007 novel were snapped up by producer Peter Spears, whose husband, Brian Swardstrom, is Chalamet's manager. Spears had attained some notoriety for writing and directing the 2001 short *Ernest and Bertram*, which imagined romantic tensions between Bert and Ernie, the cohabiting male puppets from the beloved children's show *Sesame Street*. Those tensions were then filtered through a retread of the climactic scene of William Wyler's 1961 lesbian drama *The Children's Hour*, adapted from Lillian Hellman's 1934 play about two female teachers accused of having an affair – Bert in the Audrey Hepburn role, belatedly cottoning on to his friend's feelings for him, and Ernie as Shirley MacLaine, overcome with shame at the gossip which has forced his hand and exposed the truth. 'Maybe I love you *that* way,' he admits late one night, after Miss Piggy has squealed to the press, prompting a *Variety* cover splash on the puppets' relationship. 'The way they say I love you.'

Ernie ends up killing himself, just as MacLaine as Martha does in Wyler's film. The dialogue in *Ernest and Bertram* was repurposed from Hellman's play, which Wyler had previously filmed in 1936 as *These Three*, with the plot heterosexualised to conform to the strictures of the Hays Code. In the stage version of *The Children's Hour*,

Martha describes to her beloved Karen the experience of waking up to her own sexuality: 'There's something in you, and you don't do anything about it because you don't know it's there.' She admits: 'I do love you . . . I couldn't call it by a name, but maybe it's been there ever since I first knew you.'

Despite the echo of that line in its title, *Call Me by Your Name* is as far as it would be possible to get from the angst and agonising of *The Children's Hour* (or, indeed, *Ernest and Bertram*). There is no shame, no homophobia, not even a disapproving adult to be tiptoed around. The words 'gay' and 'homosexual' are conspicuous by their absence. Any jeopardy pertains only to the characters' inner emotional conflicts and trepidation. After decades of movies addressing coming out, living in torment in the closet or dealing with the hysteria of the straight world, its uncomplicated embrace of pleasure may have been some way short of rigorous, but it was a tonic all the same.

The film could have used a spoonful of medicine to help the sugar go down. Marcel Gisler's 1998 *Fögi Is a Bastard* embraces the more unsavoury aspects of young love in its story of a Swiss teenager's infatuation with a rising local rock star. It marches boldly into Fassbinder territory as the lad is demeaned and pimped out by his idol, who has a smack addiction to fund. Also released that year was Lukas Moodysson's *Fucking Åmål*, aka *Show Me Love*, which began life not as the scratchy, unsettled coming-out yarn it became but as the story of sisters living next door to a serial killer. Somehow that idea morphed into a tale of two teenage lesbians – a shy misfit coming to terms with her sexuality and a brash, popular schoolmate in denial – who are desperate to flee their Swedish backwater. The film only arrives at its triumphant screw-you climax via genuinely distressing material (bullying, ableism, self-harm).

Complaints about the frictionless tenor of Guadagnino's picture are not hard to find. 'I confess that since I saw the wretched *Call Me by Your Name*, I've tended to avoid contemporary gay films made for a popular audience,' says William E. Jones. The broadcaster Tom Sutcliffe questioned 'this absolute picture-perfect household with the picture-perfect mother, the picture-perfect academic dad, and they sit [outside] and have their breakfast – and that's perfect, too. I just became exasperated with it. I thought: "There must be *wasps* here."'

An absence of wasps at the height of summer *is* odd. More realistic in Europe in 1983 is the lack of any references to AIDS. It crops up fleetingly in Aciman's novel, which is narrated by the adult Elio as he looks back on his teenage affair. The film's screenwriter, James Ivory, made passing references to it in an early draft. 'It didn't matter to me that they were dropped,' he said. 'They didn't say or do anything terribly important.'

Among Ivory's numerous films with his late partner, the producer Ismail Merchant, is a measured 1987 screen version of E. M. Forster's gay love story *Maurice*, released at the height of the AIDS crisis and on the cusp of Section 28. 'Ismail wasn't as driven as Jim to make *Maurice*,' explains Stephen Soucy, director of the 2023 documentary *Merchant Ivory*. 'But Jim's dogged determination won the day. They'd just had this global blockbuster with *A Room with a View*, and he knew it could be now or never. People would pull aside Paul Bradley, the associate producer, and say: "Why are they doing *Maurice* when they could be making anything?" I give Jim so much credit for having the vision and tenacity to make sure the film got made.'

Merchant Ivory tend not to loom large in surveys of queer cinema, though they are a notable part of its ecosystem, and not only because of *Maurice*. Ron Peck, who made *Nighthawks*, was an assistant director on their adaptation of Henry James's *The Bostonians*. Andrew Haigh landed his first industry job as a poorly paid assistant in Merchant's Soho office in the late 1990s. In Haigh's 2011 break-through film *Weekend*, one character admits to freeze-framing the naked swimming scene in *A Room with a View* and masturbating over 'Rupert Graves's juddering cock'.

Producer and director may not have been publicly out about their lifelong relationship (the *Guardian*'s obituary of Merchant in 2005 concluded: 'He did not marry'), but the pair were open to those in their immediate vicinity; as early as their 1963 debut, *The Householder*, the crew referred to them as 'Jack and Jill'.

Ivory was hired in 2014 to adapt *Call Me by Your Name* by Spears and Swardstrom, who were also his neighbours in Claverack, New York. The original idea was for Ivory, who was then eighty-six, to co-direct with Guadagnino. 'And then I was dropped. I was never told why I had been dropped, by Luca or anybody else.' He wasn't the only person elbowed out. When Shia LaBeouf read for the part of Oliver opposite Chalamet, Ivory reported, 'Luca and I had been blown away. The reading by the two young actors had been sensational; they made a very convincing hot couple.' Without explanation, Guadagnino cast the sleeker, more antiseptic Hammer instead. (Both actors later underwent public falls from grace after allegations – and, in LaBeouf's case, legal action – relating to coercive and abusive behaviour towards women.)

When Ivory won the Oscar for Best Adapted Screenplay, Guadagnino was among those he thanked, though he never downplayed his rancour over the picture's compromised approach to sex and nudity. His screenplay specified that Elio and Oliver would be shown naked, and that Elio's bare foot would move rhythmically over Oliver's left shoulder as the older man fucked him. 'When people are wandering around before or after making love and they're decorously covered with sheets, it's always seemed phoney to me and I never liked doing that,' said Ivory. 'And I don't do it, as you know. In *Maurice*, the two guys have had sex and they get up and you certainly see everything there is to be seen. To me that's a more natural way of doing things than to hide them, or to do what Luca did, which is to pan the camera out of the window toward some trees.'

Guadagnino playfully dismissed Ivory's objections. 'Old age doesn't bring wisdom,' he said. 'That's one of the reasons why I love James Ivory, because he's not wise. He has the soul of a kid who always wants more. Maybe when you get more, you become spoiled or you have a tummy ache. But I was a bit disappointed that one of my heroes, the poet Ocean Vuong, criticised the panning because he thought it was betraying the nature of queer love. For me, it was more about a classical gesture of cinema. I wanted to be Sirkian. In a Sirk movie, lovers are left alone to love.'

When he came to adapt William S. Burroughs's *Queer* in 2024, he offered what felt like a droll rejoinder to complaints about the earlier film. *Queer* jumps from bed to window, *Call Me by Your Name*-style, in three separate sex scenes, only to cut straight back each time to images of escalating explicitness: a towel on the floor bearing a squiggle of semen; a blow job reaching the point of completion; and the actors Daniel Craig and Drew Starkey making the beast with two backs, or rather one.

Liz Purchell saw *Call Me by Your Name* on opening night. 'I was in the theatre with a row of older bears next to me,' she recalls. 'One of them fell asleep in the middle of the movie. I could sympathise. The film didn't feel real to me. It was too chaste, too precious. I wanted something edgier. Think of what Arthur Bressan would have done with that material.' Those of us who haven't seen Bressan's 1982 drama *Abuse*, about a thirty-one-year-old independent film-maker and the fourteen-year-old victim of parental abuse with whom he becomes sexually involved, can only imagine: the film is currently out of circulation and unlikely to re-emerge in a hurry.

The teenybopper popularity of *Call Me by Your Name*, which pre-empted streaming hits like *Sex Education* and *Heartstopper*, was made possible, as Purchell suggests, by its relative chasteness. If a film with LGBTQ+ subject matter is to find any purchase in the mainstream, explicit sex is out of the question. Even the transference of bodily fluids from one sexual partner to the other in *Call Me by Your Name* can only happen indirectly, via the vessel of the peach into which Elio ejaculates – and which Oliver then gobbles up.

The peach scene excuses Guadagnino from having to show or indicate oral sex. But it also serves a more legitimate purpose by concluding the film's pattern of surrogates, intermediaries and proxies. This motif is established initially when Elio receives a shoulder massage from Oliver while standing shirtless watching friends playing volleyball in the villa's gardens. Squirming free, he is dragged back by the older man, who then enlists a nearby teenage girl to continue the massage – the first in a series of gestures that involve puppetry of some description. The next occurs when Elio clocks Oliver's attraction to a local woman and tries to play matchmaker, much to Oliver's chagrin. When the two men eventually make up, it is through another act of puppeteering: Oliver extends the hand of friendship to Elio, though it isn't his own hand he proffers but one attached to the disembodied arm of a statue rescued from the sea. The film charts the dismantling of Elio's and Oliver's defences as they move beyond proxies and puppetry towards an ideal of intimacy.

There are enough evasions and ellipses in place, though, to ensure that audiences don't have to contemplate the granular detail of sex. No lubricant, poppers, not even saliva, nothing that might ease Elio's experience. There is no blood, no douching and no shit either – though it would be churlish to criticise Guadagnino for his discretion when so few films have dared to go there.

The queer gross-out comedy *Dicks: The Musical* riffs rather delightfully on that very absence, and the generally photogenic, wipe-clean, pain-free representation of gay sex in movies. Lying in bed together after their first strenuously acrobatic gay session, two formerly heterosexual bros talk over what went down.

'That was so hot,' says one.

'And easy,' replies his partner. 'Everything made sense and was comfortable.'

'Anal's easy.'

'Anal *is* easy.'

'It takes no practice to learn.'

'I didn't douche. Did you douche?'

'I didn't. No. I don't know what douching *is*.'

One exception is Ira Sachs's *Keep the Lights On*, where a passionate fuck suddenly gets messy. Sheets are stripped, and lust dissipates in the wake of the apologetic but matter-of-fact clean-up operation. In that case, shit hints at all the other crap that the film's deeply troubled couple (based on Sachs and his ex-boyfriend, the literary agent Bill Clegg, who was addicted to crack cocaine) must deal with during their miserable romance. *Keep the Lights On* is candid and penetrating, but drugs, misery and dirty linen don't translate into *Call Me by Your Name* money. (Sachs's film made $338,000.)

If the book I'm writing covered queer television as well as cinema, then it would be within my jurisdiction to mention the writer and actor Ryan O'Connell, who plays a gay man with cerebral palsy in his autobiographical Netflix comedy *Special*. The second series includes a moment which gets properly down-and-dirty. 'The shit-on-the-dick scene!' O'Connell exclaimed when I asked him about his character shaming his boyfriend for not having douched before anal sex. 'I kept trying to write that in season one. I was trying to fit a square peg into a round hole, as it were. I was trying to make shit-on-the-dick happen.

Sometimes when you have sex, it's on the menu, right? Whether you like it or not.'

It's a challenging scene, leaving audiences no choice but to actively disapprove of the protagonist's behaviour. 'He doesn't react with the same generosity of spirit that has been extended to him,' O'Connell said. 'I never wanted him to be this amazing virtuous figure. As marginalised people, we're allowed to exist within these very narrow slots, and I always like to challenge that. I set out to make the viewer feel annoyed at this gay guy with cerebral palsy. He doesn't have to be perfect so that you can feel good about yourself. He doesn't need to be your inspiration, honey. He can be a source of your ire and frustration.'

Having restricted myself to covering only films, however, it's frustrating to realise that I can't mention *Special* in my queer cinema book. I will need to go back over the preceding paragraphs and delete them from my final draft.

———————

At the precise moment that Elio and Oliver are making goo-goo eyes at one another in northern Italy in summer 1983, a film is on release in Europe that presents an altogether grimier but more ravenous version of a queer awakening. There is a poster for *Tootsie* in one of the town squares that Elio and Oliver wander through after dancing all night. But if these damp-eyed aesthetes could instead find a cinema in Lombardy that is showing Patrice Chéreau's *L'Homme blessé* (*The Wounded Man*), they might stumble in and have their over-educated minds blown.

Chéreau's feverish film, like Guadagnino's dreamy hit, focuses on a teenager, Henri (Jean-Hugues Anglade), discovering his sexuality through his infatuation with an older man, in this case the pimp Jean (Vittorio Mezzogiorno). Its mixture of conflicting tones, though, makes it incalculably queerer and more radical. Harsh realism, visual and verbal non sequiturs, disorientating temporal leaps or compressions, an apparently endless, fruitless series of pursuits – these are among the elements that render the film's events as confusing and mysteriously compelling for the audience as they are for its startled, shaggy-haired protagonist. Scanning the frame for hints and clues, the viewer is drawn into cruising the film just as the men on-screen are cruising one another.

Anglade, who later became a minor god in a million student bed-sits as one of the stars of *Betty Blue*, was twenty-seven when he played Henri, but easily passes for younger: scrawny, twitchy, occasionally surly, eyes constantly popping, mouth agape, he has the fragility of a featherless chick ejected from its nest too soon.

An agile and sensual actor, he is intensely physical, even whimsically Chaplin-esque in the early scenes – fidgeting outside a restaurant, he seems unsure how to operate his own hands – but as remorseless as a flick-knife by the film's conclusion. He is constantly craning his neck, gawping at his surroundings, his face swivelling around like a flower on the hunt for the sun.

It is the departure of Henri's sister for university in Frankfurt that is the catalyst for his awakening: the loss of one of the female components of the household seems to unlock some paralysed aspect in him, while in literal terms it is the trip to see her off at the train station that first plunges Henri into the vortex of his own unexpressed homosexuality. On the bustling concourse and among the crowded benches, everyone is on the prowl: clusters of lads in denim jackets call out to him, lone older men size him up. It is in the heat of their gaze that he starts to flourish. His desires are abundant without yet being legible to him; these strangers recognise what he is before he does.

Chief among them is Bosmans (Roland Bertin), a crumpled middle-aged doctor slumped in the station's waiting room wearing a camel-hair coat and an expression that could spoil any summer. He

70

reacts to Henri's presence as though he has set eyes on a wanted man. That's as good a description of Henri as any: the whole world wants him, paws him, pants after him, seems to be stripping him with its eyes. It is the attention of Bosmans, mirrored by the camera, that helps to nurture Henri, to bring him to fruition. This is no *Death in Venice*; Tadzio doesn't need Aschenbach – his beauty is insulated from the world, demanding nothing but awe – whereas Bosmans' gaze shapes the younger man, guides him towards who he is.

Henri wanders off, apparently disconcerted by the man's longing. Bosmans follows. As soon as one gets near to the other, though, the pursuer seems to change his mind and turn on his heel; they're like magnets repelling each other. Both men are simultaneously predatory and skittish. The film runs on this faulty, stuttering energy, this push–pull of conflicted lust. It is best embodied by Henri as he flings open the window at night in his mother's bedroom, exposing them both to the storm raging outside while reassuring her that he doesn't want to go out – only to then announce, 'I'm going out!'

In this fog of yearning and horniness, it is easy for the audience to lose its bearings. Not only do we not know where we are (night falls abruptly without warning, and a rainstorm leaves the streets dry), but we can barely determine what is happening. Desire has sent everyone doolally. The ceaseless electric buzzing at the train station comes to represent the sound of an urgent and festering carnality.

The nearest comparison now would be *Eyes Wide Shut*, another erotic odyssey styled as several hours of *coitus interruptus*. Stanley Kubrick's adaptation of Arthur Schnitzler's *Traumnovelle* wouldn't be released until 1999, but he was already mulling the project over by the late 1970s, when Chéreau was a good few years into hatching *L'Homme blessé*.

Since 1975, Chéreau had been toying with the idea of making a present-day version of *The Thief's Journal* – Jean Genet's autobiographical novel in which he luxuriates in his own criminality and squalor, prizing the lice in his clothes as the impoverished equivalent of a monarch's jewels. Chéreau wanted to portray 'the subproletariat of homosexuality' but discovered that Genet was 'too literary' to adapt, a problem Fassbinder would encounter on his visually delirious but dramatically sluggish 1982 swansong, *Querelle*. The book's sleaziness bled into Chéreau's film, though, as did 'the basic idea: an impossible love story between a young boy and an older guy who disappears all the time. It's the story of an apprenticeship'. Within a year, he had mapped out the characters of the wide-eyed novice Henri and the seething pimp Jean, with whom Henri becomes besotted, as well as a plot in which he could send them scurrying around like mice in a maze.

The young gay novelist Hervé Guibert, who admired Chéreau's stage work, longed to collaborate with him. Chéreau threw the kid a bone, hiring him to type and organise his notes, a job Guibert had already done for Michel Foucault. Eventually, they drifted into writing what would become *L'Homme blessé*. The title was the last thing to fall into place. It is borrowed from a Gustave Courbet painting, revised in 1854, ten years after its initial completion. The original version showed the central figure with a woman leaning on his shoulder. In the revision, the woman is gone and the figure is now injured; sleeping or unconscious, he slumps against a tree with a cutlass visible beside him. All that prevents the image from being engulfed by the gloom is his sallow face, a distant gleam of dusk or dawn, and his soiled white shirt kissed with a bloodstain. Guibert kept a postcard of the painting on his desk throughout the writing process, just as I will as I work on my book.

———

Anglade admitted that Henri scared him: 'he evolved in a very marginal world that was foreign to me . . . that I discovered little by little just like the character'. Gérard Depardieu was offered the part of Jean but turned it down, explaining that he might have accepted it if he and Chéreau 'had done some other film together first'. (Several earlier associations with Bertrand Blier must have equipped the actor to hurl himself into playing a burly gay burglar besotted with an unassuming heterosexual dork in Blier's 1986 comedy *Tenue de soirée*.) Chéreau snagged Depardieu in the end, in a manner of speaking: after casting Mezzogiorno, with his furtive skid-row handsomeness, he found the Italian actor's delivery to be too formal, too clipped. It was classroom French, whereas Jean needed to reek of the streets. Depardieu dubbed the entire role. 'When one invests someone else's body with one's voice, it's as strong as a sexual penetration,' the actor said. 'An act of love-making.'

L'Homme blessé premiered at Cannes in May 1983, where it was one of several Genet-adjacent titles in town. Giorgos Katakouzinos's *Angel*, directly inspired by Genet's writing, was there. Also in contention, and tangentially linked to Genet, was Nagisa Oshima's *Merry Christmas, Mr Lawrence*, set in a Japanese prisoner-of-war camp in Java, where the taboo attraction of the camp's commander for a pretty English prisoner becomes unmanageable and finally fatal. It was a masterstroke of Oshima to cast two members of the same exotic species in those pivotal roles: Ryuichi Sakamoto and David Bowie are both glow-in-the-dark gorgeous, and keenly aware of it, given to out-dazzling each other in queeny little pout-offs. More significantly, they are both pop performers, though Bowie had already acted widely and trained in mime under Lindsay Kemp. Sakamoto and Bowie are on the same frequency as one another, distinct from the rest of the cast. Whatever else is going on, they communicate in crackling pop-idol telepathy, just as they could transmit their charisma to audiences in the farthest reaches of the Hollywood Bowl.

The film's Genet connection came via Bowie, whose 1973 song 'The Jean Genie' riffed on the writer's name. He and Genet met briefly when Bowie let it be known that he wanted to star in a proposed screen version of *Our Lady of the Flowers* as Divine, the trans female protagonist – a role previously played by Lindsay Kemp on stage in his orgiastic adaptation, *Flowers*. (The name was given by John Waters to his neighbour and eventual muse, Harris Glenn Milstead, who was known as Divine from their first film together, the 1967 short *Roman Candles*, to their last, *Hairspray*, in 1988.) Bowie and Genet arranged a restaurant rendezvous in London, but when the Frenchman's party arrived, nobody could find the singer among the diners. It was Genet himself who spotted a woman sitting alone and identified the figure correctly as Bowie in drag.

The subsequent prevalence of AIDS made *L'Homme blessé* feel like a final lunge at depicting promiscuity before the drawbridge was raised. 'One year later I learned of the existence of the disease, when I went to present the film in San Francisco in '84,' said Chéreau. 'So one year later I could no longer make this film.' Anglade said the timing 'made it possible to enter this universe without any moral censorship'.

In the press notes that accompanied the film at Cannes, Chéreau played down its queerness, claiming instead that it was about 'the passion that an adolescent feels for another man. Yet this is not a film about homosexuality. It is the story of passion and its apprenticeship.' But the picture became the catalyst for his own public coming-out during press interviews at the festival: 'I was drunk, and after the tenth or twelfth question I finally said, "Yes, I am [gay]."'

The picture was out of step, and Chéreau knew it. 'The only reference which encouraged me in thinking that this movie isn't pure madness is Fassbinder,' he said. Perhaps that's why he cast Armin Mueller-Stahl, fresh from Fassbinder's *Lola* and *Veronika Voss*, as

Henri's father. But though the milieu recalls *Fox and His Friends*, Chéreau's command of the frame is unique: whereas Fassbinder contrives intentionally stilted tableaux, turning his actors into butterflies pinned under glass, Chéreau situates Henri in a tactile reality that just happens to be accented with surreal touches, irrational behaviour and heightened set pieces hinging on carnal pursuit. In the film's choreography of compulsion, Henri's repeated visits to the same dismal locations (train station, family home, fairground, dancehall) suggest a killer returning to the scenes of his crimes.

Fassbinder looms over the film. Henri tries to catch a train to Frankfurt – where *In a Year of 13 Moons* was shot – but the handful of coins that he dumps on the counter aren't enough to get him there; the land of Fassbinder remains beyond his grasp. *L'Homme blessé* was shot in the summer of 1982 – the summer of Fassbinder's death, that is. Chéreau had recently spent time on the chaotic set of *Querelle* and can be spotted in that film's behind-the-scenes documentary, *The Wizard of Babylon*, which includes interviews with Fassbinder recorded just hours before his death. Some of the German's belligerence seemed to spill over into Chéreau on his own press tour. He declared himself weary of films presenting an 'idyllic' picture of gay life, bizarrely picking on *A Very Natural Thing*, released nearly a decade earlier in 1974. 'I'm not sure it's beautiful to be homosexual,' Chéreau told the *Bay Area Reporter*. 'I think it's fantastic, but I'm not sure . . . I don't think it's terrible what happens to [Henri]. It's better than what would have happened if he had stayed with his family.'

In the clamour for positive images – too often a euphemism for the anodyne and homogenous – *L'Homme blessé* was never likely to find many defenders, and it may still be going against the grain today. But it's an extraordinary film: in its mix of febrile desire, saturnine intensity and scorched lyricism, it honours Genet while reproducing on-screen a convincing mood of queer adolescence in freefall. Henri is driven by an appetite he can neither contain nor comprehend, taking a bite out of the world with a mouthful of milk teeth.

Chéreau was told by journalists that his film's depiction of homosexuality made it synonymous with the pitiful and criminal. Genet would have approved, but the director protested. 'In all love stories between men and women, where things go badly and one kills the other, no one says it gives a degrading image of heterosexual love,' he said. '*L'Homme blessé* doesn't pose the question of whether homosexuality is better or worse, leading to happiness or misery. Things can turn out badly, that's all.'

———————

'Mainstream films about homosexuals are not for homosexuals,' wrote Vito Russo. 'They address themselves exclusively to the majority.' But even films not positioned for wide or sceptical audiences still face their own pressures. As the gay former HBO executive Carolyn Strauss, who was instrumental in bringing Alan Ball's *Six Feet Under* to the screen, puts it: 'When you're dealing with a sliver, there's an unfair weight on that sliver to be the best.' That partly explains the expectations heaped on *Moonlight*, directed by Barry Jenkins, who adapted the film from Tarell Alvin McCraney's unproduced play *In Moonlight Black Boys Look Blue*. In a culture hardly drowning in representations of Black queerness, it was incumbent on *Moonlight* to compensate for a historic shortfall. That it couldn't is no surprise.

McCraney's autobiographical triptych covers three stages in the life of one African American male, Chiron, growing up gay among the bullies and junkies of a seamy, sun-baked Miami. As a helpless child (Alex R. Hibbert) with a crack-addicted mother (Naomie Harris), he finds an unlikely mentor in the shape of a neighbourhood dealer, Juan (Mahershala Ali). As a guarded teenager (Ashton Sanders), he becomes besotted with a classmate, with whom he is fleetingly intimate on a beach at night. And as a scowling adult (Trevante Rhodes) with a cobblestoned torso and grills on his teeth, he crosses paths again with his teenage crush.

'At some point, you gotta decide for yourself who you wanna be,' Juan tells the young Chiron. People keep posing variations on that question to one another. Meeting his old flame as an adult, he is asked bluntly: 'Who is you, man?' The question resonates throughout the film. 'Am I a faggot?' the younger Chiron asks Juan. 'You could be gay,' comes the reply, 'but you can't let nobody call you a faggot.'

Moonlight was greeted initially with acclaim. It had on its side a hushed solemnity, a tender if chaste sensuality and a respectable cinematic heritage. The influence of Pasolini, as well as Terence Davies's autobiographical trilogy (*Children, Madonna and Child, Death and Transfiguration*), was stamped across Jenkins's visual style, especially his use of close-ups as portraiture. The script's religious allusions also cleaved to the tradition of Pasolini and Davies. The film includes a swimming lesson that is also a baptism, a reunion toasted with plastic beakers of red wine (the blood of Christ) and a Judas kiss followed by a Judas hand job.

Since the film's Best Picture Oscar win in 2018, when it beat the frontrunner, *La La Land*, there has been a partial and unflattering reappraisal. Official approbation, especially at a time when the Academy Awards were scarred by the #OscarsSoWhite debacle, seemed to make viewers suspicious of the film. No wonder the Academy voters championed *Moonlight*, the logic seemed to be, when it was made so palatable for them. In 1987, Russo had railed against 'an infantile leftist viewpoint [which has] perpetuated a loser mentality . . . This viewpoint says, if it succeeds in reaching a large general public, it can't be any good. Let's all be hippies together and keep ourselves pure for the true struggle. Consequently, radical, revolutionary thought is shared among the same few people year after year.' Engaging a wide audience, though, can mean making a bonfire of specificity.

In Danny Lee Wynter's play *Black Superhero*, which premiered at the Royal Court in London in 2023, one character accuses the makers of *Moonlight* (though the film itself is unnamed) of omitting 'all the joy' and most of the sex from Black queer life:

> They ignore the very essence of what it is to be alive and repackage my culture and sell it to me as some dirge underscored by an oboe? The most valiant drug dealer in the history of cinema? Of course whites love it, it's a neoliberal's wet dream. A lacklustre hand job on a beach? Please. How can ya make a gay film wid *no* gay sex? . . . Not showin gay sex gives a big free pass to all the squeamish straights who reject that part of our lives. A story about gay black male desire? Like, is that *all* the gay sex they can have? Are you seriously tellin me he wouldn't have fucked that guy a million ways till Sunday at the end? It was implausible. It was post-queer. I've seen versions of this story my whole life, the black victim overwhelmed by the system. Even *The Color Purple* had a few laughs, for fuck's sake! Queers ARE funny! . . . WE ARE! Society had no place for us, we had to be . . .

In defence of Juan, 'the most valiant drug dealer in cinema history', who explains to Chiron that 'faggot is a word used to make gay people feel bad', it should be noted that he is modelled on a cherished figure from McCraney's own childhood – with all the understandable idolatry that might entail. 'My mother was dating him from when I was very young,' McCraney said. 'He was always kind and generous to me. He hugged me at a time when other people were making me feel shame. I was being admonished a lot by my mother and my biological father for being effeminate. When you're growing up gay or queer you mark very clearly those times when your behaviour got you into trouble. I remember I had touched another boy out of curiosity – I certainly wasn't feeling sexual at that age – and my father told me: "If you ever do that again, I'll kill you." And yet here was this drug dealer who had no qualms with me in that way.'

The film still has its champions, such as Grace Barber-Plentie, who argues that Jenkins 'does the impossible by making a story that's so specific . . . feel universal and reach beyond an arthouse audience all the way to the Oscars, despite using more experimental film-making techniques'.

It is the picture's elision of physical desire, though, which continues to rankle for Campbell X, the writer and director of the probing, prickly 2012 comedy-drama *Stud Life*. '*Moonlight* wasn't Black queer love,' he insists over video call. He is sporting a lumberjack shirt, horn-rimmed glasses and a tufty beard; the chunky noise-cancelling headphones worn over his shaved head lend him the authoritative look of an airline pilot. 'It was a weird kind of closetry thing. The hand job on the beach? Nah. I was, like, "Miss me with that, straight man!" I knew that film was made by a straight cis man. I *knew* it. I thought, "This ain't like no gay man I know." It's very beautiful, I'm not doing it down. But straight audiences are like, "This is so radical!" And us are like: "What's radical 'bout that?" And they're *Black* as well. Black people are raw! Queer people are raw! I didn't see any rawness in that film. Where's the rawness of desire? This is a *hot* man, and I don't believe that when you finally meet that one, you're just gonna do a little *tingy-ting*.'

Then he turns reflective. 'People say we see a lot about gay men. Do we *really*? We get an avatar of gay men's representation but do we see them? 'Cos I think it's still threatening. *Call Me by Your Name*, *Brokeback Mountain*, *Moonlight* – it's a safe, marketable way of dealing with us. That has a detrimental effect because those of us who think, "Fuck, I'm not like that," start to feel shame about who we are. A lot of the journey towards ourselves is about shame. On top of that, we are made to feel ashamed of desire. Why can't we savour it?'

5

STUD LIFE

Campbell X's debut film shows every sign initially of being a love story between JJ (T'Nia Miller), a masc lesbian photographer, and Elle (Robyn Kerr), a femme sex worker. Where it begins, though, and where its heart lies, is with JJ and her gay best friend, Seb (Kyle Treslove). The first sound heard on-screen is an alarm going off. JJ sits up in bed and starts snapping away, only to be appalled that Seb, snoozing next to her, has made a tent out of the duvet with his morning wood.

Unexpectedly, perhaps, for a film sold as a lesbian romance, dicks play a big part in *Stud Life* – or, in the case of the outsized dildos that JJ brandishes during her straight-to-camera vlogs, a gargantuan part. Campbell's movie is part of a mini-wave of queer cinema from the start of the twenty-first century which showed how the Sapphic and the phallic overlap. The domesticated couple played by Annette Bening and Julianne Moore in *The Kids Are All Right* get their kicks watching gay male porn. At the start of *Appropriate Behaviour*, Shirin (Desiree Akhavan) heralds the end of a lesbian relationship by throwing out the strap-on she bought for her ex, before retrieving it from the rubbish. And the teenage Alike (Adepero Oduye) in *Pariah* is given her first strap-on by a more experienced queer friend. 'They didn't have brown?' she says, aghast at the mismatched colour.

In *The Fluffer*, made around a decade before those titles, Silver (Adina Porter) dismisses lesbian porn as ridiculous – 'All those long red nails,' she sneers – and prefers to watch dicks. 'I found that out from my lesbian friends,' says the film's writer and co-director, Wash

Westmoreland. 'Whenever I'd finish making a porn film, we'd have a little viewing party at our house. Many of my lesbian friends would come over and watch. This seemed to be an interesting intersection in the LGBTQ+ Venn diagram, so I wanted to include that.'

Putting an erection, even a concealed one, in the opening scene of *Stud Life* also serves to warn viewers that this is a departure from *Go Fish*, the 1994 New Queer Cinema comedy that established a template for lesbian cinema for at least the next decade. 'Nah, this ain't *Go Fish*,' Campbell agrees. 'This is *Go Cock*. This is *Go, Cock, Go*. Look, I used to share beds with my gay men friends and that's what would happen. Seb doesn't desire JJ but they're close. It's a closeness I found with gay men but which I never saw represented in anything, and still don't. Straight women are always the ones shown with gay men – shopping together, the whole *Sex and the City* thing. But you don't see the social relationships between queer people. I didn't write *Stud Life* as a "lesbian film". It was written as a story of friendship between a gay man and a stud.'

Any film that begins with an alarm going off must fancy itself as a wake-up call. 'You got it,' says Campbell. 'It's a wake-up call to say: these are people carving out their own lives within a structure that has not made space for them. Seb is white and Jewish; JJ is Black and Caribbean. London is rich with people who live on the edges like they do, but they've formed a bond. People tend to look at JJ and Elle as the focus of *Stud Life* – they're on the poster – but that was about marketing, capitalism, categorising. It's actually about JJ and Seb.'

The gay/stud dynamic shown in *Stud Life* is one Campbell knows intimately, having come out around gay men in the 1990s. 'Gay men have always been my fortress. I didn't find lesbians interesting until I met radical dykes. I identified with the clarity and power of gay men's desire and friendship: they educated me, showed me films I'd never seen. Some of them were much older, some my peers, which is important. I mixed with people twenty or thirty years older than me when I was in my twenties. They told me who went before, so I had an idea of lineage.'

He also became an expert reader of body language. 'I think as queers we had to. Maybe that skill is being lost now with apps because we don't have to walk the streets and check out bodies in the way we did before. Back then, we were very aware of surroundings and looks and how somebody holds a stare. Also as younger queers we had to check people's body language to know about safety – is this person safe to come out to? It's how we learned.'

There is an unusual tension in the film between the confident intimacy of JJ's vlogs and the often guarded or fearful nature of her interactions with Elle. 'That's the paradox of studness in a way,' Campbell explains. 'There's a fear of vulnerability that might bring out the woman, the female, the feminine side. It's so complicated in terms of gender. Also, if you are a feminine performer, as T'Nia is, the question is how to overcome the fear of masculinity, which is perceived as ugly in women and unmarketable in actresses. That's why I had to work very hard with her to embody the part of JJ. To inhabit the stud role – which did *not* bring her approval as she walked the streets – she had to get that into her body in some way, leaning into that particular kind of masculinity, which is scary. T'Nia said it made her think of her son, and what he goes through as a young Black man. Because that's what she was read as when she was out on the streets: a young Black man.'

It still happens to Campbell today. 'I get a lot of homophobic abuse on the street. It's because I refuse to accept the cultural norms of cis-het manhood. I wear certain clothes, behave a certain way that's perceived as "gay". But at the same time, when I'm on the Tube and there are white gay men around, they look at me with fear because they see a Black man who they think might beat them up. Those are two sides of the coin: who are you recognised by, and what are you recognised for? So they're recognising my manhood but they are ascribing certain qualities to it that don't apply.'

No wonder photography is a central component of the plot. JJ earns her living as a wedding snapper, not unlike the protagonist of *The Watermelon Woman*, who supplements her video-store job in a similar fashion. This nudges the audience to consider who is behind the camera, whose point of view we are seeing, where the power usually lies – and where it is now, when a gender non-conforming director is wielding the lens.

Scattered among the cast as walk-on parts or background per-formers are a collection of queer Black British artists: the poets Dean Atta and Jay Bernard, the film-maker Topher Campbell, the musi-cian David McAlmont. 'It's a way of saying: we are here. We show up for each other. Putting that on film is a statement of pride.' Among the film's producers is Lulu Belliveau, one of the former editors of the sex-positive lesbian magazine *Quim*; JJ and Seb preface a night on the town by chopping out lines of coke on the cover of one of its back issues. 'It's all part of the archive. I don't want us to forget. People are already forgetting figures from the 1980s: Frankie Goes to Hollywood, the Communards. These people were out. They weren't hiding in the closet.'

Stud Life took two years to make from start to first screening. 'Bam! Done! I didn't have to go through any gatekeepers because the gatekeepers had said: "Fuck off." I sent the script to Film London, which was then the BFI place you went to for London funding, and they rejected it because they couldn't see an audience for the film.' Did he know they were wrong? 'Yeah,' he smiles. 'They were right in one way, though, because they hadn't seen anything like that before. Usually they ask you to compare it to something but it's always got to relate back to the gatekeeper, who wants to somehow see themselves or somebody they know in the product. *Stud Life* represents a specific queerness that even some queer people don't have access to.'

There has been far-reaching approval for *Stud Life* – Jenni Olson and Caden Mark Gardner selected it as part of their 2023 Criterion Channel series 'Masc', alongside other films about butch dyke, AFAB (assigned female at birth) and gender non-conforming characters, including *By Hook or By Crook*. 'These are films made for us and by us, and the point is not to cross over,' said Olson. 'Queer audiences see these films and they're like, "Cool, here we are. Don't explain anything to us; just be you."'

Yet there has not been a pronounced or widespread *Stud Life* effect in British cinema, and it has taken twelve years for Campbell to make his follow-up, *Low Rider*, a road-trip movie about a Black queer femme Londoner of mixed parentage searching for her absent father through the Western Cape in South Africa with a local Black trans man. 'It's because of the cis-normative patriarchy,' Campbell says. 'In terms of gender non-conforming people, that's the biggest head-fuck because they aren't slotted into any binary. When you're gender non-conforming, people are like: "What *are* you? Why can't you just make my life easier?"' He gives a little growl to mimic their irritation. 'I don't see butch actors. I see trans actors, non-binary actors, but I'm not hearing about butch actors and femme actors. Bull-daggers and butches. Effeminate gay men – where are they? If we're talking only about trans and non-binary, then how is that helping actors who aren't that? They may be cis but resolutely non-gender-conforming. This is the challenge for us as creators when it comes to casting and storytelling: who am I – who are we – leaving out of the story? Because there's always someone.'

When I interviewed Todd Haynes in 2015, he argued that 'the easier language for legislative agendas is this "born that way", biologically determined idea of sexual orientation, and that's what also fits more neatly into trans issues as well, where there's a sort of essential idea of gender, an essential idea of sexual desire – that we just have to find and embrace and then marry and have kids and blah-blah-blah, whatever. And that isn't queer to me. What interested me so much about the glam era in the early 1970s was that whole vernacular of radical instability around identity and sexual identity. It was fluid. Androgyny was the model. That is unnerving to straights and gays alike, and I think it's easy for the straight world to accept the gay world when everybody is in their solid essential identities. "You just stay over there and I love you for your innate difference to me that will never change." But I think sexuality, just the stuff of being human, is not clean and tidy, and there's this fear of the word "choice", which is something that conservatives use or that the Left use against conservatives – that we've chosen the lifestyle. The Left wanna say, or gay communities wanna say: "No, there was no choice in the matter."'

The image *Stud Life* presents is one of magnificent flux: no one is fixed in their identity; everything is fluid and liberated. 'We all change,' Campbell says. 'We change our minds back and forth, and that's allowed.' The array of queerness, too, is diverse. Elle refers to 'the lesbian buffet', but the film represents more of a queer food court. 'I used to go to parties with queers, trans people and sex workers,' Campbell recalls. 'I never felt any separatism or separation. That's why I made Elle a sex worker in the film – because *we* are part of that world. Queers are sex workers and vice versa. That always gets forgotten in the march to respectability and homo-normativity – a wife and two children, a husband and two children, all that.'

Then he stops, leans closer to the screen and squints at me.

'Oh my God. Have you got a husband and children? You have, don't you? You *have*!'

Suddenly I realise how a counterfeit note must feel when it is held up to the light.

'Sort of,' I tell him.

'See? *You* are the problem!' He shakes his head in mock dismay. 'Well, I hope you guys are still cruising on Hampstead Heath.'

I'm eager not to seem like a square or a stiff in front of Campbell; I don't want to be the wrong *sort* of gay. It used to be that we had to channel our energy into pretending to be straight. Now there is pressure to shrug off the disguise we've spent our whole lives perfecting, or else risk looking like the clot who showed up at the party not knowing it was fancy-dress. You've married your boyfriend but are you sleeping around? Seeing other people? Are you truly *queer*?

'We're keeping it lively,' I reply at last, leaving the details vague but wearing what I hope is a knowing, even devilish, expression. 'Don't you worry about that.'

He nods approvingly. 'That's the thing,' he says. 'We've participated in the structure but we've found a way to bring queerness into it, haven't we? A lot of my friends who are married still have open lives, and I think that's beautiful. How can we bring that in so people don't feel locked down into the binary of "this is what marriage looks like"? Something's missing. We're being straitjacketed.'

Stud Life itself is anything but. 'The challenge of that film is it's got lesbians in it, bisexuals, queer and trans people, whereas the marketing was like, "Two lesbians. The end." But you know what? The world has caught up with *Stud Life*. Now we're all talking about polyamory and trans people, aren't we? Gender non-conformity, sex work, bam-bam-bam. In 2012, that wasn't the dominant conversation, even among queers.'

Not that he thinks the quality of representation is anything to write home about. 'What we see are blanched-out, blanded-out versions of ourselves. And then people are faced with the reality, and they become hostile to that. I don't recognise us. I'm seeing candy-coloured versions which are safe. I don't see our Ugly, our Banal, our Flawed. If we don't show our best versions, we are punished. Straight people can be anything on film, but we always have to be respectable, high-value citizens or else we're not allowed to exist. There's even a ridiculous discourse now: No Kink in Pride. It's like, *what* are you talking about? Who do you think rioted and fought for us to live our best lives all those years ago?'

6

THE WATERMELON WOMAN

Two years before making *Stud Life*, Campbell mucked in on *The Owls*. The title, an acronym for Older Wiser Lesbians, refers to a group of friends played by, among others, the film's director Cheryl Dunye and the *Go Fish* duo of Guinevere Turner and V. S. Brodie. They dispose of the body of a younger lesbian after she is killed by one of their group at a party. The violence emerges from a generational schism seldom represented on-screen: the Gen-Z arrogance, either real or imagined, which takes for granted freedoms fought for by activist boomers and Gen-Xers, and the resentment of those older queers towards these apparently oblivious upstarts.

Hooters!, a documentary about the ramshackle production of *The Owls*, shows the film's screenwriter, Sarah Schulman, explaining to a sceptical Turner the motivations behind the murder in her script. 'Some girl has power in some job where she can be out, where no one of my age and my kind ever could be,' says Schulman. 'And then I ask her for help and she treats me like shit – and I wanna *kill* her.'

As with all Dunye's work, *The Owls* has an unstable structure and an unresolved surface. The film is punctuated with talking-head interviews with its cast, some in character, others not. During the end credits, the interview format extends to its crew, including Campbell and another up-and-coming director, Rhys Ernst (who went on to make *Adam*, the 2019 film about a cis teenager who is mistaken for a trans man, then keeps up the facade). This sense of the provisional is what affords Dunye's movies their distinctive air of flux. It is as though they are being made even as we watch them, the print wet and prone to imperfections; the approach undermines the certainty that this is the definitive truth. The 'Dunye-mentary' technique of mixing fiction and mediated reality has been present in her work from early-1990s shorts such as *Janine* and *She Don't Fade*, which acknowledge the artifice of their own conception, to *The Watermelon Woman*, which is simultaneously a mockumentary, a film about its own making and a search for a figure who doesn't exist.

In that 1996 debut, Dunye plays Cheryl, a Philadelphia video store clerk and budding auteur. Her first straight-to-camera address echoes another female-directed pseudo-documentary about Black queer life, Shirley Clarke's *Portrait of Jason*, which also opens with its subject introducing himself several times using different names. In both instances, the audience is alerted to the artificiality of performance. 'I'm a . . . film-maker,' Cheryl says tentatively, sitting in front of the camera moments after she has strolled into the frame. Then she corrects herself: 'No, I'm not really a film-maker.' *The Watermelon Woman* charts her journey from this wobbly beginning to the more authoritative stance at the end of the picture, where she can look directly into the lens and assert herself: 'I am a Black lesbian film-maker,' she says, finally.

The centrality of the camera as a character is only to be expected from someone whose father worked for Polaroid, and who grew up with cutting-edge technology as part of her domestic life. As a child, Dunye, who spent her first few years in Liberia before the family decamped to Philadelphia, became fascinated by the gadgets of her father's trade. 'Little Cheryl would put the camera on the tripod, then stand in the photo and push the button on the lead, all without a timer,' she tells me. 'It was amazing. My father let me do it again and again. Everything was documented: there was this tangible signifier of our lives being lived.'

Cheryl, her character in *The Watermelon Woman*, has the same objective: making tangible her life and the lives of her forebears and those in her community. She is hunting for evidence of an African American actor – Fae Richards, known as 'the Watermelon Woman' – who appeared in 'mammy' roles dating back to early talkies. Cheryl discovers her in tapes borrowed from the video store where she works. Her curiosity piqued, she turns her search into a documentary – the one which forms part of the film we are watching – about the hunt for this embodiment of Black lesbian history.

Scenes from Cheryl's daily life, in which she is falling in love with a white customer, Diana (Guinevere Turner), and being ribbed for that attraction by her militant best friend, Tamara (Valarie Walker), are interspersed with footage from the documentary project as she begins piecing it together. The cultural critic Camille Paglia sends herself up during one interview, passionately defending the symbol of the watermelon from its racist associations. There is a cameo from Schulman as the worrywart head of the Centre for Lesbian Information Technology, or CLIT.

What dawns gradually on the viewer, and is confirmed in the end credits, is that the Watermelon Woman herself has been invented by Dunye for the purposes of the film. The apparently archival footage and snapshots are fabricated; the supposed romance between Richards and her Dorothy Arzner-esque white director is inspired by a rumour about Hattie McDaniel and Marlene Dietrich that Dunye found in Kenneth Anger's scurrilous gossip bible *Hollywood Babylon*. The figure of the Watermelon Woman symbolises all the queers of colour who have been devalued, overlooked or wiped from the records. The final title card makes plain the pantomime: 'Sometimes you have to create your own history. *The Watermelon Woman* is fiction.'

The film's revelation of its artifice mirrors the process of creating a queer identity, especially for people of colour, in a world that provides few precedents. 'I was looking for images of myself in film history and there was nothing there,' says Dunye. 'I looked in *The Celluloid Closet*: nothing. Hollywood has never embraced varied lives. They're not written about or documented. There might be biographies. Or you'll get something like *Carol*. But are there queers of colour? It's 2024 and there's *Rustin*, but the gate-keeping systems in commercial Hollywood can't allow more than one story to be in the spotlight at a time.'

What Dunye found – or didn't find – in film history contrasted with the highly visible queer milieu in Philadelphia of which she was a part. 'It was a lively scene. I was involved in being a DJ, a club host, running parties in lofts that I lived in. It was bumpin'!' As she built up her audience and refined her style through a string of video shorts, several factors enriched her ambitions. One was getting to spend time on the set of Marlon Riggs's final film, *Black Is . . . Black Ain't*, through her friendship with the poet Essex Hemphill. 'Marlon was filming a lot of stuff around then, knowing he wasn't long for this world, and that turned into the last couple of pieces he made. Essex took me to the set, and I got to be around these powerful Black gay folks who were making sure they were known and shown. That was something I took to heart in my own films.'

Her contact with Riggs was minimal. 'He was like, "Nice to meet you. Stand over there." He was busy, you know? But you were meeting an icon, someone who was doing major work in the same space you're in. He was working for what he believed in, same as Michelle Parkerson or Barbara Hammer. And he wasn't going to be around for much longer – he was working for his life.'

Seeing Riggs in action helped light the way for Dunye. 'I mushroomed out by realising there was support you could get. Marlon got grants. "Hold on, a grant? What's a *grant*?" Lots of lightbulbs went on for me.' The issue of grants for queer work was already an inflammatory one. Performance artists such as Karen Finley were having their NEA (National Endowment of the Arts) scholarships publicly attacked and overturned, leading to protracted legal battles. Riggs was pilloried for the use of grant money in making his unblinking masterpiece *Tongues Untied*; Todd Haynes was targeted by Republicans over NEA funds that helped pay for the Genet-influenced *Poison*, described by a spokesperson for the Christian Life Commission of the Southern Baptist Convention as 'perverse' and 'denigrating'.

It seems laughable that a film as frisky as *The Watermelon Woman* should be drawn into the melee. And yet it really was denounced on the floor of Congress for putting its $31,500 grant from the NEA towards a supposed gay agenda. The sex scene between Dunye and Turner might have gone unnoticed outside the queer circuit had it not been described by the journalist Jeannine DeLombard as 'the hottest dyke sex scene on celluloid', a claim quoted the following month in a *Washington Times* article querying the NEA's use of funds. The controversy never became a firestorm like the ones faced by Riggs and Haynes, or, for that matter, any number of court-vs-queer cases centring on contentious works by the likes of Pasolini, Genet, Anger and Chantal Akerman. And the proposed cut to the NEA's budget in the wake of *The Watermelon Woman* mercifully never made it to the Senate.

Looked at now, that sex scene is part of an important lineage – from Anger, Akerman and Hammer to Frank Ripploh (*Taxi Zum Klo*), Bruce LaBruce (*No Skin off My Ass*), Jacques Nolot (*Before I Forget*), Desiree Akhavan (*Appropriate Behaviour*), Xavier Dolan (*I Killed My Mother*), Isabel Sandoval (*Lingua Franca*) and Jessica Dunn Rovinelli (*So Pretty*) – of queer film-makers unveiling their own bodies on-screen in an act of self-revelation and self-possession.

'It's about us being able to see ourselves,' says Dunye. 'On a personal level, it was about me getting over myself. My first job as a young punk anarchist in Philly in the early 1980s was at the Pennsylvania

Academy of Fine Art, where you could be an artist's model for $10 or $15 an hour, when minimum wage was $3. As a Black queer lesbian nerd with glasses who wasn't happy about the way I looked, here was an opportunity for me to take off my glasses and just stand there as myself. You can see in *She Don't Fade* that I'm still uncomfortable with my body. But I wanted to deconstruct the making of a sex scene. It's fun, and funny, that certain love narratives require that to happen. All the lesbian movies that I saw before I was a film-maker included those seminal sex scenes.' She names two directed in the early 1980s by straight white men: Robert Towne's *Personal Best* and John Sayles's *Lianna*. 'I knew I had to do my own.'

Though the inspiration came from addressing a historical absence, Dunye's domestic concerns began bleeding into the script. '*The Watermelon Woman* was my own personal therapy about the very deep and powerful relationship I was in with a white academic,' she says. 'That spilled out and became fodder for some of the scenes. I realised from watching Godard that there was a way to play with this line between the myth you're making as cinema and the myth of the self. There can be power in that.'

Her presiding playfulness accommodates references within the film to *Go Fish*, even as that movie's real-life stars, Turner and Brodie, are present as fictional characters, making porous the barrier between internal and external realities. She also gives pride of place in one scene to a poster advertising her friend and contemporary Isaac Julien's S&M-accented short *The Attendant*. Julien has named *The Watermelon Woman*, along with *Tongues Untied*, *Paris Is Burning* and his own work on the lyrical drama-documentaries *Looking for Langston* and *Frantz Fanon: Black Skin, White Mask*, as part of that era's 'multi-vocal queer aesthetic'. Time has created another hat-tip, albeit one that Dunye could never have foreseen: Cheryl recommends to a customer Brian De Palma's horror gem *Carrie*, which would be remade seventeen years later, in 2013, by Kimberly Peirce, the *Boys Don't Cry* director who assisted with the archival material in *The Watermelon Woman*.

Dunye has moved in recent years into episodic television (*Bridgerton*, *Lovecraft Country*), but the collage-like Dunye-mentary style persists in her latter-day films such as *Black Is Blue*, a short about a trans man confronted by his past. The technique comes in handy when she needs to cut away from material that is either missing ('*The Owls* was a sixty-page script and only half of it was shot,' says Schulman) or not up to snuff, as in the case of her 2012 lesbian porn comedy *Mommy Is Coming*.

Schulman explains that her original script for *Mommy Is Coming* 'was a slapstick comedy with slamming doors and mistaken identities: a real film, but with seven classic porn scenes'. Then Dunye arrived in Berlin to shoot the film. 'She called me and said: "Schulman. Bad news. Germans aren't funny." The actors were having trouble with my New York Jewish deadpan humour. They couldn't land it. She had all these great sex scenes and then she had to create filler to link them because we didn't have a film.'

The title alludes to *My Father Is Coming*, Monika Treut's blasé 1991 comedy about a struggling lesbian actor in New York who pretends she is straight and successful when her father visits from Germany. 'I had history with *My Father Is Coming*,' says Schulman. 'Monika hired me to write it but she hated what I came up with. She only kept one thing: a visual joke where the girl is drinking coffee, and somebody puts a quarter in her cup because they think she's begging. Everything else she hated. So the title is my little response to that.' It also connects to the genesis of the project: she and Dunye were at the Berlinale with *The Owls* when they were approached by Jürgen Brüning, Bruce LaBruce's producer, about making a queer porn film. 'We asked ourselves, "What is the last lesbian taboo?" And the answer is: mommy.

Then there was this weird con-artist girl who Cheryl and I were both having affairs with in Berlin at the time without each other realising. When we talked about the film, she suggested *"Mommy Is Coming"*.

The Owls is a hoot. *Mommy Is Coming* has its moments. But *The Watermelon Woman* endures. 'I don't know why,' says Dunye. 'It could be the format, the underdog idea, or the create-your-own-history thing that so many communities of any race or colour are looking to do. People on the margins need strength, and that's what they see in the film when they find it. What I want is for queer cinema to be more expansive. Especially for folks that look like me, who rarely get a shot. The trouble is the gatekeepers. It's the totem pole: white straight men are at the top, Black queer people at the bottom. Being able to tell a story of difference in queer cinema, rather than saying "We're all the same", is so important. Once we become commercialised and co-opted, Ikea'd and Targeted, the magic of subversion disappears.'

7

UN CHANT D'AMOUR

The Watermelon Woman offers two lessons for how his book on queer cinema might be constructed. One is that it should occupy that same destabilised territory as Dunye's film, making the process of its creation transparent in the book itself; it feels like the natural state of any queer work, an implicit acknowledgement that identities are not stable or fixed. But perhaps there is another, more literal sense in which his book can mirror *The Watermelon Woman*. Cheryl had her romance with Diana among the VHS shelves. And though video shops have died out now, he still makes regular trips to a low-ceilinged hipster joint hidden down a cobblestoned backstreet in east London, among the fabric shops and greasy spoons, where shelves crammed with thousands of DVDs and books reach into the back of the premises and spill into the basement. He spends afternoons here on the sunken leather sofas, thumbing through the crinkled volumes with their tree-bark spines. This is where he does much of his research. This is where he comes to see *him*.

The kid behind the counter is a dead ringer for Mike, his first love, who never loved him back. Or at least how Mike looked the last time he saw him. The stern, oblivious handsomeness, the clenched jaw, the rust-coloured hair, the peppering of freckles on the bridge of the nose, the tight, secretive mouth. He doesn't know the kid's name, but he thinks of him as Mike. Mike is the name that fits.

'Undoubtedly straight' is his husband's verdict when he brings him in to give Mike the surreptitious once-over.

At school, he only ever fell for straight boys. If there were any gay ones, they weren't broadcasting it: no queer after-school clubs at his

96

1980s Essex comp, no bitchy conflabs in the playground critiquing the new soccer strip. It was agony to be caught in that thrashing whirlpool of frustration, but sublime in its own way, too, thwarted desire heady with its own perpetually delayed gratification. He became addicted to not getting what he wanted.

He's long past bothering with straight boys now. What purpose do they serve? None. But when he is standing at the counter, it's as if he is a teenager again. Ignore me, he thinks. Don't give me what I want. That's how Mike makes him feel. *This* Mike, the one who wasn't even born when he was at school in the 1980s.

'Uh, so I got, like, an "overdue rentals" email about these,' he tells Mike, straining for nonchalance as he digs in his canvas bag for the discs. There's no one else in the shop. Ghostpoet rumbles and throbs from the speakers; Chantal Akerman's *News from Home* is playing unwatched on a nearby screen. Mike stands behind the computer, bare arms folded, watching him impassively.

When they met a few months ago, the two of them got chatting about Kenneth Anger, whose films were screening that weekend in the dinky four-row cinema tucked away at the rear of the shop.

'*Scorpio Rising* blew my mind when I saw it at the Scala,' he said, shaking his head as though still feeling the aftershock.

'Really?' said Mike, eyes widening. 'That must have been awesome!'

His skin prickled with remorse. Why the fuck did he have to bring up the Scala? Sure, he was proud of having got his cinematic education at that grandly insalubrious King's Cross picture palace, where no distinction was drawn between masterpieces and monstrosities: you could see everything from *Andrei Rublev* to *Zombie Flesh Eaters*, *ABBA: The Movie* to *Z*. He took it for granted that he could hide out in that cold, musty sanctuary whenever he liked, spending whole afternoons there from the age of fourteen watching Pasolini triple bills or hardcore pairings of *Thundercrack!* and *Café Flesh*. But the place closed in 1993, for goodness' sake. He may as well have told Mike he was at Ford's Theatre the night Lincoln was shot.

There was even a documentary about the place, *Scala!!!*, which was surely a definitive sign that his adolescence had passed into history's digestive tract. For someone of Mike's unworn vintage, the Scala cinema would be indistinguishable now from everything else on the archival carousel: the three-day week, the Cuban missile crisis, the Blitz.

Scala!!! was co-directed by the cinema's former manager, Jane Giles, whom he used to write to as a teenager. His pestering correspondence ('Could you please show Truffaut's *Small Change*?') was met with a bracing lack of condescension ('*Small Change* is not well regarded so we'd be unlikely to programme it'). Before she ran the Scala, Giles wrote her thesis on Jean Genet's sole completed film, the silent 1950 short *Un Chant d'amour* (*A Song of Love*), which she had seen at the cinema in a double bill with *Querelle* before working there. She was encouraged in her scholarship by Richard Kwietniowski, her BA supervisor, who later directed *Love and Death on Long Island* and fed traces of Genet into his short film *Ballad of Reading Gaol*, narrated by Quentin Crisp.

Un Chant d'amour interweaves the fantasies of a sadistic guard, those of the prisoners he spies on and the solitary erotic lives of the inmates. The influence of its tripartite structure and hothouse prison fug on Todd Haynes's *Poison* would be obvious even if Haynes hadn't named one of his characters 'John Broom'.

Genet's film is characterised by permeable barriers, and not only between imaginative freedoms and the physical kind. Comparing the cell-wall sketches of male genitalia with the prisoners' tattoos, Giles notes that 'like tattooed skin, the graffiti . . . is a sublimation of sexual energy and the eroticisation of a boundary'. One of those dense walls is penetrated suggestively by a long, thin straw, poked through by a prisoner in the adjacent cell. It's a spectacle more erotic than any of the film's shots of penises, erect or otherwise. 'The cinema can open a fly and search out its secrets,' said Genet, but *Un Chant d'amour* is hottest when it sticks to hints. There is an ongoing visual rapport between the motif of holes (spy-holes in the cell doors, the hole in a prisoner's sock, the aperture in a wall plugged by a moist finger) and a series of answering images, such as the leather belt which flops lazily towards the camera like a tongue or a drooping cock. Cigarette smoke blooms from the end of that jabbing straw and into the waiting mouth of the young inmate played by Genet's bruised and puppyish lover, Lucien Sénémaud. Both literal and lyrical, this is cinema's sexiest blow job.

It's possible that Genet was inspired by Anger's *Fireworks*, which he saw in 1949 at the Festival des Films Maudit in Biarritz, where Jean Cocteau ensured it took home a prize: 'It touches the quick of the soul,' Cocteau said. Anger's revolutionary short, made in 1947, when he was twenty, is a fifteen-minute wet dream that depicts the fledgling director being ravaged by sailors. It speaks the same language of metaphor, poetry and innuendo as *Un Chant d'amour*, albeit with a more confrontational accent. Even Genet decided his own film was 'too bucolic and not sufficiently violent'. Anger, on the other hand, shows a spitting, sparking Roman candle protruding from the front of a sailor's trousers, and depicts his own torso torn apart by his attackers, exposing a compass where his heart should be.

He insisted the mob were real sailors, a claim disputed by his friend Ed Earle, who said: 'That's a wonderful illusion . . . They were people dressed up. They were tricks who had no inhibitions . . . They all got high and instead of having an orgy, they made a movie.' But then myth-making was Anger's stock-in-trade, if not his raison d'être, and it's only fitting that he considered *Fireworks* to be, as Earle puts it, 'his own autobiographical fantasy'.

99

Both shorts were prosecuted in the US for obscenity; *Fireworks* was exonerated but *Un Chant d'amour* was not, despite defence witnesses including Susan Sontag. Genet was blasé about the ruling ('I believe I saw something about it in the papers,' he said) but never directed another film. Meanwhile, Anger came to Paris at Cocteau's behest and went on to conjure a formidable reputation on the strength of several hours of celluloid, two volumes of *Hollywood Babylon* and more than seventy years of arch, self-mythologising interviews, before his death at the age of ninety-six.

'Will Kenneth Anger be in your book?' asked Mike during that first conversation.

'Of course,' he replied, then started complaining about how critics always felt the need to highlight Anger's influence on better-known film-makers. It was almost as if the value of this queer alchemist could only be measured by the number of prestigious straight directors, such as Martin Scorsese and David Lynch, who deemed him worthy of imitation.

It's true that the use in *Scorpio Rising* of pop music to adrenalise the images did have a pervasive effect on cinema. Even now, its innovations feel radical: the Crystals singing 'He's a Rebel' over images of Christ lifted from a religious instructional film; the tenderness of Bobby Vinton's 'Blue Velvet' softening the montage of bikers getting dressed, but also intensifying its queerness. As they strap themselves into their prophylactic leather skins, the buttons and buckles all a-gleam, Vinton seems to be serenading them directly, happily risking a sock to the jaw.

But if *Scorpio Rising* is going to feature in his book, he is determined to celebrate the film on its own merits. He won't even mention Scorsese and Lynch, or anyone else who raided Anger's box of tricks. Omitting them will help prove that queer film-makers don't need validation from straights.

Rummaging in his bag now, he produces the latest batch of overdue discs, which he used as research for the first section of the book: *Nitrate Kisses* and *History Lessons* are in there; *Funeral Parade of Roses*, too, and *In a Year of 13 Moons*. Then he takes the discs he needs to watch for the later sections and puts those in a separate pile, ready to be checked out.

'Bringing *these* queer ones back' – he pushes the old titles across the counter to Mike – 'and taking *these* queer ones out.' He nods at the new pile, which has *The Erotic Films of Peter de Rome* on top. 'Work, work, work.'

His comment, intended to sound off-the-cuff, has the ring of an artificial icebreaker contrived on the walk from the station.

Tapping the details into the system, Mike gives a lopsided smile. His cheek dimples as though prodded by an invisible finger.

'Oh yeah, you're writing a book, aren't you? Remind me what it's about.'

It's only been two months since he told him. How has he forgotten already?

'Uh, queer cinema.'

'Cool. So how are you doing it?'

'I'm not sure. I've made a rod for my own back because I want the structure of it to be queer somehow. I don't want to do "fifty films to see before you die" or "ten great directors". And I'm not arranging it chronologically. So I know what I *don't* want it to be. But I'm not sure what it is.'

'Wicked. That'll come.'

'Maybe,' he says, not letting on that he still doesn't feel queer enough for the job, no matter how many DVDs he watches. 'Just wait, I'll probably have a nervous breakdown by the end of the year.'

Mike slides the discs back to him.

'I'll have the coffee ready for then,' he says.

This is perfect, he thinks. His pursuit of Mike can be a thread running through the book, a refrain to come back to in between the other chapters. Their conversations could comment on and even unpick the text as he's writing it. Mike already asked him how he is planning to do the book, but if he were to ask, say, '*Why* are you doing it?' then that could help him articulate what he is hoping to discover. Not just about queerness and cinema, but about himself.

The next few times he stops by, however, his visits don't coincide with Mike's shift, and he can't think how to ask the other employees when Mike will be there without looking like a stalker. It is only when Will, one of the friendlier members of staff, strikes up a conversation with him a month or so down the line that he feels able to enquire after Mike.

'Where's the other guy who worked here? The Kenneth Anger fan. The one who . . .'

He's not sure how to describe him without drooling.

Will wrinkles his nose. 'Young? Square jaw?'

'That's the one.'

'Oh, that's Eric. He left to make his own films. He's actually a brilliant cinematographer.'

'Wow, that's so cool,' he replies, feeling nothing of the sort.

His dreams of a *Watermelon Woman*-style subplot are dead, and with them has gone this twenty-first-century Mike, thoughtlessly killed off by Eric. But maybe Eric could still trigger a segue in his book into the two important things that happened in 1984.

8

THE SECRET POLICEMAN'S BALL

Two important things happened in 1984: the boy admitted to himself that he was in love with Mike, the original Mike, and then he saw *The Secret Policeman's Ball*. Those events bleed and blur together now, though the first one was a gradual dawning that took a few months to zing into focus, while the second was sudden and nasty, like a poke in the eye.

Mike had a kind of austerity about him: the knifed lines of his cheekbones, his monastic stillness. He only moved or spoke when he had to, but he never stayed where he didn't want to be. He would step off the train just as the doors were closing or jump from the back of a Routemaster bus and be gone, melting into the traffic, and you wouldn't see him again until school on Monday. One breaktime, amid the detritus of sandwich foil and Tupperware lunchboxes, Mike leaned back in his chair and said, 'Cry for me.' And that was that: the boy had to make himself cry. He would have done far worse. Didn't Mike know he would have licked a toilet bowl if he'd asked him to, just for the privilege of sharing a milkshake with him and drinking through the same straw?

He wondered how you got to be the sort of person who could demand someone else's subjugation. Everybody knew Mike's parents had split up. There were stories doing the rounds. His mum changed the locks and his dad smashed a window. Shouting, fighting, neighbours, sirens. People in doorways in dressing gowns. What a palaver. Maybe this was how Mike ended up that way, his features lit from within by scepticism and mistrust. He had been through something. That's what you looked like when your mum and dad didn't insist on staying together, boringly loving each other, the way the boy's parents did.

Even at thirteen, the boy liked to think of himself as the fruit of movie-star stock. His mother was the spit of Jane Fonda as Barbarella, or at least the way she looked on the cover of his *The Geoff Love Orchestra Plays* Star Wars *and Other Space Themes* album, with her zero-gravity copper hairdo. His father was like Oliver Reed in Ken Russell's *Tommy*: a pair of sideburns on strutting legs, all mouth, all trousers, all the time, with more chest hair than there was chest for it to grow on. Dad introduced him to every movie he knew and loved – from the Marx brothers and Fred Astaire to *Get Carter* – and the boy tried to return the favour, even if it can't have felt much like a favour to his father. It was foolish of him to expect Dad to share his passion for *The Warriors*, the stylised thriller set among New York's impossibly spiffy gangs, when Dad was, after all, half Italian and half cockney, formed by the intersecting mythologies of the Mafia and the East End. Dad liked his thugs kitted out in greatcoats and porkpie hats, not leather vests, baseball pumps and clown-face. *The Warriors* was as far from his world as *The Red Shoes*.

Comedy was their sanctuary, their neutral ground, and the boy was intimate enough with his father's enthusiasms to be able to flatter him by taping *The Secret Policeman's Ball* from a midnight Channel 4 screening. The film, a fuzzy 16mm recording of a late-1970s Amnesty International benefit concert, was a compendium of sketches and stand-up routines performed by comics his parents loved, including most of the Monty Python team, with the laughs punctuated by the odd musical interlude.

Once his younger brother and sister were in bed, he and his parents settled down to watch it: the boy at one end of the sofa, still in his school uniform, Mum at the other with her cup of tea, Dad in the armchair with his impress-me look. The opening sketch had John

Cleese reading a newspaper on a park bench. Peter Cook was sitting next to him clutching a red notebook, from which he kept reeling off unsolicited facts mangled by misremembering – 'Do you know an Arab can live for a whole year on one grain of rice?' – while Cleese tried to ignore him. It was silly and smart at the same time; you had to be clever to spot what a buffoon Cook's park-bench dullard was being. He got that fact about Arabs muddled up, for instance, because, as he put it, 'they're next door to one another in the dictionary'.

'What are?' Cleese demanded.

'"Mosquito" and "mosque".'

Halfway into the film, a sketch with Cleese as a manic game-show host ended, and the screen cut to black. Then the camera began panning down from high in the rafters, eventually reaching an illuminated stage. Right before the camera found what it was looking for, a croaky male voice started singing, earnestly but with a hint of cockiness. The voice belonged to a bushy-haired young man, planted at the microphone in a donkey jacket, denim shirt and flared jeans. Isolated but fearless, he strummed his acoustic guitar against a black void that stretched in every direction. As the camera zoomed in slowly, the lyrics rang out crisp and clear:

> British police are the best in the world
> I don't believe one of these stories I've heard
> 'Bout them raiding gay bars for no reason at all
> Lining the customers up by the wall
> Picking out people, knocking them down
> Resisting arrest as they're kicked on the ground
> Searching their houses and calling them 'queer'
> I don't believe that sort of thing happens here.

The boy couldn't breathe, couldn't move. No one was looking at him yet it felt as if everyone was – he was boiling under a billion eyes, his skin sizzling like the time Mike held a magnifying glass to his face while he was dozing on the playing field. This was all his own doing: he had plonked his parents in front of the television and served them this outrage. How stupid can you get? He wanted it to end, to protect his parents from what they were hearing, from what they might find out about him. He needed some way to distance himself from the singer's taunting words and demeanour, except he couldn't think of anything to say. Every possible mocking or mitigating comment died in his throat before he could rehearse it. He wanted to pick up the remote and rewind the evening back to when his parents were laughing.

Now he sensed Dad stiffening through the Benson & Hedges fog, and Mum sighing into her tea, but he didn't dare turn his head to check what they were doing, so instead his eyes flicked from side to side like polygraph needles as he tried to read their reactions. The boy was nothing more than a pounding heart, his body like a shrivelled balloon. All he had to do was stay still and the song would eventually be over.

After the first verse, the singer paused. 'You don't have to be gay to sing on this chorus,' he muttered. 'But it helps.' Laughter from the crowd. Silence from Mum and Dad. And then the unignorable refrain:

> *Sing* if you're glad to be gay
> Sing if you're happy that way, hey,
> *Sing* if you're glad to be gay
> Sing if you're happy that way.

The words sounded triumphant: the 'i' in the second and fourth 'sing' was stretched out interminably. The singer's face, though, was set in a bitter sneer. He was saying 'sing' and 'glad' and 'happy', but he didn't look like he wanted any kind of party. It was the first time the boy had witnessed a gay person expressing fury or bitterness about how they were treated. Until that moment, he had thought being gay, and seeing how hostile and uncomfortable it made other people, was something you muddled through. Weren't you meant to lump it?

Here, though, was a different response. The singer wasn't going to shrug it off or smile along. He was making a scene.

Even though the boy was praying for the song to end, hating it and loving it and cringing simultaneously, he could chart the changes in the singer's rhetoric: there was a part that was gentle and sad, and a staccato section where he hacked up the words with brusque, axe-like strums, then finally a blast of rage ending on a note of agitation in the last verse. 'The buggers are legal now,' he said in his speak-singing voice. 'What more are they after?'

Then it was back into the chorus, and that syllable – 'gay!' – over and over, impossible to explain away as anything other than the incriminating torchlight, searchlight, *floodlight* of a word that it was. If people like the singer would only shut their cakeholes, there'd be none of this trouble. Then a boy who secretly loved Mike could go on enjoying the film with his parents, not letting on that the song had anything to do with him.

Once it was over, there was a commercial break. Nobody moved at first. Dad's arms looked unnaturally stiff, two big right angles with balled-up fists on the end like cartoon boxing gloves. The boy watched his father lift himself from the armchair and plod into the kitchen, then heard the click of the kettle going on.

'Who was that, anyway?' Mum called after him. 'That singer?'

'What-siz-name, innit,' Dad grumbled over the roar of boiling water. 'Tom something. That bloody – Tom Robinson.'

'Oh yes, that's him. Such a nice-looking fella.' Mum shook her head sadly. 'What a waste.'

The rest of the film rolled on but it wasn't the same. Tom Robinson had cast a pall over the remaining half-hour, and nothing seemed funny any more.

At school, the boy asked his friend Jan if she had seen the film. She was three years older than him, a sixth-former already part of the adult world. She drank tea and knew everything. They met through the school youth theatre group – she was in the orchestra and sometimes rehearsed with the actors. Her instrument was the violin; her arm moved lightning fast, faster than his eyes could keep up with. A bumfluff-faced lad from her class told him she was like lightning in bed, too. What did that mean?

'She'll make every bit of you stand on end,' the lad said with a leering wink.

But she didn't. The two of them just leafed through the *Cult Movies* book together, and she promised to take the boy to see *The Rocky Horror Picture Show* and *Pink Flamingos* one day.

Some lunchtimes, she would sneak him into the sixth-form common room. The boy wasn't supposed to be in there, what with him being only thirteen, but no one was going to argue with Jan.

'*Secret Policeman*?' she repeated, unscrewing her flask and splashing tea into the lid, which was also a cup. 'Yeah, love it. Got the album. I should lend you the Derek and Clive ones. Just don't play them in front of your gran. Not unless she's a filthy old bint.'

He laughed uncertainly, steeling himself for the question he wanted to ask.

'Did you see that singer, though?' he said. 'The . . . gay one?'

'Tom Robinson?'

'Was that his name?' He pretended to be mulling it over. 'Yeah, I think that was it.'

'I've got his album,' she said. Jan had everyone's albums. 'He's brilliant. Proper political. What did you think of him?'

The boy tried to come up with the least exposing comment he

could muster, one that wouldn't draw any attention to him. What did people say about Tom Robinson? What did they say when they had nothing to hide?

'He was alright,' he said. 'But, you know. What a waste.'

Every chance he got after that, he watched the 'Glad to Be Gay' bit from *The Secret Policeman's Ball*. It got so that there was a little crimp in the tape just before Tom Robinson came on stage, where it went crackly and the picture hiccupped. He scrutinised every curl of the singer's lip, every acidic inflection. He loved how you couldn't take the '*siiiiing* if you're glad to be gay' bit at face value, because what was there to be glad about when the police were raiding gay bars for no reason at all, lining the customers up by the wall?

He had heard there were gay bars (*Time Out* magazine said so), but he'd never given much thought to what might happen in them, never allowed himself to wonder. Now Tom Robinson had pushed open the door of a world he knew nothing about; he imagined peeking through it, into the bar, and spying on all the gay movie characters he had collected in his head. He had filed them away over the years, keeping them to himself, but now he filled the place with them. The room was *heaving*.

There was Mr Wint and Mr Kidd, the assassins from the James Bond film *Diamonds Are Forever*, who skip off into the desert together holding hands.

Who else? Colin, the gay gangster sliced up at the start of *The Long Good Friday* while he is cruising at the swimming pool. He imagined Colin was in the bar, too, right as rain now, getting to know Mr Wint and Mr Kidd. Maybe they'd all skip off together afterwards, the three of them clutching hands.

There was Sonny, the doomed bank robber played by Al Pacino in *Dog Day Afternoon*, who is only carrying out the heist in the first place to pay for gender-affirming surgery for his lover (Chris Sarandon). Rod Steiger was there, too, as a serial killer with a mother fixation in *No Way to Treat a Lady*. Sometimes you had to work out who was gay because it wasn't always obvious. James Mason in *The Seventh Veil* protected his masculine household so fiercely that there was surely something fishy about him. When his young ward (Ann Todd) comes to stay with him, he tells her: 'This is a bachelor establishment. Do you know what that word means? It means that I don't like women about the place. When I came to live in this house I promised myself that no woman should ever enter it. So far none ever has. You're the first.'

The boy loved Geoffrey in *A Taste of Honey*: the pinched Pierrot face of the actor Murray Melvin, how he flapped and flitted like a moth. (Dirk Bogarde told Melvin that his performance had done more to advance the cause of homosexuality than the entirety of *Victim*.) Geoffrey is thrown out by his landlady for canoodling with a fella. Jo (Rita Tushingham) treats him like a museum exhibit at first. 'Why do you do what you do?' she asks, half intrigued, half repelled. Later, he begs to marry her. Wasn't that the only option? You found a girl you could have a laugh with, and you shacked up together. You certainly couldn't live with another man. Could you?

Clint Eastwood and Jeff Bridges were like secret sweethearts in *Thunderbolt and Lightfoot*. Eastwood notices Bridges' beautiful blue eyes. 'We gotta stop meeting like this,' they tell one another. Bridges dresses as a woman. He really throws himself into the part. That's something gays liked to do. You couldn't stop them.

There was the flasher in *High Anxiety* who exposes himself to a psychiatrist (Mel Brooks) in an airport toilet, then chastises him when he runs off. 'Don't be so gauche,' he calls after him. 'We're all doing it!'

And the theatre director Roger DeBris (Christopher Hewett) in an earlier Brooks comedy, *The Producers*. Max (Zero Mostel) and Leo (Gene Wilder) stop by his apartment, only to find him in sparkly earrings and evening gown.

'He's wearing a dress,' hisses Leo under his breath.

'No kidding,' says Max.

Roger's assistant, Carmen Ghia, is played by Andréas Voutsinas. He was a friend of Peter De Rome, the gay British fighter-pilot-turned-pornographer whose flickering Super 8 films and 1974 feature *Adam & Yves* never shed their prelapsarian air, no matter how explicit they got. (*Adam & Yves*, the first international gay porn feature, included footage shot from an apartment window of Greta Garbo walking along First Avenue in New York – technically her final movie appearance.) Voutsinas can be seen (clothed) on top of the Arc de Triomphe in De Rome's 1972 short *The Second Coming*, which climaxes with a Christ figure on the cross spattering himself with ejaculate. But the boy didn't know any of that then. He only discovered it once he was an adult and had begun researching his book about queer cinema.

The joke in both those Brooks comedies is on the prissy, uptight straights. They're self-conscious, scared of what anyone else might think. The queers, meanwhile, are living it up. Leo in *The Producers* and the psychiatrist in *High Anxiety* look as repressed as Inspector Clouseau (Peter Sellers) in *The Pink Panther Strikes Again*, directed by Blake Edwards, who made the jubilant cross-dressing comedy *Victor/Victoria*. During his investigations, Clouseau visits a secret nightclub where everyone is light in the loafers. It looked like the sort of place that Kenneth Williams and Charles Hawtrey, the boy's *Carry On* favourites, might have blundered into by accident, only to find themselves enjoying it. When Clouseau dances with another man, you aren't meant to find it romantic, just daft. And while the club is a grotesque caricature, everyone but him is having a blast. Then again, Clouseau lives with the athletic Cato (Burt Kwouk), who leaps out and surprises him with martial-arts ambushes whenever he gets home. Two cohabiting men who spend their time together play-fighting.

There was so much in the Monty Python films that was gay, none of it hidden or shameful. He kept rewinding the parade ground exercise in *And Now for Something Completely Different*, which begins with the sergeant barking orders at his soldiers ('Squad! Camp it *up*!'), before their limp-wristed, precision-drilled mincing is accompanied by chanted catchphrases: 'Ooh, get her' or 'I'll scratch your eyes out'.

The best bit came later, though, in the film's most low-key sketch. Michael Palin is the flustered man who approaches a police inspector, played by John Cleese, in daylight on an empty suburban street to report that his wallet has been stolen from his coat. 'Well, there's very little we can do about that, sir,' says the inspector. There follows eight or nine seconds of silence as the man looks dejected, then furtive. Eventually, he asks: 'Do you want to come back to my place?' There is a pause while the inspector thinks this over. 'Yeah, alright,' he replies finally. They walk out of shot, and the film cuts to the next, unconnected sketch. The tension that should have been released by a punchline is left agonisingly undischarged.

All the US comedies he loved seemed preoccupied with gays. In *The Blues Brothers*, it was only safe for one Nazi to tell another that he was in love with him once their car had fallen off the edge of a bridge and was dropping through the sky, a certain death awaiting them.

In *Stripes*, the army recruiting officer asks Bill Murray and Harold Ramis: 'Are either of you, uh, homosexuals?'

The friends gaze at one another in mock tenderness.

'No, we're not homosexual,' says Ramis finally. 'But we *are* willing to learn.'

'Yeah,' Murray agrees. 'Would they send us some place special?'

Their easy-going vibe didn't make him feel tangled up, the way he did after seeing Eddie Murphy in *48 Hrs.* and *Trading Places* and *Beverly Hills Cop*. 'Faggots' was what Murphy called people like him. The word sounded hostile but also silly. 'Faggots aren't allowed to look at my ass on stage,' Murphy announces at the start of his stand-up set in *Delirious*. 'That's why I keep moving when I'm up here.' He was wearing a bright red leather suit with the zip open to the navel, but he didn't want the fags' 'imagination flowing' when they saw him. Too late for that. The boy kept a shirtless photo of Eddie Murphy, torn from a film magazine, in a tobacco tin under his bed.

He imagined bringing him to the gay bar in that sexy suit. They could gawp at the biker from *Mad Max 2*, the one with the mohawk and harness whose angelic boyfriend gets sliced in the forehead with a metal boomerang. Monty from *Fame* might be there, too: the milk-faced, Walt Whitman-quoting loner who is, implausibly, the only gay pupil at the New York School of the Performing Arts. And there would be Michael Caine as Maggie Smith's gay husband, fussing around on Oscar night in *California Suite*. It was Caine, too, kissing Christopher Reeve – Superman! – in *Deathtrap*: the first time the boy had ever seen one man's lips on another. Gay was big in the year *Deathtrap* came out (1982), what with *Personal Best* (sporty lesbians) and *Making Love* (a married man, secretly gay), but it was the Caine–Reeve smacker that was all over the press.

The only character he didn't want in the bar was the seedy Uncle Ernie, played by the Who's drummer, Keith Moon, panting as he molests his disabled nephew in *Tommy*. It was one thing to write the character as a pervert. But why did he have to be shown with his nose in a copy of *Gay News*?

Without Uncle Ernie, the gay bar was still crowded. No one present, though, expressed their sexuality with quite the force on display in *The Secret Policeman's Ball*. Put up or shut up had always been the order of the day, but Tom Robinson wasn't having it, he wasn't bloody well having it. The chorus of 'Glad to Be Gay' might have been littered with upbeat words, but he spat them out as though they were the bones of his enemies. The camera choices only consolidated the song's power. Most of it was shot in tight close-up, so there was no escape, no possible release. The singer was in your face in both senses.

'Thanks for your kind words. And yes, that performance was a pivotal moment for me personally, as well. If you like, we could meet tomorrow for lunch before I go away on tour for a few weeks. Also (long shot this) if you have nothing better to do this evening, my band are playing a rare London show at Nell's Jazz & Blues in West Kensington and I'd be happy to put you on the guest list . . .'

The split-level club is a sea of pink-faced heads, most of them white-haired or balding. He stands near the bar clutching a pint, but once the musicians amble on stage, he joins the bodies milling at the front. All at once, the band is tearing through numbers that made his teenage bedroom shake; he had to weigh the stylus down with a blob of Blu Tack so that the thump and crash of 'Bully for You' and 'Up Against the Wall' didn't jog the needle on his lightweight turntable. If it did, the aching lilt of 'War Baby' would kiss it better. The band plays all those tonight, as well as a cover of Steely Dan's 'Rikki Don't Lose That Number' in the glam style of Roxy Music.

When they finally launch into 'Glad to Be Gay' in the second half of the show, the track sounds mellower, like it has buried the hatchet for good. The years have stripped its chiming chords of their former rage. Nothing like the last time he heard Robinson play it live, on a stage in Jubilee Gardens in south London following the Gay Pride march from Trafalgar Square earlier that day. That was 1988: a week shy of his seventeenth birthday, and less than a year before he stumbled onto the straight and narrow.

———

The story of 'Glad to Be Gay' began in the mid-1970s. 'I wrote it when I was with my previous band, Café Society,' explains Robinson the following day, as we pick at our salads in a deserted pub opposite Wandsworth Common. He is seventy-two, his hair silver now, his once scratchy voice smoothed out from decades working as a radio DJ. 'We never performed it live because the other two in the band didn't want to be tarred with that brush. Then, when I formed Tom Robinson Band, it was part of the repertoire from day one. We signed to EMI and tried doing a studio version of it. But it didn't have the same energy, so we just put out a live recording. That was on an EP with the number of Gay Switchboard on the back. Capital Radio played the bejasus out of "Glad to Be Gay", and it was voted number one on the listeners' hotline for six weeks. That's what made the ban from Radio 1 seem so retrograde. BBC management thought the public weren't ready for that song. Commercial radio knew that they were.'

From its opening lines, the song crackles with a lacerating sarcasm that feels Dylan-esque. 'Well, I was listening to a lot of Dylan,' he admits. 'Especially *Desire*. I was feeling very wound up and knew I had to write something, but I didn't have a tune so I wrote it to the melody of "Sara".' Right there at the table, he launches into that first-draft version of the song, singing it in Dylan's croak and tapping his foot to keep time, sending *Jurassic Park* ripples across our beers. 'I woke the next day and thought, "What melody can I sing that isn't that?" And I realised it would work as a Kinks-y kind of "Dedicated Follower of Fashion" thing. I was signed to the Kinks' label at the time, and I'd learned all my stagecraft, such as it was, from watching Ray Davies, so there was a lot of that music-hall side in what I was doing. That Kinks style seemed a natural way to write the song.'

He and Davies later had a falling-out, and Davies recorded the B-side 'Prince of the Punks', a diatribe against the unnamed Robinson which questions his personal and musical integrity. He smiles magnanimously when I mention it. 'It's an honour to have a song written about you by Ray Davies,' he says. 'It's just a shame that it's such a shit one.'

At Gay Pride in 1976, Robinson played an acoustic version of 'Glad to Be Gay', the choppy, insistent rhythm lending itself to the solo guitar. When Amnesty's producer Martin Lewis asked him to perform on the bill for *The Secret Policeman's Ball*, there was a personal and political incentive for him to accept. 'At that time, there was concern in the gay community because Amnesty didn't count anyone who was in prison for being gay as a political prisoner. Their excuse was: it's not political, it's just their lifestyle choice. Many of us felt a huge injustice was being done to people who were in prison through no fault of their own, and that Amnesty should support them, which it subsequently did. So I knew it was important to show up, but I had no idea it was going to be captured on film until I got there.'

There was a gay-themed sketch on the bill, too: Peter Cook's torn-from-the-headlines monologue, in which he scathingly lampooned the judge's biased summing-up in the recent trial of Jeremy Thorpe, the MP accused of hiring a hitman to kill his lover, Norman Scott. (The case was adapted for the BBC in 2018 as *A Very English Scandal*, with Hugh Grant as Thorpe and Ben Whishaw as Scott.) Tellingly, the Thorpe sketch in *The Secret Policeman's Ball* follows 'Glad to Be

Gay' in the film's running order. 'That was very thoughtfully done,' says Robinson. What was his reaction when he saw the film in a cinema? 'I thought, "Ooh, thank God they caught me on a handsome day. One without jowls."' It was a decisive moment for the song, as well as for him. 'Until that point, it was associated with the Tom Robinson Band version, and we had just broken up at the time of the film, which is why I showed up solo with the acoustic guitar. That marked me claiming the song back on my own from the band. In some ways, that's the definitive version.'

The lyrics have had to change down the years to correspond with shifts not only in society (age of consent, marriage equality) but in Robinson's own life. In 1982, he met Sue Brearley, who remains his wife today. 'For many years, I added a verse that said: "If gay liberation means freedom for all/ Then a label is no liberation at all/ I'm here and I'm queer and I do what I do/ And I'm not gonna wear a strait-jacket for you." Then the generation of people who were upset by the changes in my life gave way to a generation that didn't remember any of it, or care.' Now the song ends with the lyric: 'Whatever your shade on the rainbow today/ We're here and we're human and happy to say/ Sing if you're glad to be gay . . .'

The first time I heard that Robinson was dating a woman was in 1988, when *Time Out* ran a diary item about a mix-up involving his phone number. 'Could this be Dorothy's Revenge on Robbo for stepping out with a member of the opposite sex?' the magazine asked. Robinson is sanguine about the response he received in those days. 'When I first started going out with Sue, I didn't want to be singing "Glad to Be Gay" on stage, then going home to a secret girlfriend, so I very deliberately mentioned it in interviews with *Capital Gay* and the *Pink Paper*.'

The reaction from the gay press amounted to a collective shrug. 'It took two years before the *Sunday People* got hold of it and thought,

"What a story!" They ran a centre-page spread under the headline: "Britain's Number 1 Gay in Love with Girl Biker". They fabricated quotes which implied I was disowning my queer identity and had somehow "gone straight". This was at the height of the AIDS crisis. We were losing friends and former lovers in terrifying numbers: a whole generation of young men suddenly getting sick, withering away and dying horribly. No wonder people in our community started wondering, "What's he playing at?" Then, when our first kid was born, the same journalist rang up and said, "We want to come and take pictures of your baby." I said, "You're fucking dreaming." He threatened to run a smear story unless we co-operated, so we were forced to get our own baby pictures taken to give to the other tabloids – homophobic rags like the *Daily Express*, the *Mail* and the *Sun* – just to kill his story. The coverage was broadly sympathetic, with inevitable "Glad to Be Dad" headlines, but the community went, "Has he totally lost the plot?" I even got booed at Pride.'

It caused a shift in his own thinking. 'When I considered myself to be a full-scale, card-carrying gay man, I believed bisexuality was just a cop-out for people who couldn't come out properly. So when it happened to me, it was quite hard to come to terms with. I never stopped liking men – as far as I was concerned, I was just a gay man who happened to be in love with a woman.'

He knocks back the last of his beer.

'*You* know what that feels like,' he says.

9

TRASH

Alongside Tom Robinson and all the queer characters in the boy's imaginary bar, there was someone else – a lad just a few years older than him, fifteen or sixteen, standing on the threshold, sort of there and not there at the same time. The boy had read about him in the novelisation of the horror sequel *Damien: Omen II*. Novelisations were widely impugned (Woody Allen dismisses the form as 'truly moronic' in *Manhattan*), but those tie-in books gave generations of underage viewers tangential access to movies they weren't yet old enough to see. The novelisations of the first two *Omen* films made an indelible mark on the boy. A literal mark, in fact: flush with excitement after reading about Damien, the son of the Devil, he drew tiny clusters of 666s on himself with a biro, in imitation of the child's demonic birthmark. The young actors in the *Omen* films even looked like him, with their boot-black hair and coal-smudged eyes.

Animals went nuts whenever Damien was nearby; he literally frightened the horses, along with the dogs and the monkeys and everything else. The boy was only just starting to comprehend his own difference, but here was a phenomenon with which he could identify. Like him, Damien was born with some core element innately warped, causing suspicion and panic in the adults around him.

By the time of the second *Omen*, the character had grown so much in power that any kinship the boy felt previously had dwindled. No wonder he was drawn to a more marginal figure in the sequel. In Joseph Howard's novelisation of *Damien: Omen II*, a reporter named Joan Hart becomes convinced of Damien's diabolical lineage and turns up at the military academy where he is a student. The pupils are playing football on the field when she arrives. She goes over to the touchline.

> Joan Hart noticed a young boy who was obviously a cadet from his uniform, but who was watching the scrimmage instead of playing in it. Her trained eyes sized up the situation instantly; the boy was scrawny, he had pimples, and he wore glasses with lenses as thick as plate-glass windows. His attention was riveted on the field. Perhaps he felt an adolescent, semihomosexual attraction to the lean youths out there. Obviously, one of them was his hero.

There are shades here of Aschenbach observing Tadzio and his playmates on the beach and realising that the teenager has a social supremacy which equals (and is made possible by) his beauty: it is Aschenbach who notes of Tadzio that 'his was the name oftenest on their lips, he was plainly sought after, wooed, admired'. There is something similarly satisfying about the experience of the reader watching Joan Hart as she watches the nameless closeted cadet watching Damien – a layering of voyeurism which animates the scene's queerness.

Save for the spectacles, it was as if the boy had found himself in a movie, or the novelisation of one. He wasn't expecting anyone gay in those pages and yet here was this teenage alter ego: a minor character on the margins of the action whose sole function was to have his unrequited longings speculated on by a passing journalist.

When he was finally allowed to watch *Damien: Omen II*, taped from a late-night showing on ITV, he looked everywhere for that yearning adolescent spectator. But the weedy, carbuncular, half-blind cadet ogling the dreamy football players had failed to make the leap from page to screen. Was he written into the script and never filmed? Were there a few seconds of him on a strip of celluloid in a 1970s landfill somewhere? Or was he invented solely for the book? It didn't matter: he wasn't there.

The boy rewound the videotape, combed the scene frame by flickering frame, scrutinised the bystanders, hunted for this figure who had been part of his private imaginary cut of the movie for so long – but he didn't exist.

Queer viewers learn to work with absence. The excision of queerness can even leave behind a smudge, as it does in Billy Wilder's 1972 comedy *Avanti!* The film shows Wendell Armbruster Jr (Jack Lemmon) arriving in the Bay of Naples to claim the body of his father, who has died in a car accident while on holiday. There, Wendell meets the jolly Pamela Piggott (Juliet Mills), whose mother perished in the same accident. Their parents, it transpires, had been conducting an affair for many years.

Wilder's original idea was bold for its day. 'Now what I really wanted to do was, the father is a homosexual, and he had a *bellhop* with him,' he said. 'That was the first thing that I thought of – wouldn't it be funny if an elderly man who goes every year to take the baths is actually having an affair with the bellhop? But of course [the studio] talked me out of it.'

Though Wilder abandoned the notion that Wendell's father is 'a homosexual [who] only does it in Europe', the film's wordless and enigmatic opening is still coloured by its original queer impetus. As the picture begins, Wendell is on the golf course, when he is summoned to fly to Italy. Once on the plane, he persuades the stranger in the neighbouring seat to join him in the cramped bathroom. (How he persuades him, and why, is hidden from the audience at first.) The crew and the other passengers seem mildly perturbed at what appears to be a rather brazen meeting of the mile-high club. It is not until the two men emerge from the bathroom having traded outfits that the lira finally drops. Wendell is now wearing the man's suit, which looks appropriately sombre for a son arriving to identify his late father's body. Meanwhile, the stranger is kitted out in Wendell's garish red golfing togs.

The rest of *Avanti!* unspools in the lingering shadow of that gay tease, which is apt considering the brushes with disinhibition that Wendell will experience once he falls into the company of Pamela, who tempts him into a spot of skinny-dipping and nude sunbathing. Lemmon had form in muddying the waters sexually at Wilder's behest: along with Tony Curtis, he spends most of *Some Like It Hot* in drag, though it is Lemmon whose character commits fully to the masquerade, even indicating, in one of Hollywood's most casually outré endings, that he is perfectly happy to stay that way.

Not all queerness leaves a trace. Richard Curtis wrote and shot a lesbian subplot for *Love Actually*, his 2003 selection box of rom-com doodles and vignettes, but it was one of the first elements to be junked in the editing. No hint remains now of either of the actors: not Frances de la Tour, who played a stern headteacher, nor Anne Reid as her terminally ill lover.

Gay and lesbian characters haven't had an awful lot of luck in Curtis's movies. In *Four Weddings and a Funeral*, Simon Callow and John Hannah are the gay couple who pop up at three of the film's four nuptials, with Callow's sudden expiration supplying the non-marital get-together promised by the title. The actor declared himself 'grateful' that his character, Gareth, 'died of Scottish dancing. When [the film] came out in 1994, AIDS was rampant... He died from an excess of joy and generosity, which was a wonderful thing.'

Felicity, played by Katherine Parkinson in Curtis's pirate-radio comedy *The Boat That Rocked*, isn't killed off, or snipped from the finished film, though much of her dialogue refers to the fact that she is a lesbian, just in case anyone should cease defining her by her sexuality for a moment. Next time Curtis writes a gay character, he might look at the stop-motion animation *ParaNorman*, which is both bold and nonchalant in its approach to sexuality. One of the hero's more macho friends is casually revealed in the final moments of the film to have been gay all along. Bad news for any homophobes duped into rooting for him.

A Nightmare on Elm Street 2: Freddy's Revenge is a more unusual case. That horror sequel's closeted young star, Mark Patton, found himself shouldering the blame for what audiences and critics at the time regarded as the film's deficiencies – but which now make it one of the most thrillingly tangled queer horror films. In a departure from the logic of the original 1984 hit movie, where the monstrous Freddy Krueger (Robert Englund) can only reach his victims through their nightmares, the sequel's hero, Jesse (Patton), has Freddy inside him – and trying to 'come out'.

This queer allegory would be compelling enough even without the other hints dropped: the homoerotic interplay between Jesse and his best friend; the male nudity (rather than the female variety typical of the horror genre); and one scene set in a leather bar, where Jesse encounters his PE teacher. Later, the teacher is dragged into the showers, where he is stripped, his bare buttocks whipped with towels, before being killed. Jesse looks on, both witness and voyeur.

David Chaskin, the film's screenwriter, admitted that his own motives were coming from a place of bigotry: 'There was certainly some intentional subtext but it was intended to play homophobic rather than homoerotic . . . There were certain choices that were made like casting that pushed the subtext to a higher level and stripped away whatever subtlety there might have been.'

In other words, if only the pesky Patton hadn't been cast, then the movie could have carried on being straightforwardly homophobic, demonising queerness rather than propagating it. The actor, who had already played a pre-transition trans woman in Robert Altman's stage and screen versions of *Come Back to the 5 & Dime, Jimmy Dean, Jimmy Dean*, vanished from the industry soon after, wounded by the homophobic criticisms of the movie. He resurfaced decades later to capitalise on its emergent cult appeal, and to parlay his desire for closure into a 2019 documentary, *Scream, Queen! My Nightmare on Elm Street*.

———————

There exists a minor tradition of actors playing gay even when the script hasn't demanded it, such as in Gus Van Sant's *Finding Forrester*, which stars Sean Connery as a reclusive novelist mentoring the wayward sixteen-year-old Jamal (Rob Brown). 'It wasn't in the script,' Van Sant said. 'The studio didn't want us to advertise it. But Sean wanted to play that part as gay.' There are clues that seem initially to present Forrester as a gay voyeur. When we first meet him, he is standing at his apartment window, peering through binoculars at the park opposite. 'What we have here is an adult male,' he purrs. 'Quite pretty.' But the joke is on us: what has captured his attention is a Connecticut warbler. Forrester is a watcher of birds, not boys.

When Jamal breaks into Forrester's apartment as a dare, he accidentally leaves behind his rucksack; the novelist later hangs the bag in his window as a taunt to the intruder, but it could easily be regarded as the first of their primitive courtship rituals. The youngster comes to retrieve his bag and finds the notebooks inside daubed with encouragements.

Contrary to Van Sant's assertion that the subtext was Connery's idea, the actor pleaded something close to ignorance. 'On the issue of the gayness and whether that's in the movie, that's Gus's cross to bear,' he said. 'I suppose there could be undercurrents that [my] character is closeted.' Either he was playing hard to get or his choices were buried so deep that even he forgot about them.

Not every actor who supplies their own queer backstory is so circumspect. Robert Carlyle played Begbie, the psychotic hard-nut in *Trainspotting*, as gay, a decision supported by Irvine Welsh, author of the original novel. Begbie's violence, Carlyle argued, came from a 'fear of being outed'. Harrison Ford used gayness to fill a vacuum when he played a mildly sinister corporate PA in Francis Ford Coppola's thriller *The Conversation*. 'There was no role there until I decided to make him a homosexual,' the actor said. Sexual orientation remains a private matter between Ford and his character, unless you count the home-baked Christmas cookies he has brought into the office. They may be as much of a giveaway cliché as the incriminating bottle of Perrier left beside two dead jocks in the black comedy *Heathers* to suggest that they died in a gay suicide pact.

Actors developing interior lives for their characters isn't news: it's what they do. The difference in the case of sexuality is that this kind of choice has traditionally been regarded as needlessly risky. A factually inspired gay encounter in a prison shower in *Midnight Express*, for instance, was nullified on-screen to make it appear as if one man were rebuffing the other. 'I wish that they'd let the steam in the shower come up and obscure the act itself instead of showing a rejection,' complained the author, Billy Hayes, and with some justification: *Midnight Express* was based on his life, so he knew what had really gone down.

Reality isn't always a film's best friend. The writer–director Bruce Robinson used the it-really-happened defence to justify the cartoonish depiction of Uncle Monty, played by Richard Griffiths, in *Withnail and I*, his squalid buddy movie about two out-of-work actors (Richard E. Grant and Paul McGann) in late-1960s London. In a 1987 *Evening Standard* interview with the subheading 'Is it still fair to poke fun at gays?' Robinson says of the character of Monty: 'I think homosexuals probably wouldn't like it...But who knows? Why shouldn't homosexuals be funny? Wilde was one and he was a bloody laugh. Monty also has great dignity in a way that is supportive to homosexuals. What they don't like about it is that he is predatory. When I was a young man I suffered, and that's not too strong a word, from predatory homosexuals.' (Monty's manoeuvres were inspired by the unwelcome attention that Robinson received as a young actor on the set of Franco Zeffirelli's *Romeo and Juliet* in 1968.)

Staunch defenders of *Withnail and I*, who proliferated in the lads' mag/Britpop era, have given the film a free pass on account of its obvious virtues, but it can be an uncomfortable watch for anyone not in the boys' club. There were early signs that it wasn't only gay audiences who would feel that way, regardless of Robinson's predictions about what 'they' would object to. When Paul McGann was briefly sacked from the role of the budding actor Marwood due to his inability to hide his native Liverpudlian accent, Robinson offered the part to Michael Maloney. He turned it down on the grounds that the script was 'anti-Black, anti-Irish and anti-gay'. McGann was given another shot.

Finding the early rushes 'about as funny as lung cancer', the producer, Denis O'Brien, pressured Robinson to crank up the camp excesses of Monty, who loans Marwood and Withnail his country cottage, only to show up in the middle of the night and attempt to insinuate himself into Marwood's...well, into Marwood. ('I mean to have you,' he pants, 'even if it must be burglary!') It was a pressure the director likes to believe he resisted – 'I'm most certainly not homophobic in any which way ever' – though it is Griffiths who deserves the lion's share of any credit for the character's vitality.

Homophobic or not, it's striking how incurious the film is about who Monty might be. As far as Marwood is concerned, he is a menace who wants only to ravage him. (He thinks the whole of London is after his butt. 'I fuck arses,' reads the graffiti on the lavatory wall of a north London boozer. 'Who fucks arses?' wonders Marwood, then steals a glance at the snarling drunk in the saloon bar. 'Maybe *he* fucks arses.') Monty, a simpering, plus-sized queen in trowelled-on eyeshadow, is the locus of the gay panic in *Withnail and I*, but his real function is to throw us off the scent about the main characters' relationship.

There's more to him, though, than the grotesque and ridiculous. Think of where he fits in the social chronology. Homosexuality was partially decriminalised in England and Wales only two years prior to the action of *Withnail and I*, and Monty is in his mid-sixties when the film takes place, so not only is he more lawless, and more of an outsider, than either of the film's title characters, but there would be for him a bittersweet aspect to the change in the law. Society was at last making slow progress in its grudging acceptance of people like him. Except now, he was old and over the hill: an Aschenbach in a world of Tadzios.

He must have seen *Victim* on its release in 1961. Kenneth Williams, the *Carry On* stalwart, certainly did, accusing it of being 'superficial and never knocking the real issues'. What was Monty's take? Whether he ever crossed paths with Bogarde, he would have known the actor was gay. Those in the business and on its fringes did. Strolling past a poster advertising Bogarde and Michael Redgrave in the wartime drama *The Sea Shall Not Have Them*, Noël Coward remarked: 'I fail to see why not. Everybody else has.'

Monty is a theatrical pretender, so perhaps he hobnobbed with the theatre crowd of the day. John Gielgud was a contemporary. Did Monty idolise him? Did he encounter him while cottaging? Monty must have felt twitchy, as many gay men would have done, when Gielgud was arrested in 1953 for 'persistently importuning male persons' in west London. The actor could not have foreseen that, three decades later, he would be playing Uncle Willie in the 1984 comedy *Scandalous*, loitering in a nightclub wearing the clone outfit of black leather cap, vest and trousers. He marvels at the post-punk outfit Bow Wow Wow ('They're all the rage, my dear') as they clatter through a rendition of 'Where's My Snake'.

After being collared for cottaging, Gielgud got off with a £10 fine and a slapped wrist from the judge, who called his conduct 'dangerous to other men, particularly young men'. He still had to withstand the opprobrium of newspapers such as the *Sunday Express*, which referred to his kind as 'human dregs'.

––––––––––

Disparaging images can be argued with and contested. Being overlooked entirely is harder to withstand. How to account, then, for Mike Leigh? It is no hardship at all being a queer fan of Leigh's films, and not only because many of them are tremendous, suffused with compassion and affinity for the outsider. Leigh works so diligently in the area of marginal lives that there is never any shortage of misfits, renegades and oddballs for a queer viewer to latch on to in his work. And yet he can find no place for any character who isn't avowedly heterosexual. Why isn't he interested?

It would be infantilising to suggest that queer audiences require ceaseless like-for-like representation. Gena Rowlands in *Opening Night*, the women in *The Women*, Judy Garland in anything – these have served as figures of identification for queer viewers regardless of sex or gender identity. The film-maker Jenni Olson has spoken of feeling a bond with James Dean in *Rebel Without a Cause*, and with Terence Hill, the laidback star of Italian comic westerns of the 1960s and 1970s. 'He was a complicated protagonist,' Olson said. 'He's a guy, he's very masculine, and I've had my gender identity "stuff" for as long as I can remember. Identifying with him made me feel heroic and aligned.'

And it would be a pity if movies came to resemble those personalised children's books produced using find-and-replace software, in which the main character bears the name of the gift's young recipient. That way madness and narcissism lie. 'Sometimes you see a movie and someone like you isn't in the movie and that's OK,' said Julio Torres. 'Representation matters, but not everything's about you, you know?'

Absence in a body of work spanning more than half a century, however, can only look conspicuous. And the manner of Mike Leigh's process makes the omission even more baffling. It's well known that he begins each project not with the written word but by selecting his actors and meeting with each of them individually to pick over a list of people they have known or met, several of whom will provide the spark for a potential character. That list, which can total a hundred or more names, is then whittled down to a handful. Once each character has been built up through solo improvisation and discussion, they are then brought together in group improvs, from which a narrative, and a film, eventually emerge.

One might point out that Ken Loach, Leigh's conscientious counterpart in British cinema, has shown an equal indifference to queerness in his films. But Loach's actors are not engaged at the stage of conception, since he works from screenplays originating with a single screenwriter. The peculiarity of Leigh's movies, on the other hand, is that each of them without exception is nurtured in close collaboration with around ten actors at a time, the avenues of creative input unrestricted by the vision of a single screenwriter. And yet no queer character has materialised.

That amounts to fourteen films, from *Bleak Moments* in 1971 to *Hard Truths* in 2024. Multiply this by around ten actors a-piece, each of whom will have suggested as many as a hundred or more possible inspirations for each role they've played, and the scale of the erasure begins to look astonishing. The situation as it currently stands is that Clint Eastwood has engaged more directly with queerness – whether demonising gays in *Magnum Force* and *Sudden Impact*, wallowing in homoeroticism and homophobia in *Heartbreak Ridge* or celebrating a drag queen, The Lady Chablis, in *Midnight in the Garden of Good and Evil* – than Leigh, one of the foremost chroniclers of contemporary life.

There is evidence, however slim, that he is aware of the existence of queer people, or at the very least, of gay men. He has certainly employed gay actors, such as Francis Lee, who was cast in *Topsy-Turvy* as a backstage dogsbody. Lee went on to direct a brace of earthy, hard-scrabble gay love stories: *God's Own Country*, which was, as he put it, about 'two queer lads on the side of a hill in Yorkshire in bad weather'; and *Ammonite*, which imagined a lesbian relationship between the nineteenth-century palaeontologist Mary Anning (Kate Winslet) and a married younger woman (Saoirse Ronan) of higher social standing.

In the space of two films, Lee has presented four detailed queer characters, whereas in fourteen of Mike Leigh's features, there is only one unconfirmed contender: Natalie, the young plumber played by Claire Skinner in *Life Is Sweet*, who presents as masc-leaning. The critic David Sterritt noted in Skinner's performance 'a hint of ambiguous sexuality that adds another dash of spice to the household'.

For *Naked*, his next film after *Life Is Sweet*, Leigh concocted with the production designer Alison Chitty a typically thorough history for the London flat that is being looked after by a minor character billed as 'Café Girl' and played by Gina McKee. (In Leigh's work, every location has its backstory.) His biographer, Michael Coveney, wrote that Leigh and Chitty had decided the place was owned by 'an upper-working-class, slightly pretentious gay couple called Dave and

David, who liked going to opera, travelling (especially to Morocco) and cooking with woks'. One of them worked at the Vehicle Licensing Office in east London, the other in the now-defunct Keith Prowse ticket agency. 'Nobody else knew about Dave or David,' said Chitty, 'though of course I did send mail to that address.'

Though never seen, or even mentioned by name, the couple still become a minor laughing stock. Sport is made of their decorating choices. A poster for Verdi is tacked to the wall with pins; a wok hangs over the oven. Imitation Greek knick-knacks are scattered willy-nilly around the flat, and there are Hockney-esque postcards on the mantelpiece. Pride of place on the bookcase goes to a large black-and-white glossy of Rock Hudson, once the most bankable star in Hollywood, who was outed a few months before dying of complications from AIDS in 1985.

To drive the point home, the anti-hero Johnny (David Thewlis) asks whether the absent owners are 'homo, er, sexual', to which Café Girl replies: 'What do you think?' Johnny makes it clear that he isn't being 'Homer-phobic. I mean, I like *The Iliad*. And *The Odyssey*.'

If you were hunting for a silver lining, you might argue that this proves Leigh's films take place in a world where queerness exists, even if it can be broached only tangentially. Mocked and absent Dave and David may be, but they also provide the sole suggestion in *Naked* of a romantic relationship not blighted by violence, dysfunction or misery. It's a little-known fact that movie characters continue living their lives after the end credits have rolled, and the same can be true even of those fictional figures who never quite make it in front of the camera. Watching *Naked* now, Dave and David are more vivid than some of the characters we can actually see, just as the plaintive unnamed cadet in *Damien: Omen II* still seems to be there, somewhere, yearning on the touchline.

Anyone who loves Leigh's films can only be puzzled by this uncharacteristic timidity. Even if he had accommodated a queer character in 1971, the year he made *Bleak Moments*, he wouldn't have been any kind of outlier. There were a lot of them about.

It was the year of *Death in Venice*; the Belgian lesbian vampire film *Daughters of Darkness*; the prison drama *Fortune and Men's Eyes* (tagline: 'What goes on in prison is a crime'); Pasolini's *The Decameron*, which is the middle panel in his bawdy 'Trilogy of Life'; and *A Season in Hell*, about the gay poets Arthur Rimbaud and Paul Verlaine, later played by Leonardo DiCaprio and David Thewlis in *Total Eclipse*.

It was the year of *Sunday Bloody Sunday*, starring Peter Finch as a gay doctor sharing his lover (Murray Head) with a divorcée (Glenda Jackson). Early in the film, the doctor casually plants a bold smacker on his boyfriend's lips. The director, John Schlesinger, fresh from the fascinatingly conflicted *Midnight Cowboy*, went straight for a tight two-shot. It was intimate, brightly lit, with both actors in profile. No musical editorialising, no ambiguity, no cuts. In another scene, a surly, bowl-haired Daniel Day-Lewis, with a red bandana knotted around his neck, scratches a parked car with a broken bottle as he slinks along the street. Such hooligan behaviour makes it possible that this is, in fact, a younger version of the ex-National Front bully-boy whom Day-Lewis would go on to play fourteen years later in *My Beautiful Laundrette*, set in a different patch of south London and another corner of the Queer Cinematic Universe.

1971 was also the year of *Badnam Basti*, or *Neighbourhood of Ill Repute*, the first Indian film to suggest, if not depict, a love affair between two men: Sarnam (Nitin Sethi), an ex-bandit toiling as a truck driver, and the young cleaner Shivraj (Amar Kakkad). Adapting the 1957 novel by Kamleshwar Prasad Saxena, published in English as *A Street with 57 Lanes*, the director, Prem Kapoor, had no choice but to handle the subject with kid gloves worn inside oven mitts and held at arm's length. There may be nothing here as emphatic as the kiss in *Sunday Bloody Sunday*, but *Badnam Basti* still crackles. In one scene, Sarnam stands over the sleeping Shivraj, a pair of globe-like pendants dangling suggestively from his neck as he strokes the young man's head. A cut to the next morning reveals Shivraj getting dressed beside the bed while Sarnam, under the covers but naked from the waist up, sleeps on. Later, Sarnam tells him: 'I thirst for you.'

This was the year, too, that James Bidgood's *Pink Narcissus* was finally released: the visually succulent, polymorphously perverse adventures of a hustler in a kitsch fairy-tale landscape. Bidgood, a photographer, former dressmaker and East Village drag performer, began work on the film in his Hell's Kitchen apartment in 1963. He lived inside the elaborate sets he was constructing, foam-board urinals and all, and built a funhouse-mirror version of Times Square in a loft loaned to him by the producers; the film sprang up around him, even devoured him, as the shoot dragged on and on. When it surfaced in 1971 in a cut not sanctioned by Bidgood, it was credited to 'Anonymous'; his identity remained undisclosed for almost another thirty years.

Released in the same year was Rosa von Praunheim's confrontational semi-documentary *It Is Not the Homosexual Who Is Perverse, But the Society in Which He Lives*, which provoked anger among many gay activists. 'It was a very critical film on gay subculture and gay unpolitical behaviour,' the director said. 'It asks gay people to be open, to be political, to be on the side of other political causes and this was a big scandal.' Von Praunheim was a contemporary of Fassbinder, but the rallying spirit of his film (which ends with the slogan 'Out of the toilets and into the streets!') couldn't have been further from that director's bleakness. 'His philosophy was "life is shit" and he showed that in his films. That's a message I couldn't support.'

Fred Halsted was still in the process of shooting *LA Plays Itself*, but its path had already been cleared by the success of Wakefield Poole's revolutionary hardcore porn classic of 1971, *Boys in the Sand*. The title of Poole's film alluded to an earlier queer landmark, Mart Crowley's 1968 play *The Boys in the Band*, which was filmed in 1970 by William Friedkin (and would be again fifty years later by Joe Mantello).

Fassbinder, who could make a movie in the time it took other directors to unscrew the lens cap, released four in 1971, as well as premiering the stage version of *The Bitter Tears of Petra Von Kant*, which he filmed the following year. After *Whity*, his deranged queer western, he plunged straight into *Beware of a Holy Whore*, his behind-the-scenes portrait of a chaotic film shoot. It was inspired by the explosive production of *Whity*, where he had invested time and money into wooing his beloved (and married) star, Günther Kaufmann, who was slow to play ball and put out.

By 1971, the macho landscape of British gangsterland was already in touch with its own queerness – unsurprisingly, perhaps, for a milieu that had been presided over by the Kray twins. *Villain*, released that year, starred Richard Burton as Vic Dakin, a sadistic, Ronnie Kray-like gay crime boss. (Burton had sought Kray's counsel before making the film, as had James Fox prior to playing a hoodlum in *Performance*.) Ian McShane, one of the stars of the original production of Joe Orton's *Loot*, was Vic's handsome driver and plaything. Three decades later, McShane did his bit to restore queerness to the British gangster movie in *Sexy Beast* and *44-Inch Chest*, following a few years in which Guy Ritchie had overrun the genre's kinkiness with dreary straight-boy vulgarity.

For obvious reasons, Britain has never cornered the market in westerns. Its gangster films, though, are spur-deep in homoerotic text and subtext. From *Performance* to *Mojo*, *Gangster No. 1* to *I'll Sleep When I'm Dead*, there is as much queerness there as you'll find in any western since Montgomery Clift and John Ireland admired one another's pistols in *Red River*. *The Long Good Friday*, from 1980, goes as far as to make sexuality both a plot point and part of the furniture. The pugnacious East End mob boss Harold Shand (Bob Hoskins) is devastated when his gay childhood friend Colin (Paul Freeman), a member of his criminal gang, is fatally stabbed. Colin was slain by the poolside stud he was cruising at the time: a near-wordless walk-on part for Pierce Brosnan, exactly fifteen years before he was cast as James Bond, the queerest straight man in cinema.

In *The Celluloid Closet*, Vito Russo argues that the film only makes Colin gay 'so that he can be dramatically murdered while cruising... His sexual desire leads him to death.' A less simplistic take might be that the casual depiction of Colin's sexuality puts the film in step with both the tenor of the British gangster flick and the Genet-esque association between queerness and criminality.

For LGBTQ+ people of the 1960s and 1970s, 'the Krays and the police... were not at the moral polar opposites they might have been for [their] straight contemporaries', writes the journalist Hugo Greenhalgh. 'For many queer men – and the few exceptionally brave trans women – the police were very much the enemy; criminalised due to their sexuality or gender identity, one can understand the sympathy and perhaps greater understanding they had for fellow outlaws such as the Krays.' You would look for some time at *The Long Good Friday* before finding the homophobia that Russo saw. What the film shows is the sort of casual acceptance of queerness that would never have happened if these were cops instead of robbers.

If there was a reigning queer queen of 1971, it was Holly Woodlawn, seen whooping it up with her trans sisters Candy Darling and Jackie

Curtis as members of the insurrectionist group P.I.G. (Politically Involved Girls) in Paul Morrissey's *Women in Revolt*. That film came hot on the high heels of her career-launching turn in his movie *Trash* the previous year. To claim that Woodlawn had been discovered by Morrissey would be to suggest a misleading degree of passivity on her part. No one who lies to the press about being one of Andy Warhol's prized superstars – when the truth is that her only connection to him was being rumbled after trying to charge a $2,000 camera to his account – can accurately be described as a wallflower. Woodlawn was an off-Broadway hoofer when she boasted falsely that she was a Factory girl. Her audacity appealed to Morrissey, though, and he invited her to star in his next film without having met her.

He had been pondering the shape of *Trash*, which was to be a picaresque account of the life of a drug addict. The figures in Warhol/Morrissey films suggest the lovers described by Tennessee Williams in the poem 'Life Story': 'rag dolls a bored child dropped on a bed'. But now Morrissey asked: what if the typically apathetic central character, to be played by the ravishing but somnambulant Joe Dallesandro, was involved with his temperamental opposite? This would be a woman who, as Morrissey put it, was 'hellbent on survival instead of destruction, someone who lied and stole and cheated to get something out of life, as opposed to someone drifting inexorably down the gutter to death'. This could be Holly Woodlawn.

Sure enough, she is the special sauce that gives *Trash* its kick. Her incorrigible, scare-haired vitality contrasts joyfully with Dallesandro's concussed stupor; she flaps and soars, crackles with sarcasm, conveys emotional nuance, while he performs his usual beautiful, hypnotic, slow-motion swan-dive into oblivion. She was, said Morrissey, a 'volcano-like mountain of energy and positivism, a powerful but always good-natured life force that just shrugged off every kind of horror and adversity'.

Remarkably, Woodlawn's performance broke through to the Hollywood establishment. Bette Davis complimented her when the pair met at a party; George Cukor lobbied unsuccessfully for her to receive Oscar recognition.

Soon, Woodlawn was being courted by Ismail Merchant and James Ivory, who offered her a part in *Savages*, their 1972 satire on civilisation and primitivism; she declined in favour of the musical *Scarecrow in a Garden of Cucumbers*, which paid more. In a performance punctuated by slapstick and soft-shoe shuffles, she is, says Liz Purchell, 'like a live-action version of her fellow trans icon Bugs Bunny' – a reference to the pansexual wabbit who kissed countless male co-stars, dressed in drag more than forty times between 1939 and 1996 and self-identified queerly as 'a rabbit born in a human world'.

Woodlawn fielded dinner invitations from Fellini. 'We hit it off famously!' she chirped. 'I picked up the fork, he picked up the tab.' A smattering of other roles followed, including the short film *Broken Goddess*, directed by Peter Dallas and originally conceived as a vehicle for Bette Midler, whose shows at the Continental Baths (or 'the Tubs', as Midler called them) Dallas had lit. Woodlawn also briefly became a cabaret star in New York's West Village. It wasn't long, however, before her screen career – fittingly for someone who had named herself after a Bronx cemetery – appeared to be dead.

10

NIGHT VOLTAGE

It was September 1995, and Peter Strickland had given up the ghost. For several hours, the twenty-two-year-old student had been waiting hopefully in Arrivals at Newark Airport, craning his neck over the crowds to try to spot the woman he was there to meet. He would notice if she tottered past – this was not the sort of person to blend in with the suits and the holidaymakers. Every time another batch of incoming travellers had thinned to nought, he would vacate his post temporarily and dash to the nearest payphone to try once more the Los Angeles number in his wallet. Now it was dawning on him that his underground dream might be over.

Five years earlier, he had been captivated by a black-and-white still in Danny Peary's book *Cult Movies*, which showed Holly Woodlawn lounging in a bomb-site room. Above her was an empty picture frame, as though the canvas inside had absconded rather than try to compete with her for the viewer's attention. A rusting birdcage, also empty, was suspended above her head. 'That whole junkyard aesthetic was so utterly new to me,' Strickland says now. 'It sounds facile, but it was very different from my middle-class life.'

His unlikely portal to the queer film underground was the Reading branch of the newsagent WH Smith. 'I worked there in my teens. Weirdly, they stocked the VHS tapes of *Flesh*, *Trash* and *Heat*, so I got those at a nice discount.' Around the same time, he started taking the train from the Thames Valley suburbs to the Scala cinema, nicknamed 'the Sodom Odeon', in King's Cross, where the streets were paved with shattered glass and vomit. The documentary *Scala!!!* is sticky with tales of the sort of sex, drug-taking and debauchery routinely conducted in the glow of the beer-stained screen. Strickland's experience was nothing like that. 'I was very young,' he says. 'I was a virgin. I was at the age where I would've welcomed something happening to me there, some older woman seducing me, but nobody ever did.' The closest he came to going wild at the Scala was buying a bottle of poppers en route to the cinema. 'But I just ended up with a headache.'

Strickland was studying fine art at university and had written his first narrative short film, *Bubblegum*. 'You could go away in term time, when it was much cheaper to travel, if it was for a project,' he explains. 'It was $200 to get to New York, I had free accommodation there with family, so this cocktail of factors made it possible.' While writing *Bubblegum*, those Warhol/Morrissey films were much on his mind. 'What I love about them is the mischief and affection. You never felt Morrissey was looking down on his characters or judging them. As well as it being quite free-flowing and outrageous, there's a lot of warmth.'

He still counts *Trash* as one of his favourite films. 'I love Joe Dallesandro's insouciance. His absolute apathy. People are being blown next to him and he doesn't care. He's even more like that in *Heat*. Everyone's after his body and he can't be bothered. It works so well. There's also no mention in *Trash* of Holly being trans, which feels so liberating. It's like in Fassbinder's *Fox and His Friends*, when he invites his boyfriend for dinner with his parents. There's no moment of: "Oof, it's a guy. . ." It's all just taken for granted.'

Strickland had the idea of casting Woodlawn in *Bubblegum* after seeing a BBC documentary about the figures immortalised in Lou Reed's song 'Walk on the Wild Side', including her, Dallesandro and Candy Darling. He offered Woodlawn the part of a supermarket cashier who has a chance meeting with a con artist posing as the rock star with whom she is infatuated. She agreed to star in the film for expenses alone. Strickland paid for her flight, arranged a hotel for the duration of the shoot and took an airport bus to Newark from the home of his Greek Orthodox aunt and uncle in Woodhaven, Queens, to pick her up. And then: no show.

'She wasn't there. I was calling and calling. A day later, I eventually got this bleary, half-asleep response from her: "What? Where am I?" I had to wire her the money for another flight.'

Having cancelled her hotel booking, he put her up with him and his relatives. 'My uncle was hardly around, as he was a taxi driver. But my aunt, a very straightlaced, devout Greek Orthodox lady who worked at Waldbaum's supermarket, got on with her, strangely enough. She just thought Holly was one of my friends. She had no idea she'd had a trans person in her bed until after Holly left. She was a bit taken aback but very open-minded.' Wait – where was his aunt sleeping? 'Oh, she was on the couch. The Greeks always offer their beds.'

Even today, he sounds astonished to have been in the orbit, however briefly, of the queen of *Trash*. 'It was kind of amazing. Here I am sharing a house with someone I idolised. She was a big singer in the shower, too; it was quite comical. Then, by the end of it, I couldn't wait to get rid of her. We were getting on each other's nerves. But, you know, I could be an arsehole as well. When Holly was going back to the airport, I thought: "She can take the bus like anyone else!" We got into an argument about that because she wanted a taxi. I accused her of being spoilt. I met John Waters afterwards through Holly, and he had a quiet word with me: "You've got to pamper your stars until they're sick." I took that advice.'

She was a breeze to direct. 'Really easy. I was restoring the sound on *Bubblegum* recently, and I thought: "God, she's so good. Why didn't more people work with her?" I mean, I *know* why: because she was such a pain in the arse. She'd disappear and I'd have to cancel stuff. It was so stressful. I was warned about her. I'm not making light of her capricious character – she'd had a few suicide attempts, and the poor woman was a bit of a mess. She had a cocktail of trauma from so many of her friends dying young and tragically; so many drugs, not just illegal ones but pharmaceutical drugs, messing up her system. She could be adorable one minute, then she could turn in a flash, not just to me but to strangers on the street. But she was a natural.'

As the object of her desire, Strickland cast Nick Zedd, the founding member of the Cinema of Transgression, who directed the 1979 punk cannibal movie *They Eat Scum*. Zedd never left home without his scowl. 'He could be very argumentative. But his eyes lit up with Holly. He knew everything about her and was constantly mining her for stories.'

Strickland later inserted a tribute of sorts to Woodlawn, and to the final scene of *Trash*, into his 2014 film *The Duke of Burgundy*. This rapturous study of a lesbian sub/dom relationship was shot by Nic Knowland, who also photographed Tony Palmer's 1981 television version of Benjamin Britten's opera *Death in Venice*, and set in a luxurious fantasy world apparently devoid of men. Cynthia (Sidse Babett Knudsen) is the reluctant dominant who would occasionally prefer simply to lounge around in her pyjamas or snuggle up with Evelyn (Chiara D'Anna), the tenacious submissive who demands unrelenting punishment. The women are consumed by their sexual role play, though it is integral only to one of them. Evelyn wants no quarter to be given, but in the long run it is Cynthia who is smarting, and even suffering, because of the demands put on her to play a role she doesn't want.

'I wanted to make it about love and compromise and how you negotiate differing sexual needs in a relationship,' says Strickland. 'Is it right to suppress your own desires to give someone else a peaceful life? Should that happen? Or should you do something you're uncomfortable with to satiate the other person? It's tricky in a long-term relationship, but I didn't want to offer any answers.'

One of the pleasures of the film is how it functions like a culinary reduction, distilling complex sensations into intense hits of flavour. Banality co-exists with breathless passion, each ingredient heightening the other. That's where the tribute to Woodlawn comes in. 'I loved Holly's last line in *Trash*, when she really needs to suck Joe's cock,' Strickland says. 'It was flippant, crude and irreverent, but you could feel how important and cathartic it was to her. I copied that when Evelyn asks Cynthia to sit on her face.'

A few months before I call Strickland, my friend Ben and I spot him in the foyer of the British Film Institute with his children. 'What's the deal with Peter Strickland?' asks Ben in a decent imitation of a Jerry Seinfeld routine. It's common knowledge that the director is straight, and yet his work is steeped in queerness. Not the cuddly Love-Is-Love sort wrapped in a rainbow flag either, but the full-on, no-cologne, sweat-and-leather, fudge-packing, jock-strapped, cum-stained kind. His affinity for queer culture ripples through *The Duke of Burgundy* and is the lifeblood of two short films: *Blank Narcissus (Passion of the Swamp)*, in which a fictitious ageing porn director delivers a doleful DVD commentary over the lyrical, *Pink Narcissus*-style gay fairy-tale he made as a younger man; and the 3-minute *GUO4*, which uses stop-motion freeze frames to render a charged balletic tussle between two naked dudes in a locker room.

Clinching his queer credentials beyond any doubt, though, is a film that doesn't exist yet. Strickland has been trying since 2012 to drum up the funds to make *Night Voltage*, his sexually explicit screenplay set in New York's thriving gay clubs in 1980, just as AIDS began scything through the landscape. The young Greek American protagonist, Nondas, is a promiscuous up-and-coming synth wizard in the mould of Patrick Cowley, the producer and musician who died of complications from AIDS in 1982 without knowing he had the disease.

'The catalyst for me was Cowley being sent home repeatedly by the doctors, who were allegedly saying nothing was wrong,' Strickland explains. 'This idea of someone who thinks he's in the clear provides a euphoric ending for the character but a tragic one for the audience, so I worked backwards from that. I'm interested in the bit between Stonewall and AIDS – this ten- to twelve-year period where you could finally be free, and there was this explosion of creativity and art and sex.'

The budget for *Night Voltage* still hasn't come together after all these years. 'The times have changed a lot with #MeToo, which I completely understand. A lot of urgent concerns about criminality, though, have become conflated with portrayals of pleasure. I often get flak for stuff I've done – being a bit of a pervert and so on – but no one ever gives you flak for showing suffering on-screen. If I said I was going to make torture porn, I'd probably get funding right away.'

He's under no illusion that his movies – which also include *Berberian Sound Studio*, a workplace drama in *giallo* clothing, and *In Fabric*, a high-street horror about a killer dress – are for everyone. 'I respect an individual saying, "This is not for me." A lot of my Greek relatives wouldn't go near my films. But I do have an issue with people passing judgement on desires that are consensual.' He mentions Operation Spanner, the criminal prosecution in the late 1980s of sixteen British men for acts of consensual sado-masochistic sex. A sobering reflection on the case, in which the State made chilling incursions into the queer body, can be found in Charlie Shackleton's 2018 short *Lasting Marks*. As one of the interviewees in Monika Treut's 1999 documentary *Gendernauts* puts it: 'My body belongs to me and I'm going to do what I want with it to make me happy. This flesh here is mine. I live here. I don't have to pay a damage deposit.'

The period setting also makes *Night Voltage* a costly proposition. 'Budget-wise, it will be extremely heavy on the production design and costume departments,' says Strickland. 'There's one nightclub where everybody's naked, but still . . .' Then there is the content. 'Most A-list actors won't go near the material.' One Hollywood star expressed an interest in playing Nondas before dropping out. Then Strickland found the perfect actor, but he wasn't bankable. Funding has come and gone. Christine Vachon's Killer Films, which produced the bulk of the New Queer Cinema of the 1990s, along with everything Todd Haynes has made since *Poison*, is on board. So, too, is the producer Tristan Goligher (*Weekend*), who has been there from the start, and Film4. On the day Strickland and I speak, there has been interest from a new source which might nudge *Night Voltage* into the light of day.

I've been hearing whispers about the project for so long now that it has become a kind of dream movie flickering dimly in my mind like something I saw on a corroded print at the Scala back in the day. Building up to ask if I can read the script, I experience a tingling sensation as if I were Evelyn summoning the nerve to beg Cynthia to lock me in a chest or sit on my face.

How would he feel about showing it to me?

'Yeah, sure,' he says casually. 'I'll send it.'

Later that day, the PDF file drops into my inbox. I open it and scroll down a few pages, feasting on the words flashing past, the smoke from the dry ice in the New York nightclub swirling around my feet like tendrils, enveloping me as I sit at my desk.

```
3. INT. NIGHTCLUB CORRIDOR. NIGHT.

Pounding music floods in from the main dance
floor, which isn't visible from the corridor.
Nondas is kissing a half-naked man amidst a
```

throng of other men making out with each other. The lighting is low and moody. Just as the man lowers himself to fellate Nondas, the lights come on in full brightness and the music stops, resulting in a loud collective groan.

DJ (*off-screen through the loudspeakers*)
Show's over, everyone. Time for bed.

A succession of penises that are sticking out of glory-holes retract almost in unison.

'Someone asked me why *The Duke of Burgundy* was about two women,' Strickland says. 'Why not a man and a woman, or two men? Of course, I was saving the men for *Night Voltage*, which I thought at the time would be my next film. My male one.'

The Duke of Burgundy is informed in its plush, Euro-sleazy aesthetic by the discredited softcore daydreams of 1970s eroticists such as Jesús 'Jess' Franco, whose 1974 film *Lorna the Exorcist* Strickland had briefly considered remaking before he took a sideways swerve into paying homage instead. It is a near-namesake of that Spanish film-maker, though, who springs to mind for my friend Ben when he is mulling over Strickland's predilections that day at the BFI. 'All the gay stuff,' he says. 'What is he, the British James Franco?'

What Ben is alluding to is that species of straight artist who co-opts queer iconography, seemingly for the cachet. Any such complaints about Franco pale alongside the allegations which subsequently emerged of his sexual misconduct. (The actor was accused in 2018 of inappropriate and sexually exploitative behaviour; in 2021, he paid $2.2 million in a class action suit.) But for nearly a decade before he ran out of road, he encouraged speculation surrounding his sexuality.

In front of the camera, his gay paydays include *Howl* (where he played Allen Ginsberg), *The Broken Tower* (another poet, Hart Crane) and Gus Van Sant's *Milk* (Harvey Milk's ex-lover, Scott Smith). He also starred in two factually inspired queer films directed by Van Sant's protégé Justin Kelly. In *I Am Michael*, he was Michael Glatze, the former gay activist and founder of *Young Gay America* magazine, who embraces religion, renounces his homosexuality and adopts a 'turn or burn' credo. In *King Cobra*, the actor was memorably sleazy as a gay-escort-turned-porn-producer who murders a rival for control of a twink superstar.

As director, Franco has been piggybacking, or barebacking, on the queer canon for years. He co-directed and starred in *Interior. Leather Bar*, a featurette about the shooting of explicit scenes which were snipped from *Cruising* on the orders of the MPAA – a loss that the film's director, William Friedkin, described as 'butchery on a scale comparable to *The Magnificent Ambersons*'. In 2011, Franco assembled *My Own Private River*, an alternative and even more River Phoenix-centric cut of Van Sant's *My Own Private Idaho* using only unseen out-takes from that film. (He and Van Sant took co-directing credits on the supplementary project.) In the same year, Franco directed *Sal*, about the melt-in-the-mouth misfit Sal Mineo from *Rebel Without a Cause* and *Who Killed Teddy Bear?*

Any serious queer intent in Franco's body of work risked being jeopardised by the sniggering peek-a-boo games surrounding his bromance with Seth Rogen, which he expressed variously through the guise of characters, in *Pineapple Express* and *The Interview*, or as an exaggerated version of himself in the apocalyptic comedy *This Is the End*. It's a running gag that doesn't run very far, beginning and ending with the notion that Franco might have the hots for Rogen. That sexual ambiguity was one component of an act which seemed to keep the media, if not audiences, on tenterhooks for years. He dragged up for the magazine *Candy* and told a journalist: 'Maybe I'm just gay.' Baiters gonna bait.

Perhaps the world got a James Franco because it didn't yet have, or couldn't yet handle, a fully formed Kristen Stewart. No other modern performer of comparable calibre and status has expressed queer sexuality so emphatically through their choice of roles. There is Justin Kelly's *JT LeRoy*, in which Stewart plays Savannah Knoop, the artist who helped perpetrate a notorious literary hoax: Knoop agreed to pose as the (male) author of a brace of edgy queer novels, which were in fact the work of their older sister-in-law, Laura Albert, played in the film by Laura Dern. Stewart was also revelatory as a diffident night-school teacher, pined over by a timid student (Lily Gladstone), in Kelly Reichardt's *Certain Women*, and as a queer steroid-pushing gym boss, daughter to a vicious gangster, in Rose Glass's lurid B-movie-style romp *Love Lies Bleeding*.

Much of the frisson in Stewart's two films with Olivier Assayas derives from the effect of her being not quite tangible, or just out of reach. In both instances, she plays a peripheral or ephemeral figure: a curious position for one of the world's most photographed faces to be in. She is Valentine, the PA providing succour to a formidable but insecure stage actor (Juliette Binoche), in *Clouds of Sils Maria*; near the end of the film, she vanishes into thin air. In *Personal Shopper*, she is Maureen, another dogsbody of sorts, who dashes across Europe to choose this snazzy dress or those stiletto-heeled boots for her supermodel boss. Maureen's identity is nebulous at best. Speeding through Paris on her motorbike, she is reduced to a blur. Arriving early at a photoshoot, she is asked to be a stand-in for her employer, which rather sums her up. A journalist for *Vogue* tells her she has 'a stupid job' and offers her work, which she turns down. A magazine called *Vague* might be more to her taste.

In the film's key scene, Maureen steps into an ensemble – harness, sheer underwear, transparent dress – which resembles an X-ray in fabric form, to complement the literal X-rays (an ultrasound, a security scanner) to which she is subjected elsewhere in the movie. The tension between a character who barely exists unless she is wearing someone else's clothes, and an actor whose presence could scarcely be more vividly human, is thrilling. Give Stewart a scene of plain exposition and she renders it natural, even nutty, with her halting delivery and twitchy, provisional gestures. Ask her to evoke inner desolation, as she does in the film's final shot or throughout her performance as Princess Diana in *Spencer*, and she will stare down the lens with all the dread of the last woman on Earth.

Personal Shopper, JT LeRoy and *Spencer* all provide Stewart with fastidious scenes of dressing and undressing that hint at the divestiture or cultivation of layers, defences and secrets. The sense here is that the actor is exposing some unseen inner dimension, expressing her own queerness through a series of masks. Now that the world has Kristen Stewart, the phenomenon of James Franco may never need to happen again.

It's true that Nicholas Galitzine, who identifies as straight, has trooped merrily through various gay or bisexual roles, including *Handsome Devil, Red, White and Royal Blue* and *The Craft: Legacy*, a twenty-first-century reboot of the 1996 teen horror *The Craft*, itself a queer favourite largely for Fairuza Balk's deranged turn as a witch who is a lesbian in all but the letter of the script. Josh O'Connor has gone the Galitzine route, too, seemingly without ruffling too many parade feathers, in the likes of *Hide and Seek, God's Own Country, Challengers* and the 2017 short *The Colour of His Hair*.

When Sean Penn claimed in 2024 that he could not play Harvey Milk today because of 'a timid and artless policy toward the human imagination', he overlooked the ease with which actors such as Galitzine, O'Connor, Daniel Craig and Drew Starkey (*Queer*), Paul Mescal (*All of Us Strangers*) and Sterling K. Brown (*American Fiction*) have been accepted in gay roles, or the absence of any outcry when Joaquin Phoenix suggested to Todd Haynes that they collaborate on a sexually explicit gay drama set in 1930s Mexico. (There was more of an outcry when Phoenix got 'cold feet' and quit that project in August 2024, five days before shooting was due to begin. '[I]f you are tempted to finger wag or admonish us that "that's what you get for casting a straight actor" – DON'T,' wrote Christine Vachon, a producer on the untitled film, a week after it collapsed. 'This was HIS project that he brought to US.')

No straight actor other than Franco, however, has turned the performance of queerness into a multi-disciplinary art project that spills off the screen and into galleries and press interviews.

I'm still not sure, though, if my Franco Couldn't Happen Now theory stands up. Fortunately, I have the perfect friend to try it out on: Justin Kelly was not only editorial assistant on *Milk*, in which Franco and Penn played lovers; he also directed Franco in *I Am Michael* and *King Cobra*, as well as Kristen Stewart in *JT LeRoy*.

Justin and I met in 2008 when I was sent to Los Angeles to interview Gus Van Sant. I breezed into the screening room where Van Sant was in the middle of viewing a rough cut of *Milk*, and promptly tripped over his Australian Shepherd, Milo, who was snoozing in the dark. Justin was minding the dog that morning, so in some small but unshakable way I will always blame him for my spectacular stumble, as well as the burning embarrassment I feel whenever it comes to mind.

It was Van Sant who first drew Franco's attention to a newspaper report on the real Michael Glatze and his dramatic volte-face. And it was he who suggested that Justin might direct *I Am Michael* after Franco had optioned the story. 'I never saw James's performances as him "pretending" to be gay,' Justin tells me from among the jaunty cushions in his mother's guest bedroom in Prescott, Arizona, where he has stopped off on a road trip. 'I just saw him as being interested in playing all kinds of characters. He knew he could help these cool queer movies get made and give someone like me a chance to direct. When we were doing press for *I Am Michael* and *King Cobra*, journalists would throw him some shade, and I'd be, like: "He's bringing these incredible queer stories to the screen, so what's the problem?"'

The term 'queerbaiting' wasn't in circulation when *I Am Michael* opened in 2015. 'Once it started floating around, I became very irritated by it,' Justin says. 'I think it's fucking bullshit. Since before Stonewall, gay people have been asking the straight world to accept us and not treat us differently. And now we finally have these huge names – actors, musicians – telling the world that not only should you not be homophobic but that maybe it's fucking cool to be gay . . . and people are *mad*? I'm, like, "What is wrong with you?"' He is laughing and spluttering. 'That's what we've been asking for all this time!'

Times change, and so does the discourse. 'In Franco's era, it was oddly normal to ask, "Are you gay?" The difference today with Nicholas Galitzine and Josh O'Connor is that we've entered an age where you don't really ask any more. Or you're not supposed to. Look at what happened with Lukas Gage, who's a friend of mine.' When a Twitter user suggested in 2022 that Hollywood should 'stop hiring non LGBTQIA+ actors like Lukas Gage to play LGBTQIA+ characters', Gage, who starred as the cabana boy getting rimmed by his boss in the first season of *The White Lotus*, replied: 'u don't know my alphabet'. (The actor, who is gay, later said: 'Let me [come out] when I'm ready.')

Objections to straight actors playing queer roles may be guided partly by the misapprehension that, in doing so, they are snatching work away from LGBTQ+ talent. 'Dare I veer into a controversial example?' asks Justin. 'Scarlett Johansson was going to play a trans character, then people raised hell, so she dropped out.' He is referring to the still-unmade *Rub & Tug*, in which Johansson was cast as the real-life trans male gangster Dante 'Tex' Gill, before stepping down from the film in 2018. 'It would have been a great story to get out there. Who knows how many people it would have inspired? But it fell apart. And now that movie is gone. I think queer people should feel bummed about that. I mean, imagine ScarJo at the Oscars for playing a trans man: that would've been major. The important thing to remember is – guess what? – famous actors get indie queer films financed. And we need visibility.'

His approach has been to cast queer where possible. 'If I've ever cast straight actors in gay roles – which hasn't been that often because I've been lucky with Kristen, and with Zachary Quinto in *I Am Michael* and Garrett Clayton in *King Cobra* – then I'll get people saying, "Oh, I wish you'd cast a gay actor." For a studio film, I agree they should try harder to cast gay actors, because they have the power and money to do so. But that's not how independent films work. You have to attach the actor first. That's how you raise the money. Without James, my first two movies wouldn't have been made.'

Attaching Kristen Stewart to *JT LeRoy* was nothing short of a coup. She came out publicly in her opening monologue on *Saturday Night Live* in 2017, during which she was greeted with cheers after describing herself as 'like, *so* gay'. Justin had met her a few years earlier to discuss the script, which he and Knoop adapted from Knoop's book *Girl Boy Girl: How I Became JT LeRoy*. 'Kristen made it clear that she'd brought her girlfriend with her, and I remember thinking: "Ooh, I know she's gay and no one else does!"'

She signed on before *Personal Shopper* was released. 'After I saw her in that, I thought: "Everyone will want her now. I hope she doesn't drop out of my movie."' It took several years to secure financing, even with Stewart on board. So why did she hang on? 'She was very connected to the material. I brought it up one time when we were shooting in Winnipeg. We would go to this small-town gay bar where everyone would stare and send over drinks. I told Kristen, "I'm so glad it all worked out. Part of me was wondering if you were gonna get 5,000 other great offers and bail." And she said: "I would have done this movie at any point. I was afraid it might never happen because it's such a cool story that it could have been too cool for people to put money into, or to understand.'"

The timing couldn't have been better. 'Since she wasn't officially out when she signed up, she jumped at the opportunity to play Sav, who was not just a lesbian but a queer woman who now identifies as non-binary – but at that time did not. There are already non-binary aspects to the character in the movie, though, in all the going back-and-forth between being a boy and a girl.'

During hair and make-up camera tests, Stewart experimented with the character's voice and physiognomy. She wedged earplugs inside her jaw, right at the back of her mouth, to give herself a more masculine look and to alter her voice, Brando-style.

She also worked closely with Knoop. 'Kristen and Sav really hit it off. Sav's a true artist: their whole style, their clothing. They wear the weirdest shit, it's fucking incredible. Kristen was so into them as a person. One of the things she brought, I think, came from not being out at that point. Sav, the character, was pretending to be JT while also in the closet about being potentially trans and potentially non-binary, and not knowing how to put that out into the world. And Kristen was going through a similar thing: at that level of fame, you're potentially gonna get attacked or ostracised for coming out. That idea of hiding part of one's identity was something she wove into the character so beautifully in these very quiet ways. You can see in a lot of her roles she's dealing with identity. As Princess Diana, she's trying to figure out who she is as someone who doesn't want to be that famous.'

Her performance in *Love Lies Bleeding*, though, is the one that Justin maintains is the closest to the Kristen Stewart he knows. 'In *JT LeRoy*, she was playing someone so different from herself, even though there was that connection of both having a secret. Whereas I saw more of Kristen in *Love Lies Bleeding*, more of the real person in terms of being a badass bitch. I think it was a chance for her to do so many things she's always wanted to do. To play a version of herself and to be super-fucking-gay. To have those sex scenes, the stuff about fingering, the "I wanna spread you" line, licking the protein shake that spills on her girlfriend's body, taking men down. All things that I believe she was dying to put out there.'

Looked at from this distance, *I Am Michael* and *JT LeRoy* play like cracked mirror images of each other. Both are inspired by real-life identity crises and capitalise on the actors' off-screen baggage. Just as Stewart's experience of being in the spotlight while hiding parts of herself informed *JT LeRoy*, so Franco's vagueness over his sexuality enhanced *I Am Michael*, which hinges on the sincerity or otherwise of Glatze's doubtful conversion. A gay man trying to convince the world he is straight was being played by a straight actor hinting that he might be gay. 'I don't think I was conscious of it at the time,' says Justin. 'But now you bring it up, it probably did help. We're watching this guy question his sexuality. It might also have helped him play the character as well. I don't know whether James is gay or not.' He smiles. 'I mean, everyone's a little bit gay, so . . .'

Peter Strickland is unconvinced about Franco's gay fixation. 'What he was doing with *Interior. Leather Bar* is exactly what I *didn't* want to be like – a straight guy seemingly posturing as gay,' he tells me. 'Whether or not it was his intention, it's as if he uses gay as this kind of totemic thing that's cool, which is not the reason for me.' Then what is? 'A lot of interesting stuff was going on creatively in those different gay scenes, with all these fertile connections between pornography and disco and avant-garde and ballet and painting. It felt organic.'

Pink Narcissus and its like had a catalytic effect on Strickland: 'Seeing those films for me when I was younger was like a budding musician hearing the Ramones and realising they didn't have to be a virtuoso with expensive gear.' Most of the work that inflamed his imagination was gay. Did he ever suspect he might be? 'No,' he says, sounding surprised and almost appreciative. 'I was always told I was, though. I was bullied in Year Nine at school for supposedly being gay. Just because of the way I looked.' Which was? 'Unintentionally androgynous.'

If he thought the matter of his sexuality had been put to bed once he became a director, he was wrong. 'When *The Duke of Burgundy* came out, I was asked about it a fair bit,' he says. 'At the time, I kept it quiet. I loved the ambiguity of the 1970s, not just Warhol and Paul Morrissey but Bowie. Even Prince into the 1980s. It broke down boundaries. Whereas in the early 2000s, I met someone who said, "I like Kenneth Anger – but I'm not gay!" That defensive thing. With *The Duke of Burgundy*, I very much *didn't* want to be that guy. Now I can see the situation has flipped. People are being coy about their sexuality because they don't want to be found out as straight. So now I'm, like, "Fuck it. I'm straight."'

That still doesn't quite explain the intensity of his penchant for queer culture. He delves beyond the significant but obvious landmarks such as *Cruising* or *My Own Private Idaho*, spelunking into the sub-cultures of experimental cinema, the S&M legends of clubs like the Mineshaft and the Anvil, or the porn of Poole and Peter De Rome. 'Those guys just made the best stuff,' he says. 'Maybe this is too much information, but porno doesn't turn me on. Gay porno, on the other hand, has so much other stuff going on in it: the lyricism, the poetry. Whereas straight porn is aggressive.'

In the days after we speak, he inundates me with all manner of valuable ephemera: vintage ads for gay clubs and saunas from the 1970s and 1980s, the sleeve notes for the soundtrack to the 1982 bathhouse porn *Turned On*, which stars Al Parker and features 'auto-fellatio and double-jointed auto-sodomy on an elevated glass-top pedestal'. It is the cloth from which *Night Voltage* will be cut. Whether Strickland is gay or not seems by the by. Kinship, he insists, is not delineated by sexual orientation.

'You can be straight but have other modes of sexual expression which make you an outsider,' he says. 'Like being into bondage or being a submissive. My mode, my desires, it's all seen as a bit embarrassing; you have to be coy about it, which means you can relate to someone who is gay. In fact, I'd argue that being gay is more acceptable than being into dominance or subservience. Just because you're not gay, it doesn't mean you can't have a valid idea of what it feels like to hide what turns you on.'

11

ALL THE COLOURS OF THE WORLD ARE BETWEEN BLACK AND WHITE

The list of films by straight directors that have won the Berlinale's Teddy Award for LGBTQ+ cinema is not lengthy, but nor is it short on noteworthy work. It includes Lukas Moodysson's *Fucking Åmål*, aka *Show Me Love*, Richard Eyre's *Notes on a Scandal*, Sebastián Lelio's Oscar-winning trans story *A Fantastic Woman*, and two gays-and-God dramas: Antonia Bird's *Priest* and Małgorzata Szumowska's *In the Name Of*. Heiner Carow's *Coming Out* is on the list, too. The first and only East German film about homosexuality, it premiered on 9 November 1989, the night the Berlin Wall came down. Tickets for the gala event had sold out, but when the movie began, the auditorium was still half empty – or, depending on how you look at it, half full.

All the Colours of the World Are Between Black and White won the Teddy in 2023, catapulting Babatunde Apalowo into the ranks of straight directors honoured for queer-themed work. 'I'd never heard of the Teddy Award before,' admits the thirty-seven-year-old film-maker from Ado Ekiti, Nigeria. He is speaking today from Bradford, in the north of England, where he stayed on after completing a Master's in artificial intelligence and data analytics at the city's university. Broad-shouldered, sweet-natured and quick to laugh, he looms over his laptop in a black shirt with a white Hawaiian-style floral print. A smoke alarm seems to hover above him like a UFO. 'I didn't know how big the Teddy was in the queer community,' he says. 'When I realised, I thought: "I need to be worthy of this."'

Intimidatingly, he is now in the company of many of the defining queer film-makers of post-war cinema. Derek Jarman, Isaac Julien, Marlon Riggs, Jennie Livingston, Cheryl Dunye, Stanley Kwan, Monika Treut, Barbara Hammer, Lisa Cholodenko, Céline Sciamma, Todd Haynes, Tsai Ming-liang, Gus Van Sant and Pedro Almodóvar are all Teddy-winners. A worthy recent addition is Levan Akin, who won in 2024 for the humane and inquisitive *Crossing*, about a retired teacher searching for her transgender niece among the queer communities of Istanbul.

What an odd position to be in for Apalowo, who never set out to tell a queer story. *All the Colours* was intended instead as an uncomplicated tribute to Lagos: its initial idea was to follow a young man as he sets out to recreate photographs of his parents taken during their youth. When Apalowo learned that a former friend from his early years at university in Benin City had been lynched in a homophobic attack in Lagos, however, the appeal of shooting any kind of love letter to the city began to dim.

Who was the friend? 'I'd like to keep his name private,' he says. 'He was someone I shared a room with in a hostel during my third year of university. I thought he was quite peculiar but I didn't realise he was queer.' Peculiar how? 'Different. Introspective. I don't know if that was connected to his sexuality, but he was more sensitive than the rest of us. He obviously didn't trust me enough to tell me what was going on in his life. Maybe I wasn't a good listener or wasn't paying attention.' It sounds like he has regrets. 'I do. I keep thinking, "What would've happened if we talked?"'

Has he arrived at an answer? 'Knowing myself back then, I might have said, "You'd better keep this to yourself." I don't know if I had the capability to support him.'

Homosexuality in Nigeria is punishable by up to fourteen years in prison, an attitude reflected in the titles of the precious few Nollywood films that tackle the subject, such as *Hideous Affair* and *Dirty Secret*, both from 2010. 'The problem is not legality,' says Apalowo. 'What the law does is encourage legalised violence against queer people. Someone I used to be friends with told me he would rather his daughter was raped than for her to be a lesbian. Another time, I turned up at a friend's house and he was harassing a man outside. I asked what he had done. He shrugged and told me, "He's gay." My position was always to maintain neutrality, don't say anything. Now I realise I was giving a voice to homophobia.'

Shades of Apalowo – or at least his 'neutral' former self – are evident in the character of the dispatch driver Bambino (Tope Tedela), who eats lunch in the street while a homophobic attack takes place behind him. 'It was going on around me and I wasn't seeing it,' the director says.

After the murder of his friend, the script morphed into a fearful, slow-burning romance between Bambino and Bawa (Riyo David), a younger man more confident in his sexuality. The photography motif survives: Bawa is an amateur snapper documenting life in Lagos. Apalowo's own visual style is plain, unadorned, patient, with one stylistic wrinkle: aside from the two lovers, and a young woman with whom Bambino seeks solace in escaping his gay feelings, the characters are reduced to off-screen voices, or have their faces obscured by the limits of the frame. The effect is to narrow the film's focus without occluding the context of life in Lagos, evoking the isolation experienced even amid the city's hubbub.

No surprise that the film was a struggle to make. Apalowo relied on his own savings, as well as loans, credit cards and private investors. Was there any physical risk to him making the movie in Nigeria? 'Nobody would put a fatwa against me for directing it,' he says. 'Whereas if I was on the street holding hands with a man, that would cause problems.' He briefly considered trying to find a queer film-maker to direct his script. Now he thinks such a director would have courted jeopardy. 'If you were queer, and you made this film, you would have lit the touchpaper for yourself. Everyone would see who you are.'

Actors willing to play the leads were in short supply. A major Nollywood performer originally cast as Bawa dropped out with only a few days' notice. 'For obvious reasons,' sighs Apalowo. Now he can see that casting David as his replacement oxygenated the central relationship. 'Having the original actor as Bawa made that character older than Bambino. It might have seemed predatory when he tries to convince Bambino to love him. Now there is a different dynamic. Bawa is younger but more confident: an example to Bambino of how his life could be.'

International acclaim for the film didn't count for much back in Nigeria. Apalowo was never under any illusions that it would be released theatrically there, but he still sounds incredulous as he recounts the catalogue of disasters surrounding its African premiere: the initial 2 p.m. weekday screening that was switched to 10 p.m. when Apalowo complained to the organisers, then the change of venue at less than twenty-four hours' notice. Two nominations in the African Movie Viewers' Choice awards were not converted into wins. 'We decided you were pushing an agenda,' a jury member told him privately.

If he was expecting succour closer to home, he was out of luck. When his mother visited him recently in Bradford, he asked her to watch *All the Colours* on his laptop. 'I came back into the room after a while, and she was watching YouTube. Thanks for the vote of confidence! She claimed she finished it.' What was her verdict? 'She said: "You tried."'

For all the film's bravery, the absence of intimate physical contact between Bambino and Bawa is surprising. 'People have suggested this was because we were shooting in Nigeria,' says Apalowo. 'No! The reason I chose not to show physical intimacy is that I didn't have that experience myself. I've never kissed a man. I don't know how it feels,

159

so I can't authentically direct that.' Has he never even known anyone queer in his life, apart from the friend who was murdered? 'The only other person was a boy who came out to me at secondary school. I had no idea how to deal with it. We had a special friendship. We had boys' curiosity.'

Several times, he goes to start his next sentence, then stops himself and looks directly into the webcam. 'I'm going to tell you something now. But I will tell you by explaining how I wrote it in the script. There was a scene that didn't make it into the film where Bawa says, "Are you circumcised? I'll show you mine if you show me yours." Bawa did it, but then Bambino couldn't go through with it. The reason we didn't film it was because it felt too juvenile for them as adults.'

And this is what happened with your friend? 'Yes.' The other boy showed his penis but you didn't fulfil your end of the deal? 'Unfortunately not,' he says, laughing as he rubs his face, as though trying to wipe away the embarrassment. After that, they drifted apart. 'I think we are friends on Facebook. I'm pretty sure we both moved on.'

As Apalowo tours the world promoting *All the Colours*, most people assume he is gay. 'I'm flattered! It happens all the time. Especially at queer festivals. I don't want to be dishonest so I always try to find the appropriate moment to mention it.' Now he has outed himself as straight, will he continue to engage with queer themes and characters? 'A lot of contacts I've made are related to queerness. And I will always champion queer characters. But I'm not sure.'

In other words, we've outlived our usefulness now that he has his Teddy. 'Not at all!' he laughs. 'I think winning that award is the reason I don't want to make a queer film next. I don't want to contribute to an untruth. The film changed my life, changed my perspective. I'm bolder and more emphatic now about issues surrounding queerness. Ideally, you make a film for other people, but I see now that I made *Colours* for myself. To become a better person.'

12
NIGHTHAWKS

The coincidence of gay issues dominating the news in the mid-1980s gave the boy the illusion that his sexuality was somehow triggering this proliferation. Likewise, it could only have been his frantic hormones that were generating so many gay films in those years when he began going to the cinema on his own. *My Beautiful Laundrette*, *Desert Hearts*, *Shadey*, *Prick Up Your Ears*, *The Angelic Conversation*, *The Last of England*, *Caravaggio*, *Maurice*, *Mala Noche*, *Noir et Blanc*, *I've Heard the Mermaids Singing*, *The Fruit Machine*: they all came tumbling out faster than he could catch them, like the jangling jackpot from a one-armed bandit.

Whatever else was coming down the pike, there was always *The Rocky Horror Picture Show*, which had been playing at the same cinema on Baker Street for five or six consecutive years before he made his first visit. At fourteen, he was too young for midnight screenings of the kind that had secured that film's reputation in the late 1970s; by the time he was old enough to be up past the pumpkin hour, he felt he had outgrown *Rocky Horror*, in the same way that he was now too old to send twee Purple Ronnie greetings cards or use the word 'skill' as a superlative. He occasionally went to see *Rocky Horror* on his own, straight from school, changing out of his blazer and tie on the way. Or he and Jan, his sixth-former friend, would schlep into town at the weekend: she dolled herself up as Magenta in a maid's outfit, while he wore an undertaker's coat, with strands of custard-coloured hair glued to a joke-shop bald wig, as the butler Riff-Raff.

They marvelled at the audience, who even in those early-evening screenings would often scatter confetti and rice around the cinema during the wedding scene or put newspapers over their heads to mimic Susan Sarandon's character during a thunderstorm. 'Buy an umbrella, you cheap bitch!' chorused the regulars. It was all part of the parallel script that ran in tandem with the film. 'Describe your balls!' hollered a woman in the front row, a split second before the narrator observed the gathering clouds to be 'heavy, black and pendulous'.

He didn't tell his parents about the trip until a few weeks later. While Mum was clattering around in the kitchen after dinner, he mentioned to Dad, who was slumped in front of the TV, that he had been to see *Young Frankenstein*. It wasn't a lie: Mel Brooks's fond comic homage to James Whale was on the bottom half of the double bill with *Rocky Horror*.

'Fan-*tas*-tic,' Dad chuckled, eyes still fixed on the telly.

Then he told him about the main attraction, the one he and Jan had really gone to see. The boy watched his father's smile fall away like one of his own Blu-tacked film posters unpeeling itself from the wall.

'I see,' Dad said calmly. 'And you're into all that, are you?'

'Into what?'

'Geezers in suspenders. Fellas dressing like tarts. That's your thing, is it?'

'It's a laugh,' he shrugged. 'I like the songs.'

'Do you? You like the songs? Jolly good. You can 'ave the songs. You can keep 'em.'

'Don't be like that.' He wanted Dad to get it: to enjoy his enjoyment. 'It's dead popular. Honest. Loads of people are into it. There were even two businessmen sitting behind us.'

'Poofs,' he said.

'They weren't. They were wearing suits.'

'Two grown men out together at the weekend at a bloody . . . at *that*? What else would they be, eh?'

Dad had been wrong before. He'd made the same claim about the boy's new drama teacher, Mark, a groovy type who wore jeans, insisted on students using his first name and referred to his office as his 'orifice'. Dad had his number alright: 'Bent as a nine-bob note.' But it simply wasn't fair to raise his son's hopes like that, making him believe that Mark might lavish some physical affection on him when he was interested only in women.

During the school holidays, the boy knocked at Mark's flat en route to the Tube station.

'I'm going to see *My Beautiful Laundrette*,' he said, his voice too high to sound casual. 'I wondered if—'

He suddenly saw how odd it was: a pupil inviting a teacher to the cinema in the hope that he might . . . Well, what?

The boy pressed on. 'Do you want to come with me?'

'It's really kind of you to ask but I've got marking up to here,' he replied, holding the front door half open with one hand and raising the other in a kind of salute to indicate the height of his in-tray.

'We could see *Colonel Redl* instead,' the boy continued, pleading slightly now. 'Or *Down and Out in Beverly Hills*. Or *Doña Herlinda and Her Son*.'

They all had gay characters in them. *Time Out* said so. That's how they'd earned a spot on his Must-See list.

Mark wasn't swayed. 'Another time maybe.'

The boy trudged off alone to the Tube, every inch of his unmolested body screaming out to be touched. Mum and Dad had told him he shouldn't go to the cinema on his own because strangers used the cover of darkness to interfere with youngsters. But no matter how often he put himself in harm's way, nothing like that happened, not really – just the occasional glance. According to his parents, practically everyone in the world was gay, which made it even more frustrating that none of them crossed his path.

Nighthawks was originally released in 1978, though it didn't enter his orbit until Channel 4 screened it late one night in 1985, a year after *The Secret Policeman's Ball.* The channel was the go-to place for adult, inflammatory or transgressive cinema. It was here that the boy first saw Derek Jarman's 1976 debut *Sebastiane*, which opens with Lindsay Kemp spraying cream from a giant phallus (a scene that was added by Jarman only because the movie was running too short), before giving way to the languid eroticism of the main sun-bleached body of the film. *Nighthawks* was a predictable target of hysteria from the UK tabloids long before its Channel 4 screening. 'Child Porn Row Looms on Gay Film' ran one spurious headline.

'Glad to Be Gay' was mortifying enough, but watching *Nighthawks* with his parents was out of the question. There was already one *Nighthawks* which they liked: the 1981 thriller starring Sylvester Stallone as a cop on the trail of a terrorist, played by Rutger Hauer, that suave Dutch ice pick who seemed actively bored by his own allure. 'Our *Nighthawks* had by then run commercially in America,' recalled Paul Hallam, who co-wrote the script with Ron Peck. 'Universal asked whether we would restrict our screenings to the arthouse circuit, so as not to confuse Stallone fans.' They agreed: a token payment changed hands between the distributors.

At the end of Universal's *Nighthawks*, Hauer's character creeps up on Stallone's girlfriend in her kitchen late at night while she is standing obliviously at the sink with her back to him. Given the killer's past form, it seems unlikely he is there to help with the washing-up. As he closes in, his intended victim spins around and reveals 'herself' to be Stallone in a platinum wig and silk dressing gown, holding not a sponge but a gun, his bushy black beard making him look like a member of the Cockettes.

The other *Nighthawks*, named after the Edward Hopper painting, is about Jim (Ken Robertson), a lonely gay geography teacher at a London comprehensive school. His life consists of drab days at work and nights spent mournfully scouring gay clubs and bars until he finds someone new with whom he can strike up a version of the same old conversation. This *Nighthawks* makes persuasive stylistic points about harmful patterns of behaviour. Like Peck's dominant influence, Chantal Akerman's *Jeanne Dielman, 23 Commerce Quay, 1080 Bruxelles*, it's big on routine and repetition. Every club plays the same pulsing electronic loop (it is even heard at Jim's work party). Certain shots are repeated throughout the film, especially driving shots, with the camera stationed on the back seat as Jim drops yet another one-night stand at the Tube the next morning. The picture is urging him to make a decisive move, and to break the cycle.

This he does in the most remarkable scene in the film. Challenged in class by his pupils ('Are you bent? Are you queer?'), he comes out to them and answers their questions with equanimity and directness.

'Do you wear women's clothes?' asks one boy from the back of the packed classroom, which is as rowdy as a cattle auction. 'Do you carry a handbag?'

'I don't carry a handbag,' Jim replies.

Someone yells: 'He carries a cucumber for a quick one up the bum!'

'What do you do in bed?' asks a teenage Teddy boy in cardigan and cravat.

'Quite a lot of things,' he says coolly.

That jeering voice again: 'He sticks a cucumber up his bum!'

The staging guarantees that the action, which was shot over the course of two days and cut together into one five-minute episode, is heated but never hysterical. Jim doesn't appear in the scene at all, save for the opening shot of him standing at the blackboard as he asks the class to settle down. Instead, we are squarely in his shoes: the camera is in his stead so that the pupils are hectoring and haranguing us directly, with Jim relegated to an off-screen presence. Yet, when he speaks, it feels as if one is hearing one's own inner voice. As he tells the pupils to get on with their work, someone hollers: 'Bollocks, we ain't working for a queer!' The position of the camera ensures it is we who receive the invective.

Despite the line about gay men and cucumbers, watching *Nighthawks* had taken the boy only so far. It was thanks to AIDS that he learned about the nuts and bolts of gay sex. People at school said the acronym stood for Arse-Injected Death Sentence, but he was slow on the uptake and still didn't twig.

Time Out had started running stories about the disease. They began as bulletins in the news section, spreading through the magazine until they colonised the features pages. As part of a three-page splash ('AIDS: THE VICTIMS'), the magazine reprinted an American poster by the Gay Men's Health Crisis. At the top of the poster in big letters it said: 'Great sex! Don't let AIDS stop it.' The best part was the column on the right of the poster, occupied by what seemed to be a series of road signs. Inside the first one, which was a circle with a bar across it, like the *Ghostbusters* logo, one of the men had his eyes closed and his lips parted while the other man stood behind him, wearing a blissful expression, one hand on his partner's shoulder. 'Don't let him come in your ass,' said the text beside the first road sign. 'Don't come in his.'

The second one was another prohibitive circle, this time showing a bum with two hands on it, and one of the men bending down in front of his partner's genitals. 'Don't come in his mouth,' said the caption. 'Don't let him come in yours.' That was easy enough to understand;

he had imagined sucking Mike's cock even before they had become friends. But he hadn't known that penises could go into bums until he saw that poster. It was the third road sign, also with a diagonal bar across it, that really stumped him. It showed one of the two men looking wide-eyed in the foreground, and the other leaning naked against the lockers in the background, his back to us. Next to the picture was a warning: 'Don't rim.' He read those two words repeatedly, but they wouldn't surrender their meaning, and it wasn't as if he had anyone to ask. He couldn't get to the bottom of it.

The last two road signs were encouragements rather than prohibitions. 'Jacking off is hot and safe,' said one caption, next to a picture of the two lovers happily masturbating. In the final image, they had their arms around each other, alongside the message: 'Affection is our best protection.'

Nighthawks pre-dated any of that; the only blight in the film is loneliness and shame. Watched in 1985, though, the approaching spectre of AIDS couldn't help but haunt the edges of the frame. The boy had hardly any sexual experience, and the characters on-screen had so much. Yet it was he who was ahead of them in another way: he knew what was coming.

In the mid-1970s, Peck placed ads in the gay press to set out his stall and invite collaborators; this was how he met Hallam, credited as co-director of *Nighthawks*. (Hallam later co-wrote another pivotal British queer film, Isaac Julien's 1991 *Young Soul Rebels*.) Those who got in touch were invited to suggest locations, appear as extras or generally contribute in some way to the texture of what was intended as a truthful portrait of gay life in London. Peck wrote to the *Sunday Times* and received a mention from the critic Dilys Powell in her column.

He sent the script to film-makers, who offered their advice. Lindsay Anderson and Michael Powell were among those who replied; the latter told Peck not to be afraid of showing 'the male looking at the male' and said: 'Don't be above (or below) plot. We are storytellers not scientists.' Powell expressed a preference for renaming the film *Cruising*.

Derek Jarman offered help and locations – his Butler's Wharf apartment is used in one scene – and can be glimpsed in the film loitering enigmatically in a club. Life and cinema began to blur as Peck's friends were drafted into the cast. 'There was a real confusion in my mind about whether people were playing themselves or acting out characters,' he said. The point of the film, though, was never in doubt: 'It was to put up on the screen something of that life which I and others were living.'

Not that it was the only way the story of a closeted teacher could play out. In 1980, Frank Ripploh directed and starred in *Taxi Zum Klo*, his own debut film, tonally distinct from *Nighthawks*, about a gay teacher, also called Frank, who is hooked on cruising (the title translates as *Taxi to the Toilet*). Despite the signals of seediness transmitted by its moody electronic score, the tone is disarmingly blithe. The German actor–writer–director is well named: he is a very frank Ripploh indeed, permitting the camera access to everything from his bowel movements ('You see me shit in the morning, at the very start of the film, because this is how I start my day') to water sports ('It shows that if you trust somebody, you are willing to try *anything*') to his own rectal exam. The vibe is anal-warts-and-all.

As with Jim in *Nighthawks*, Frank's sexuality makes waves at work: he is sacked after rolling into class in drag after the previous evening's queer shindig, delighting his primary-school students but appalling his employers. The film arose from a similar work/life conflict for Ripploh, who taught in schools in Berlin and starred in underground movies using the name Peggy von Schnottgenberg, some directed by Rosa von Praunheim. When Ripploh came out as part of a feature in *Stern* magazine in 1978, his employers brought disciplinary procedures against him on the grounds that he had 'disseminated [himself] inappropriately sexually as a public servant'. He sued them and won.

'Out of the toilets and into the streets!' is one of the slogans with which von Praunheim concludes *It Is Not the Homosexual Who Is Perverse, But the Society in Which He Lives*; Ripploh, however, is happy to remain in the *pissoir* in *Taxi Zum Klo*. In one scene, he absconds from a hospital where he is being treated for hepatitis and visits a nearby public toilet for sex. He was quick to clarify that 'in real life when I escaped, I didn't go to the loos; I went to Pasolini's *Salò*, and then I went to a gay bar and had a Coke'. The film's sex scenes caused some headaches with distribution. It was a success, though, wherever it could be seen. Why? 'Because it's not a "problem" film, like, for instance, *Nighthawks*,' Ripploh told *Gay News* in 1982. '*Nighthawks* is a very good film, a very important film. But it's also very English, very serious, very sad – there's no humour in it.'

For all their differences, the two pictures utilise the school setting as a ready-made crucible for crisis, revolution and change. No wonder so many other queer films play out against a backdrop of education. A teacher who tries to suppress his gay desires by marrying a woman forms the basis for *Coming Out*. A lesbian PE teacher bumps into one of her own students in a gay bar in *Blue Jean*. One member of the love triangle in *Passages* is a teacher, and the film's emotional climax shows a highfalutin film director on his knees in a school corridor, reduced to tears. Jean Vigo's *Zéro de conduite* and Leontine Sagan's *Mädchen in Uniform* render the rhapsodic, heart-trampling headiness of life in a single-sex boarding school. The historic homophobic argument that positions LGBTQ+ people as a danger to children turns the school setting into an instant moral battleground and a safeguarding nightmare. But it is also the case that children may not have the same compunction as adults when it comes to asking awkward questions or forcing an issue, even forcing a teacher's hand. That's excellent news for drama. Without nosy kids, the coming-out scene in *Nighthawks* might never have happened.

———————————

An email I send to Ron Peck receives no reply; I figure the address must be defunct. It turns out, though, that he has been ill with cancer. His health declines so fast, in fact, that he dies without ever having seen an oncologist. Mark Ayres, with whom Peck ran a production company originally set up to facilitate his 1987 film *Empire State*, invites me to the funeral in east London, not far from where Peck had lived since the mid-1970s. It is a week before Christmas, and the previous day's snowfall has hardened into ice. Trudging up the thin spit of tarmac with graves on either side, the white sky grubby as if passed between unwashed hands, I reach the small knot of mourners who have congregated outside the crematorium's chapel. Smoke balloons from our mouths like speech bubbles in the cold air. We all stamp our feet and rub our hands as though we are in a film about a winter funeral and are determined to play our parts to the hilt.

Patsy Nightingale, the production manager on *Nighthawks*, tells me about collecting donors' anonymous contributions in brown envelopes to put towards production costs. David Hockney and Elton John gave generously after a fundraising dinner held by John Schlesinger, who was one of the film's most ardent supporters. Freddie Mercury remained unpersuaded, so Peck followed up with a personal call. 'An additional visit is made the day after,' Peck wrote in his diary, 'but he is arguing with his boyfriend over some missing jewellery and is not very responsive.'

The service is brisk. One of the eulogists points out how delighted Peck would have been at the recent news that *Jeanne Dielman* has been voted the greatest film of all time in the *Sight & Sound* magazine poll, which is held once a decade. (That makes it one of three queer films in the top ten, alongside Claire Denis' *Beau Travail* and David Lynch's *Mulholland Drive*.) It wasn't only that Akerman's picture influenced *Nighthawks*; Peck also called on her in Paris during his time there in August and September 1977, when he was trying to raise funding for the film, which at that stage still hadn't been cast. Richard Dyer was the main candidate for the lead role, though he was known not as an actor but as the National Film Theatre programmer who had staged the Gay Film Season in 1977 (incurring the wrath of Mary Whitehouse's right-wing Christian 'Festival of Light' movement), as well as the author of a clutch of seminal gay cinema books. 'After some encouraging video tests, [Dyer] pulls out as his partner (an actor?) is extremely jealous,' Peck wrote.

Upon arriving in Paris, Peck went to see Akerman's *News from Home*, which comprises images of New York City shot by a predominantly static camera; on the soundtrack, she reads the plaintive letters that her mother, Natalia (or 'Nelly'), wrote to her while Akerman was living there in the early 1970s. Peck then found a cinema showing her debut, *Je tu il elle*, which she made at the age of twenty-three and later described as 'foolhardy'.

13

JE TU IL ELLE

When Ron Peck reached Chantal Akerman's apartment, it was as if he had strolled onto the set of *Je tu il elle*. 'There it is . . . the mattress on the floor and a mess of things everywhere,' he wrote. He had come seeking help and advice, armed with the *Nighthawks* script as well as a précis written to rustle up funds at the Cannes Film Festival. '[Akerman] doesn't know what to suggest: Truffaut, Malle, Duras, even Eustache (drunk every night at the café, unable to activate himself at all) . . . probably useless. But, after reading the Cannes synopsis, she felt the film could be a commercially viable project.' Akerman mentioned that Karl Lagerfeld was 'putting money into the arts and has a lot to play with'. But after Lagerfeld came to London as Schlesinger's guest, this proved to be a dead end. Soon, Peck was returning disconsolately to Akerman's apartment to retrieve the script before he left for the UK; he had so little money, and photocopying costs were so steep, that each copy had to be accounted for.

'A key is left under the mat. I let myself in . . . and glance around the rooms . . . still in a mess, a <u>worse</u> mess even. When I pick up the script, papers fall to the floor . . .'

Though Akerman is the star, as well as the writer and director, of *Je tu il elle*, from 1974, she is identified in the cast list as 'Julie', generally assumed to be her character's name. The film is carved into three sections. In the first, Julie, an urchin-like presence, is alone in her room, which she gradually divests of furniture until there is almost nothing left but a mattress. Though the picture is shot in black and white, a dark rectangle dominating the top half of one white wall suggests interior design by Rothko. (The painter had committed suicide four years earlier, at the age of sixty-six; Akerman was sixty-five when she took her own life in 2015.) How long Julie is there for is unclear, though at one point she says 'twenty-eight days', then sleeps for what seems to be one further night in the room. That makes twenty-nine – one day for each year between 1945, the end of the Second World War, which was so central to her sensibility and cinema, and the film's release.

As she writes a letter, filling untold pages with her scrawl, she spoons sugar into her mouth from a paper bag. Pages from the letter are then strewn across the floor, along with the sugar. She stands by the window, she lies on the mattress, her action jarring repeatedly with how she describes herself: in her voiceover, she tells us she is naked, yet we can see she is fully clothed at that point. Either she is out of sync or we are. Is it even a letter that she is writing? She could very well be scribbling the script for the film we're watching; Akerman, after all, wrote the original text while alone in just such a room in Paris.

The second section begins after 33 minutes with a cut to a wide shot of Julie hitchhiking at the side of a busy road. A truck driver (Niels Arestrup) picks her up, and she serves as a mute audience for him as he eats, talks, shaves and encourages her to masturbate him – though not all at the same time. Perhaps the strangest element here is how her doting tenderness towards him is reciprocated. He introduces her to four men of his acquaintance lined up in a roadside bar, and later sits smirking and smoking across from her at a café table – a promotion from an earlier dinner scene in which the pair are side by side, staring at an out-of-frame TV set rather than each other.

After she finishes watching him shave, he gives her a tap on the nose, much as one might a pet or a child. And Akerman *does* look like a kid in her stiff, shiny mac, which she has comical difficulty zipping up. If he sees her as a filial figure, that fits with the way he sexualises his own children: first, he remarks on the way his baby son's 'little Peter' springs to attention, then admits that he sends his eleven-year-old daughter to bed if she appears before him in her nightdress because 'she's quite a dish'. It is hard to discern Julie's expression in the murk of the truck's cab – she is in profile, pushed to the extreme left of the frame, while the nameless driver, in his gleaming white Brando-in-*Streetcar* T-shirt, hogs the screen – but she appears to be enjoying his quasi-incestuous monologue.

Julie's voiceover dominates the opening section, and there is background chatter in the second part. But it is the driver who first speaks at length to another person, a full 48 minutes into the film, when his instructions for Julie on how to masturbate him blend with the running commentary of his fantasy: 'You obey but you're afraid,' he pants. Later, he delivers a nine-minute monologue as he drives, concluding with an image which he says guarantees a hard-on for him whenever he conjures it: 'A woman crying in the corner. A woman crying works every time.' It's an admission made matter-of-factly, without malice or menace, but it transforms the sudden cut a few minutes later, from the shaving scene to the shot of Julie standing outside her girlfriend's apartment at night, into a welcome reprieve – and an escape.

Now at last Julie gets to address another human being, albeit initially via an intercom. Her words are delivered casually but that doesn't stop this from feeling like a moment of self-realisation. More than an hour of the picture has elapsed, and she has finally made her first non-narrated, present-tense declaration – which turns out to be a statement asserting her place in the world and announcing her identity.

You might say the whole film is leading up to this moment, crystallised into those two words, or even that *Je tu il elle* exists just so that

Akerman can announce herself to the world in this manner: 'It's me,' she says.

Before sex comes sandwiches. 'I'm hungry,' Julie says once her lover buzzes her into the apartment. It is hunger, too, which launched her on this journey in the first place. Near the end of the opening section, alone in her room, Julie had said: 'I wondered what was happening to me. I realised I was hungry.' Now here she is wolfing down her grub and clearing her plate. She'll need it for what lies ahead.

Je tu il elle is the first instance of explicit lesbian sex in a mainstream feature, but the approach and effect are markedly different from Barbara Hammer's experimental short *Dyketactics*, which was released the same year. The sex in *Je tu il elle* might be euphoric for the characters (it's hard to tell), but structure and composition keep the temperature cool. Over the course of ten minutes, there are a mere three shots; the camera is static – give or take an infinitesimal tremor – and restrained, holding the bodies at a distance. Even as they tumble around together like clothes in a washing machine, any heated identification is kept intriguingly at bay.

Compare that to *Dyketactics*, which in the space of just four minutes contains around 110 cuts. The shots of women frolicking and dancing in the countryside are followed by close-ups of kissing, stroking, licking and sucking, all laid one on top of the other like bodies at an orgy, each image melting and dissolving into the next. (The double-printing of the negatives was directly influenced by Shirley Clarke's 1958 short *Bridges-Go-Round*.) The beeping Moog soundtrack, improvised by Hammer and suggesting a flute getting busy with a synthesiser, transports us into the realm of ecstatic fantasy. It wasn't the director's first choice of music: she had originally used a composition by the folk singer, lesbian activist and then-separatist Alix Dobson, who withdrew permission when she discovered that Hammer couldn't guarantee that no men would ever see the film.

It was Hammer's intention that the viewing experience should be not merely sensual but tactile; she wanted the audience to feel *Dyketactics* in their bodies, just as she understood her own sexuality to be a physical, sensual entity. Sex with a woman had woken her up following her marriage to a man. Sex, she said, is 'what brought me out as a lesbian. It wasn't an intellectual idea.'

Hammer's film was shot, she told Cheryl Dunye, on 'witches' land: in other words, land that was owned in Napa County by self-proclaimed witches'. Over one weekend, she and around thirteen friends 'camped there and made this film celebrating our bodies and ourselves in nature'. Looking over the footage later, Hammer saw that all the shots 'had the sense of touch in them' – a woman putting her foot in a hot tub, combing hair, touching trees, feet walking in the grass. Then she realised: 'Oh, I'm leaving out lovemaking. The biggest sensual experience that I knew of, and that had changed my life.' Hammer enlisted the cinematographer Chris Saxton to film her and her lover, Poe Asher, having sex, asking her to 'stroke us with the Bolex, as if she were petting us'. Then she and Asher set the camera down in between them as they caressed one another. 'So you have this long, cave-like shot of two women's hands moving along their bodies – and nobody behind the camera. I love that shot.' The era, she said, felt like 'sort of the beginning of the lesbian revolution'.

Chantal Akerman would very likely not wish to be included in my book, or in any book with 'queer' or 'gay' or 'LGBTQ+' in the title. She refused to allow *Je tu il elle* to be screened in programmes of gay cinema, telling the organisers: 'I won't be ghettoized like that.' In Marianne Lambert's 2015 documentary *I Don't Belong Anywhere: The Cinema of Chantal Akerman*, made shortly after the death of Akerman's beloved mother but not finished and released until after she, too, was dead, she says: 'Each time I was asked to present my film in a gay film festival, I would say "no." I don't want to take part in gay or women's film festivals. I don't want to take part in Jewish festivals. I just want to take part in regular festivals.'

Sarah Schulman paid no heed to those objections when she and Jim Hubbard sought out Akerman's work to show at MIX NYC, the festival of gay and lesbian experimental film that they co-founded in 1986, and which launched a year later. 'We always programmed her films but she would never agree to be in a gay festival, so we had to obtain them illegally,' Schulman tells me. 'We'd order them in some crazy ways and have them shipped from other countries. And we showed a lot of them. Everything we could find.' They had no qualms about disobeying Akerman's intentions. 'It was only for marketing purposes that Chantal didn't want to be in those festivals, but these were lesbian films. I mean, c'mon – what's *Je tu il elle*?'

Its inclusion is now commonplace. In 2023, *Je tu il elle* was part of a 'Sapph-O-Rama' season at Film Forum in New York City, alongside the 1922 *Salome*, Almodóvar's *Dark Habits*, Jamie Babbitt's *But I'm a Cheerleader* and Technicolor Hollywood queer-outs like *Johnny Guitar* and *Calamity Jane*.

In 2009, Schulman presented Akerman's picture as part of Ira Sachs's Queer/Art/Film series in New York. 'I got in trouble at the screening,' she says, looking uncharacteristically sheepish. 'I was happy to have the chance to introduce it and share my love for the film. First, it's so bold in terms of its durational issues. She makes you sit with everything in this incredible way that we were not used to at the time. It's so daring for such a young person. And she takes off her clothes! She's fearless – intellectually, aesthetically and personally.'

Once Schulman had said her piece, a woman in the audience raised her hand. 'I call on her, and she says: "I am Babette Mangolte"' – Akerman's cinematographer, that is, on films including *Jeanne Dielman* and *News from Home*. 'I thought, "Oh shit." She said, "Chantal Akerman is *not* a queer film-maker. She is a *film-maker*." It was horrible.' Schulman and Akerman did end up being Facebook friends – if 'friends' isn't stretching it. 'Chantal was a very radical Zionist, so she would send me messages about my politics concerning Palestine, which she did not appreciate,' Schulman says. 'And no, she would not want to be in your book.'

Je tu il elle has its origins in Paris in the winter of 1968. Akerman was eighteen and living on the rue Bonaparte in an unheated room with ice-encrusted windows and no running water. She had with her a small lamp that she placed on her belly to keep herself warm, and she slept on a mattress three centimetres thick. Her cousin in the city paid her a pittance to look after her baby daughter, and Akerman saved valuable centimes by walking everywhere rather than taking the Métro.

She left Brussels for Paris in the first place because it was 'the city of dreams, the city of writers, and I wanted to write in Paris in a maid's chambers'. What she wrote there was a novel, *Je tu il elle*, into which she fed the experiences of her life at that time: hitchhiking back to Brussels to see Claire Wauthion, who plays her lover in the film, and having 'all sorts of adventures with the truck drivers who picked me up. It was dangerous. But that's how we lived at the time.'

Three years earlier, Akerman had seen Godard's *Pierrot le Fou*, the film which lit the fuse for her: 'I walked out of the theatre thinking,

"I want to make films, too." By 1968, she had done just that: the larky twelve-minute *Saute ma ville* is set entirely in a cramped kitchen, where she eats, cleans furiously and dresses in the 1960s housewife drag of headscarf and mackintosh, all the while humming to herself on the soundtrack. In the final shot, she calmly blows the apartment, and herself, to smithereens.

In the early 1970s, Akerman moved to New York City, where she worked as a cashier in a gay porn cinema and frequented the Anthology Film Archives, soaking up the durational, experimental work of Jonas Mekas, Michael Snow and Andy Warhol. She showed *Saute ma ville* to Mekas, who made approving noises. He was a champion and defender of queer artists, and didn't baulk at putting his money where his mouth was: not only had he stumped up the cash to print Jack Smith's scandalous cine-orgy *Flaming Creatures* but he had defended it in court against obscenity charges and stormed the projection booth at a Belgian avant-garde festival that had refused to show the film. Mekas also employed the irrepressible, confrontational Barbara Rubin, who made *Christmas on Earth*, a deranged queer jumble of naked bodies, mostly in close-up. (Its original title was *Cocks and Cunts*.) In New York, Mekas received a six-month suspended sentence for screening *Flaming Creatures*, though he escaped with a ticking-off for allowing Genet's *Un Chant d'amour* to be shown.

This represented quite the volte-face for a man who, less than a decade earlier, had expressed reservations about queer film-makers such as Kenneth Anger and James Broughton; he wrote that most avant-garde cinema was marred by 'the conspiracy of homosexuality that is becoming one of the most persistent and most shocking characteristics of American film poetry today'. Maya Deren considered suing him; Willard Haas spat in his face. After being confronted by Deren, Mekas recanted his remarks, though Barbara Hammer pointed out the overwhelming male bias that persisted in the selection (and the selection committee) of Mekas's Essential Cinema project at Anthology. 'I wrote Mekas a letter in which I suggested that I could help him with his research to include more women in his circle,' she said. 'I never got a response.'

William E. Jones became friends with Akerman around the time he started work on *Halsted Plays Himself*, his 2011 book about the porn director Fred Halsted, who made *Sextool*, *Sex Garage* and, most famously, *LA Plays Itself*. 'When we met, I told her I was starting to research my book, and she looked at me with utter astonishment,' he recalls. 'She couldn't believe I thought this man's films were worthy of serious reflection. Then she told me that she had worked at the 55th Street Playhouse, where *LA Plays Itself* had its theatrical run. She described the men who patronised the theatre as "so sad", and sadness was her main impression of the place until a co-worker showed her how to steal from the box office.'

Akerman, Jones tells me, 'was able to accumulate enough money to fund some of her early films'. In Lambert's documentary, she says: 'My pockets were filled with money. Like *that*!' – her hands outlining imaginary swag-bags bulging at her side. She skimmed around $4,000 from the takings of *LA Plays Itself*, which made Halsted the inadvertent midwife of her next films, *Le Chambre* and *Hotel Monterey*. Precisely how much money Halsted saw from that New York engagement, Jones was never able to determine.

In 1973, Akerman reconfigured *Je tu il elle* from a novel into an outline and shot it in a week on the fly. She approached Arestrup one evening and asked him to play the truck driver. There was no money or script. 'When do we shoot?' he asked. 'Right now,' she replied. The crew was waiting nearby with the vehicle.

Her plan to shoot it on 16mm had been abandoned when she came across piles of dusty boxes of 35mm black-and-white film in the corridor of a Parisian processing lab. She lugged them home along the avenue du Maine and hid them under her bed. 'I was very scared that the police would come,' she said. Shot on stolen stock, *Je tu il elle* is an outlaw film down to its very last sprocket hole.

Akerman didn't act again in any of her own fiction features, but she did cast Aurore Clément as her surrogate in *Les Rendez-vous d'Anna*, her fourth film, in 1978. Clément plays the title character, a film-maker born in Belgium to Holocaust survivors, who travels from city to city accompanying screenings of her work in between trysts in hotel rooms. As if the proximity between director and character was not explicit enough, other clues flag up the overlap. Anne was Akerman's middle name, while the fortuitous casting of Clément creates a mirror image in the initials of actor and director: AC as CA.

Anna's mother is played by Lea Massari, who was only twelve years older than Clément but may have been cast as much for her symbolic associations as for her talent. Massari, after all, was best known for creating her own enigmatic Anna: the free-spirited holidaymaker who cries 'wolf' – or rather 'shark!' – shortly before vanishing during a yachting trip near the start of Antonioni's *L'Avventura*. It is her disappearance which sets the rest of the film in languorous motion. As Anna's mother, Massari is a phantom presence for a chunk of Akerman's movie, too, albeit a different chunk. When Anna arrives at the first of the various biscuit-coloured hotels on her tour, there is a message waiting for her from her mother. 'How did she know I was here?' she wonders aloud, looking faintly haunted.

After being reunited, mother and daughter rent a hotel room, though they have been warned it has no bathroom. No phone either, which Anna only discovers when she wants to call 'a girlfriend'. They climb into bed together: Anna is completely naked, her mother dressed in a slip, the pair of them under the covers but visible from the shoulders up as the elevated camera tilts down at them, framing them in an unbroken two-shot for the next six minutes or so.

She tells her mother about an affair with a woman whom she brought back to her hotel room after going from bar to bar in a deserted city. The strangers kissed. 'I don't know how it happened,' she says. 'I felt sort of nauseous. I felt sick. It was too much. I was confused. But we kept on kissing. And then it all came very easy. I let myself go. It felt good. I never imagined it could be like that with a woman. I had no idea.' Then a scandalous admission, slipped out as if it were a mere breath: 'We stayed together all night, and for some strange reason, I thought of you. I even told her so.' The erotic frisson that has gone unspoken between the two women crackles unmistakably.

The picture was generally dismissed on its release in 1978, though its reputation seems surer now, and can only benefit from the sharp rise in acclaim for (and availability of) Akerman's other work, not to mention the homages paid to her by other film-makers.

A towering example of the Akerman-esque static-shot-with-voiceover can be found in *Beyond Hatred*, Olivier Meyrou's 2005 documentary about the homophobic murder of twenty-nine-year-old François Chenu in Léo Lagrange Park, Reims. In the film's most devastating scene, the victim's sister recounts the events of that terrible weekend in September 2002: her attempts to contact François, the call from the police, the journey to identify his body. Her calm recollections are heard over a static, unbroken eight-minute shot of the park where her brother was killed. It is early evening, still light, when the shot begins. We become so caught up in her words that we may not even notice dusk descending as the minutes tick away, the graininess cloaking this jogger or that cyclist. By the time the shot ends, a street lamp is glowing: a symbol of muted but stubborn hopefulness consistent with the grieving family's philosophy of forgiveness.

Akerman is not short of other disciples. Charlotte Wells based the final shot of *Aftersun*, with its methodically circling camera, on *Hotel Monterey*; Todd Field quotes visually from *Les Rendez-vous d'Anna* at several points in *Tár*, with Cate Blanchett following in Clément's footsteps as she stalks the no-woman's-land of anonymous hotel rooms and hallways. It is possible that Akerman will come to eclipse in the public's esteem the Nouvelle Vague figurehead who first inspired her. 'At one point, she told me that for her generation Jean-Luc Godard was a god,' says William E. Jones. 'I told her that my friends admired her more than Godard, and she was moved beyond words.'

14

TEAROOM

William E. Jones is responsible for one of the most profound queer films of all time, though he isn't its director, or its creator exactly. More like its emancipator. It is devoid of dialogue and music, though it was shot more than three decades after the advent of talkies. It features no stars, and no one who went on to enjoy any sort of career in movies. On the contrary, careers were ruined by it. Lives, too. There were no publicity materials to advertise the film – it never played in cinemas or went on general release, though today it can be found online without too much digging. If it *had* been released, however, there would have been at least one sensationalist poster quote to entice the prurient. 'No one who has not seen the film could believe that such depravity exists anywhere,' the *Mansfield News Journal* assured its readers, making the work in question sound like a trash classic.

The film as it now exists in its rescued form is called *Tearoom*. ('A tearoom is a public restroom used for brief, anonymous sexual encounters,' Jones explains in the handsome book accompanying the film: a *Tearoom* for the coffee table.) The recording was formerly known as *Mansfield, Ohio, Tearoom Busts*, which is how Jones happened to stumble across it in the alphabetical listings of the now-defunct LGBTQ+ website Planet Out, co-founded by Jenni Olson, where it was adjacent to *Massillon*, his own 1991 debut film. *Mansfield, Ohio, Tearoom Busts* turned out to be a degraded copy of *Camera Surveillance of Sex Deviates*, which was produced by the Mansfield police department over a three-week period in the summer of 1962 as an instructional video for other police forces preparing to monitor public toilets and to install cameras and two-way mirrors to ensnare the men who congregated there for sex.

Mansfield was quite the success story in this respect, having hauled in more than thirty men on sodomy charges during its own sting. The original film's narration lays bare the homophobia driving the whole endeavour: 'The sex pervert, in his most inoculous [*sic*] form, is too frequently regarded as merely a queer individual who never hurts anyone but himself. All too often we lose sight of the fact that he represents a social problem, because he is not content with being a degenerate himself, but must have degenerate companions, and is ever seeking the younger victim.' (Jones, who called this voiceover 'as illiterate and hateful a text as I have ever heard committed to film', scrubbed all sound from the recording when he repurposed it.) W. Kleon Skousen in *Law and Order* described 'the growth of homosexual cults throughout the country', before commending the force on making 'an important contribution to the police education field'.

Somewhat illogically, the catalyst for the original sting operation at that Mansfield restroom was the murder near North Lake Park in June 1962 of two girls, one seven years old, the other nine, by an eighteen-year-old man. In the aftermath of the killings, and with the suspect already in custody, a man was apprehended when a woman claimed to have witnessed him performing a sex act on a young boy in public. When police arrested the suspect, he 'disclosed that his immoral acts started in this restroom', as C. W. Kyler, the Mansfield chief of police, puts it in his narration on the original version. The assault on the boy had no connection to the double murder, but that wasn't about to deter the Mansfield police from using it as a pretext on which to launch a round-up of 'sex deviates', as they described the men who frequented the public toilets.

Footage recorded there was used as evidence in court to secure convictions. The minimum sentence at that time was a year in the state penitentiary. Even in the wake of these punishments, the connection between the murder of two girls and the habit of consenting adults meeting for sex at a time when their preferences were criminalised remained obscure.

Beyond the porn landscape, with its cubicle walls Swiss-cheesed by glory-holes, the toilet-based sexual encounter became in the 1980s an almost cosy staple of films such as *Taxi Zum Klo* and *Prick Up Your Ears*. Barely two months after the arrest of the singer George Michael in April 1998 for soliciting an undercover police officer in a Los Angeles public toilet, the practice was ferried into the mainstream by Michael and the director Vaughan Arnell in the video for the song 'Outside'. The promo begins in the mode of a crummy German porn film (credited, in a *Carry On*-style touch, to 'Hüu Jarss') and shows a public convenience transformed into a disco, its grimy urinals spinning round to reveal gleaming chrome versions. With its heterosexual trysts sprinkled among the gay couplings on show, the video falls short of what *Billboard* optimistically termed 'disco Fassbinder'.

Watching *Tearoom* today restores to the now-familiar practice of cottaging a sense of the risks involved, the bravery demanded; the participants glance furtively at the door, where a nebulous but ubiquitous menace lurks. Though conceived as a weapon to intimidate and oppress gay men, *Tearoom* – as it exists in its rescued form – is a work of haunting beauty, as well as a testament to the resilience of desire. Assorted blurry figures drift in and out of the frame, creating a vague spatial disorientation – we see bodies backing into, or emerging from, off-camera chambers and patches of darkness. The pleasure given is kept largely off-screen, too, but the bodies are angled in such a way as to leave nothing ambiguous.

The men on-screen become intrepid adventurers. The atmosphere is irreverent, erotic, funny and warm. There is a ghostliness, too; we can never be entirely sure if we have seen these people before in earlier shots, the more uniform fashion of men in the 1960s making it harder to distinguish between them. But it is also a fully democratic realm, with Black and white, old, middle-aged and young drawn to the same space by desire. Samuel R. Delany identifies the importance of the communal sex space as a way of liberating society from class boundaries, noting that 'if *every* sexual encounter involves bringing someone back to your house, the general sexual activity in a city becomes anxiety-filled, class-bound, and choosy. This is precisely *why* public rest rooms, peep shows, sex movies, bars with grope rooms, and parks with enough greenery are necessary for a relaxed and friendly sexual atmosphere in a democratic metropolis.'

Jones faced scattered opposition when he screened the film in public. 'The work divided audiences,' he says. 'But usually, my presentation of *Tearoom* had enough supporters that they defended my showing a police evidence film in the face of loud and self-righteous posturing.'

When Sebastian Meise came to make his prison drama *Great Freedom* in 2020, he studied *Tearoom* for inspiration for the opening sequence, which takes the form of a film-within-a-film showing footage shot secretly on flickering Super 8 from behind the mirror in a public restroom in Germany. Hans (Franz Rogowski) is meeting various strangers for sex, and the film in front of us is being watched also by the judges who are about to send him to prison for lewd conduct. Send him *back* to prison, that is. *Great Freedom* covers three of his spells inside over the course of thirty or so years. The film's exploration of the love that he finds and nurtures there is a counterpoint to the idea, promoted in movies such as *The Shawshank Redemption* and *A Prophet*, that sex between incarcerated men is only ever an expression of violence.

Narrative chronology in *Great Freedom* is constantly being disrupted, so we can't predict which era Hans will be plunged into next.

Near the start of the film, he is thrown into solitary confinement in a scene set in 1968, only to emerge from the darkness into 1945. Now he is gaunt and feeble, with a number tattooed on his forearm. In another scene, he stumbles out of the gloom of 1945 into 1957, looking healthier and sporting a modest rockabilly haircut. Trends change but homophobia never falls out of fashion.

'We were trying to find a form that expresses the world he is living in,' says Meise of the script he wrote with Thomas Reider. 'Hans's life is like a prison. He can't be someone else, he can't do time and turn into a "better" person. The punishment doesn't do anything to him because he is immediately persecuted again. Even being on the outside is a prison. That's how we arrived at our structure. We wanted to create this feeling that he is trapped in a time loop. Every time he goes back into solitary confinement, in the darkness, he is then spat out somewhere else.'

He falls foul repeatedly of Paragraph 175, an article of the German penal code that was in force for more than a century. Already established to penalise male homosexuality, it was made even more stringent under the Nazi regime and lasted far beyond the end of the Second World War: more than a third of the 140,000 men who were punished under it received prison sentences. Its persistence in law exposed a tacit accord between the Nazis – who lowered the threshold for punishment while raising the sentence – and the post-war liberating forces. (Paragraph 175 was not fully repealed until 1994.)

'The material in *Tearoom* influenced not only the opening sequence of our film – the surveillance scenes – but the whole film,' Meise says. 'When we were researching the history of Paragraph 175, I kept asking myself: Why cinema? What is necessarily cinematic about the story? When we came across the footage of *Tearoom*, I felt like I had found one of the main motifs of the film and I knew immediately that it would have to start with shots of this kind.'

The film-within-the-film activates our awareness of voyeurism on several levels. 'We're looking at a film that's being projected,' says Meise. 'In this film, there is a frame – the edges of the spy mirror. In this frame are people having intimate encounters who don't know they are being watched. We also see the camera lens reflected on our side of the mirror. At the end of the sequence, Hans is looking at himself. He doesn't know that he is actually looking at us, because on his side of the room he sees only his own reflection. Yet there is something revealing about this gaze. Without knowing it, he is watching us watching, which should make us aware of our voyeurism and our desire for exploitation – as film-makers *and* as viewers.'

The events captured in *Tearoom*, and the process of its creation, feel baked into Jones's DNA. He was born in 1962, in the period between the arrests of the men in the case and their first court appearance. Massillon, his home town, is a straight 55-mile line – an hour's drive – from Mansfield. *Massillon*, his debut film, includes a section in which he narrates his own experience of visiting a roadside rest stop renowned for sex, and of being fucked there by a stranger as he stares down at the waste piled beneath him in the rudimentary hole-in-the-ground toilets. 'I cannot say with certainty that I didn't know anything about the Mansfield tearoom busts while I was growing up,' he tells me. 'There seemed to be a pall over gay life in this region, and I knew that something was wrong, something that was perhaps unique, but I had no way of finding out the details of the whole tawdry episode. When I discovered the police instructional film *Camera Surveillance* . . . it was as though an obscure riddle from my youth had been solved.'

Though *Massillon* comprises only landscape shots, it feels close to *Je tu il elle* in its structure, its impact and its tone of self-assertion. There is the exposure of the director's sexual life, even though Jones is present in voice alone rather than in front of the camera as Akerman

189

was; the use of narration divorced from image; and the division of the material into three parts.

'The format was a matter of absolute necessity,' says Jones. 'I had little money, I almost always made films alone, and I was shooting mainly in areas where I thought people would be hostile to me if they understood what my film was about. The moment I saw a rough cut of *Massillon* with an audience, I realised that that voiceover device was very effective, and I decided to continue working that way. I also thought it was an advantage that the action of the film wasn't obvious in the images.'

During that period, film laboratories in Los Angeles would 'refuse to process and print explicit films, and gay sex was considered beyond the pale for most of their employees'. Solitude and self-sufficiency were integral to his process. 'I'm reminded of what Dennis Cooper told Robert Glück in his best, most revealing interview: "I think the attraction of writing was its secrecy, and that I could do it with absolute independence and in complete privacy." All of those qualities appealed to me, and I tried to do something similar in film-making.'

Massillon, in turn, had a profound effect on Jenni Olson. As with Jones's film, the sound in Olson's *The Joy of Life* and *The Royal Road* of a queer voice recounting their experience over apparently objective footage transforms images that would otherwise have no special queer currency. Without actors on-screen in these films, our identification with the disembodied voices is comprehensive, since there is no face to which we can connect them. Watching *Massillon* as we listen to Jones's voice, we are in his head, in his psyche; absorbing Olson's films as her narration unspools intimately in our ears, it is as if we become her, ushered through her romantic yearnings and disappointments, her history. She interweaves musings on geography, classic Hollywood cinema and her own (partly fictionalised) love life to create a new map of queer identity. In Olson's work, queerness is not segregated from the rest of society; it bleeds into the landscape, and our subconscious, regardless of our gender identity. Liberated from our corporeal selves in the dark, we become passengers on her train of thought.

When I call Olson, she is at home in Berkeley, California, the room swimming in sunlight. She has short, side-parted grey hair and ever-hopeful eyes shaped like apostrophes. Behind her on the book-shelf are pictures of her wife and their two children. She considers the moment when she saw *Massillon* at Outfest in Los Angeles in 1991 to be 'life-changing': 'I had made one short video prior to that. But *Massillon* was what made me want to make films.' She became friends with Jones after interviewing him for the *Advocate* and hired him to shoot her 16mm short *Blue Diary* in 1998 – 'the melancholy story of a dyke pining over a one-night stand with a straight girl'. It's narrated by Silas Howard, who later co-directed and co-starred with Harry Dodge in the butch/trans masc cornerstone *By Hook or By Crook*.

'Are you a boy or a girl?' asks a child who finds Howard, as Shy, sleeping in a doorway in a crumpled suit and tie.

'Both,' comes the reply.

I ask Olson what *Massillon* means to her. For a while, she doesn't answer. Then I realise she is sobbing quietly. 'I'm sorry,' she says. 'I'm having these waves of emotion.'

When we last spoke a few years earlier, in 2021, she was emotional for a different reason: she had just won the Berlinale's Teddy Award for 'embodying, living and creating queer culture' and for her 'decades of bridge-building work with which she has made queer film history visible and tangible'.

'It's important to me that I deal with my gender identity, my butch identity, in my work,' she said then. 'I'm trying to speak about that experience in a way that reaches other people like myself. In 1986, I read *The Celluloid Closet* and that was how I came out: "Wow, I wanna see these movies! I bet other people wanna see them too!" That experience of how important it is to see ourselves is what lead to my career, my life, as a film critic, curator, programmer and historian. That can be a life-saving thing. As a film-maker, being queer and being butch, I wanna show what that's like. Not in a "my life is so hard" sort of way – but where some other butch dyke is watching my films and thinking, "Oh my God, that's how I feel. I'm not alone."'

Her cinematic awakening went hand in hand with her sexual one. After reading Russo's book, she launched Lavender Images, a gay film series at the University of Minnesota, in 1987. 'You'd order 16mm prints from the companies through these catalogues: "OK, *Victim*, 1961, who has that . . .?"' The first screening was *The Killing of Sister George*, the overcooked 1968 lesbian drama with Beryl Reid as an age-ing soap star who fears that a TV producer (Coral Browne) is moving in on her young girlfriend (Susannah York). Today, it has acquired a sheen of camp fascination rooted largely in scenes that must have felt prurient or contemptuous at the time, such as Reid forcing York to eat her cigar butt.

'When I showed that film, people were so mad,' Olson recalls. '250 women had shown up, very excited. This being 1987, I programmed it without seeing it. Afterwards, everyone stomped out, like, "What the fuck did you just show us?" I was standing there crying, apolo-gising, saying: "I'm really sorry, I'll give you your money back!" *The Killing of Sister George* is an amazing film, but this was not so long after 1968, and these women were saying: "We lived through this! How could you show this?" It's easier to watch it now that it's so long ago and see the camp aspects.'

One film that hasn't been fully decontaminated for Olson is William Friedkin's *Cruising*. It was, said Russo, 'the first time gays rose up and rioted in the street in reaction to the making of a motion picture'. Part of its attraction today, Olson concedes, comes from the images of real New York S&M clubs and their clientele. 'It's so moving to see those guys,' she says fondly. 'The bar sequences make it feel like documentary at times.'

As far back as 1986, Robin Wood argued that the use by Friedkin of gay extras tempered the film's infernal tenor, pointing out that 'many of [them] look irrepressibly happy and energetic, especially in contrast to the haggard face of Al Pacino: we may ask ourselves how, if this is hell, so many people appear to be enjoying themselves in it'. Two decades later, Nathan Lee wrote that the film's 'lasting legacy isn't political but archival . . . Nowadays, when the naughtiest thing you can do in a New York gay club is light a cigarette, it's bracing – and, let's admit, pretty fucking hot – to travel back to a moment when getting your ass plowed in public was as blasé as ordering a Red Bull.'

Olson agrees that the context has changed with the years: 'Since it's further away, we can reappropriate things and enjoy them. But that's incidental. The fact is that it's gross and creepy and not on our side. It's inherently homophobic, and there's no way round that. Fuck Friedkin!'

Andrew Haigh saw *Cruising* on video in his teens. 'That's a *ballsy* film,' he says. 'I don't think it's homophobic, whatever people say. The fucked-up characters in it are either damaged deeply by straight society, or living in straight society. The people in the clubs are having a whale of a time!' And when Liz Purchell showed the movie as part of her queer series at the Austin Film Society in Texas, the screening sold out: 'People were in full gear. There was a furry bear wearing nothing but a leather jock. It was really wonderful.'

What is it about *Massillon*, then, that moves Olson to tears? 'It's like I say in *The Royal Road*: when I'm in a movie, I feel like I'm OK,' she says, dabbing her eyes. 'But particularly with the form of *Massillon* and how it holds you. It's this combination of spaces and the duration of the shots, and the sound, and the peace, and this feeling of being alone with yourself and with other people, and with this figure talking to you, with whom you're identifying. There's this whole fascinating thing about urban landscape, first-person voiceover films, which is about the viewer's identification with that character, if you will, and that voice. You project yourself onto it. And as an artwork, what it does is facilitate dropping the viewer into their own emotional state in a way that's so profound, so deep. Obviously, Bill's is a male voice, and mine is female, but men do identify with my character, and that's possible partly because you're not seeing a woman on-screen. You're not seeing anyone.'

There is a tradition of the disembodied queer voice transforming and enriching the image, from Paul Scofield as the gay flaneur in Patrick Keiller's semi-documentaries *London* and *Robinson in Space*, to the casting in Disney's animated version of *Mulan*. It must be somebody's idea of an in-joke that the two most fiercely macho characters in that picture are voiced by actors whose appearances in front of the camera have been associated with queerness: BD Wong, best known as the prissy assistant to Martin Short's exaggeratedly camp wedding planner in the *Father of the Bride* comedies, and Harvey Fierstein of *Torch Song Trilogy*. Their involvement in *Mulan* can only give credence to the movie's assertion, in its story of a girl who poses as a boy, that preconceptions are there to be overturned.

In Derek Jarman's final film, *Blue*, queer voices (including Jarman and Tilda Swinton) are woven into a kind of sound sculpture set against a screen of timeless, ocean-deep Yves Klein Blue that stains the eye. The narration drifts between reflection, poetry and ribald chants ('I am a cock-sucking/straight-acting/lesbian man!'), and includes several charged lists: one detailing the bewildering potential side effects of Jarman's HIV medication, another a roll call of friends and lovers lost to AIDS.

Olson's intricately textured 16mm essay films enable a tissue of sound and image to form in our imagination as we watch. The static camera, the extended shots, the affectless but confiding tone of Olson's narration, all conspire to cast a spell. 'Emotionally, one of the things I'm trying to do is hold the viewer in that vulnerable state of being told a story,' she explains. 'When I used to read to my kids, I remember that feeling, that state they had of being open to whatever they were hearing. I want to do that for the viewer.'

And she does. Among the choicest examples is a scene from *The Royal Road* in which the camera holds on a shot of a residential San Francisco street. What we see is a row of pastel-coloured houses, cars parked outside, a block of blue sky overhead, a line of telegraph poles shrinking into the distance like toothpicks. What we hear is Olson recounting the circumstances of arranging to see her latest crush.

I'm meeting her at that quaint French café in the Lower Haight. I will get there early. I'll be at a little quiet table in the corner window, immersed in *Death in Venice* when she arrives. This will give her the opportunity to observe *me* seemingly unguarded and vulnerable before I see her. I will appear deeply interested in something that is not her, giving the illusion that I actually care about anything else right now.

But that's not how it goes. She's on her cell phone when she arrives. She merely glances at me and taps the window to let me know she's there.

The layering effect here is sublime. Olson could have delivered her narration over a shot of the same street in the Lower Haight to which she is referring; she could have put the quaint French café itself centre-screen and allowed us to insert into the tableau the imagined figures representing her and her crush. Instead, she photographs a different street, so that we project our version of the one she is talking about onto the reality she is showing us. As she narrates what happens, we play that imaginary film over the one we are watching.

There is the knowing choice, too, of *Death in Venice* – that queer study of voyeurism and erotic yearning constructed from unreciprocated looks. Onto the memory of Mann's novella we might be mentally grafting the film version, with Bogarde as Aschenbach feigning obliviousness after he falls under Tadzio's spell. That pantomime of casualness is repeated in Olson's description of her own pre-planned spontaneity, only for the construct to slip heartbreakingly from her grasp. But there remains a defiant, triumphant quality to Olson's films. In their frankness and intimacy, they reprise the elation of Akerman speaking those first present-tense words over the intercom in *Je tu il elle*. Cinema becomes a way for Olson, like Akerman before her, to announce: 'It's me.'

15

LINGUA FRANCA

Isabel Sandoval never meant to pay homage to Chantal Akerman. '*Lingua Franca* is my third film, but it was the first time I wasn't consciously nodding to my heroes,' she says from her apartment in New York. 'Then I look at the opening and closing montages in my film, showing these isolated landscapes in Coney Island and Brooklyn, juxtaposed with a voiceover that's not in English, and – of course! – it's *News from Home*.' Heroes, like ghosts or guilt, have a habit of haunting you.

The serenely composed actor and film-maker, who was born and raised in the Philippines, made a sudden leap in sophistication with *Lingua Franca*, in which she plays Olivia, an undocumented transgender immigrant working as a carer in Brighton Beach. While paying instalments to a stranger who has promised to marry her so she can acquire her green card, Olivia grows close to an abattoir worker, Matthew (Eamon Farren), the enigmatic, feline-faced son of the woman she is looking after. Matthew's occupation is a nod, not to *In a Year of 13 Moons*, as I had supposed, with its protracted slaughterhouse sequence, but to Lino Brocka's 1976 *Insiang*. I check it out on YouTube and find that it begins with a scene of graphic, remorseless culling that makes Fassbinder's movie look vegan.

Sandoval's two previous films – the *Klute*-inspired *Señorita* (2011), where she cast herself as a trans woman in Manila juggling personae as she tries to escape the sex industry, and the eerie *Aparisyon* (2012), set in a remote convent in the early 1970s – were confident psychological thrillers with an accent on the sensual. How does she account, though, for the elevated accomplishment of *Lingua Franca*?

'I became more confident as an artist as I grew more comfortable as a person,' she says. 'My films are more visual now. In *Lingua Franca*, this emphasis on silence and interiority stands out because it's set in New York City, which we don't associate with quiet and solitude.' She used to feel suspicious of voiceover. 'But then I realised how important it can be in getting inside the mind and subjectivity of characters who are otherwise invisible or voiceless. Given who Olivia is, it's quite radical for her to be given a voiceover. Characters like her are usually peripheral in US cinema.'

Sandoval displays an uncommon dexterity with slippages of time and space as expressed through juxtaposition, such as the wide shot of Olivia standing on a train platform, which is accompanied by the sound of her pillow-talk with Matthew from the night before. The dissonance between the intimacy of their conversation and the wide shot, with its connotations of voyeurism, is eloquent in its disruptiveness. Another sequence travels in the opposite emotional direction, superimposing a difficult conversation between the lovers over carefree shots of them larking around together on the boardwalk at Asbury Park.

None of which is to suggest that her previous films are crude. *Señorita*, especially, ended up being more than just a movie. 'I think I made it to sort out questions I was asking myself about my gender identity,' she says. 'Growing up in a Third World Catholic country like the Philippines, the Madonna and the whore were the predominant images of femininity; I felt like by inhabiting a fictional version of those polarised images in *Señorita*, and seeing if it felt true and honest and right, then I would know if I was transgender after all.'

So *Señorita* was her rehearsal for life? 'In a way, yeah. I didn't think of it at the time, but in hindsight I realised I didn't feel like a fraud playing those characters. In fact, I felt stronger and braver and more powerful.'

Once she made *Aparisyon* a year later, she had decided to transition. 'I never told anyone. I said, "I'll give myself time to map out the steps I need to take." Another reason why I took so long was that in the Philippines – well, this is true everywhere – the men are more powerful, and I was afraid of losing my stature. I was partly concerned with what other people thought of me because trans women as portrayed in popular culture in the Philippines are almost always treated with derision. They're buffoons. And that was not how I saw myself. My character in *Señorita* is a repudiation of those shallow, swishy types. She's a serious double agent. After *Aparisyon*, people were talking about me as an emerging film-maker, so I said: now's the time. I took down my social media accounts and went about transitioning in a very low-key way. I laid low for two or three years and started writing *Lingua Franca*.'

Mainstream trans narratives are dominated by the coming-out, the dreaded discovery, the disclosure. *Lingua Franca* is not that movie. Olivia is way past her transition by the time it begins. 'Showing that is not a priority for me,' she says. 'That fixation is coming from a very straight cisgender perspective. Most films about trans characters made by straight directors have the reveal as a pivotal point. Not to disparage *A Fantastic Woman*, but it's the films that pander to a mainstream audience that get the most recognition, because they allow viewers to pat themselves on the back. And I don't care about that at all. There's a scene early on where Olivia is lying in bed and it looks like she's masturbating. In fact, she is dilating. But I didn't feel like I needed to explain that to the audience; trans viewers will get it. For me that's enough. I didn't make the film to educate cisgender people.'

I nod, pretending I knew all along that Olivia was dilating. Sandoval would undoubtedly understand if I told her the truth. But I don't want to disappoint her, or to reveal that my queerness is flawed and incomplete, any more than I want to admit that I gave *A Fantastic*

Woman a rave review when it came out. I hid that fact from Jessica Dunn Rovinelli when we spoke a few months earlier. I can hide it again now: I've had practice.

One notable element of *Lingua Franca* is its cast list, which contains the credit 'Introducing Isabel Sandoval' – despite this being her third acting role. 'It was my producers' idea at first,' she smiles. 'It was a way to deal with the politics of having actors whose contracts stipulate "first billing" or "second billing" or whatever. But I thought it was the most apropos way of introducing me as an actor. Although *Lingua Franca* is my third feature, it feels like my first. Not only because it's the first one I've made after my gender transition; it's my first set and shot in the US, and the first as the film-maker and artist I envisioned myself to be.'

Sandoval has two new films on the runway: *Moonglow*, about a corrupt police detective in 1970s Manila investigating crimes of her own making, and *Tropical Gothic*, set in the sixteenth-century Philippines. The future for her is about moving away from trans identity being the defining characteristic either for her or the roles she plays. 'For me, it's about writing and playing characters not exclusively defined by gender identity or sexual orientation. That will encourage both trans and non-trans film-makers not to fixate on one facet or aspect of our identity that happens to be the one that we are most oppressed for.'

She sees fecundity and potential in the very nature of queer cinema. '"Queer" is useful as a mode of artistic practice. It embodies a spirit of adventure, innovation and fearlessness that I would like to continue working in. I think the future of art and cinema can be found in that word. Films that struck me as queer in cinema were not always the ones about explicitly queer characters, but rather those that addressed desire that was suppressed, thwarted or sublimated. That's the crux or central aspect of what makes a film queer: the desire is kept hidden because of broader socio-political forces that punish its articulation and expression.'

She singles out *Beau Travail*, Claire Denis' rhapsodic take on *Billy Budd*. '*Beau Travail* is innately queer. It gets at a certain yearning and longing and desiring that is not easily satisfied or resolved.' Apichatpong Weerasethakul's *Tropical Malady* has also had a profound effect on her. 'It's an exquisitely daring way of embodying an Eastern spirituality in a medium invented in the West. He reinvented cinema in his own vision. Seeing the film was a very jarring experience. Even arthouse cinema is usually tethered to a certain understanding of time and space, but that's not how *Tropical Malady* works, especially after the midpoint.'

The fracture to which she refers marks a sudden shift from the portrayal of the tender relationship between a Bangkok soldier, Keng (Banlop Lomnoi), and his lover, Tong (Sakda Kaewbuadee), into a mythical realm where Keng is now pursuing a shape-shifting tiger through the jungle. The two halves of the film are divided by a blackout, with the second part announced by a new title (*A Spirit's Path*) and its own brief credits. Reincarnating itself, the film draws on a fresh palette of textures and colours, an infinity of greens in fact. (Some of the later jungle shots are so denuded of light and colour they are almost black-and-white; the sound design and the flecks of sunlight on the jungle floor become our only guides.) There is a clamminess here in the verdant depths; the screen itself seems to sweat. The film transitions from an external experience to a stiflingly interior one.

The same actors return from the first half, though that alone doesn't clear up any of the mystery. 'The two territories are linked by characters who the audience can take as the same or not,' said Apichatpong. 'What's essential are the memories. Memories from the first part validate the second part. Neither wholly exists without the other.' Memories flow, too, between the director's films: *Tropical*

Malady begins with the discovery of a body, which may or may not be a character whose fate was left dangling in *Blissfully Yours*. (That 2002 picture was similarly bisected – in that case by an opening title sequence that didn't begin until around the forty-five-minute mark.) *Tropical Malady* also reaches into the future to reference *Uncle Boonmee Who Can Recall His Past Lives*, a film the director was still five years away from making at that time.

Perhaps it would be more helpful to see the film's sections as tributaries flowing into the same river. Tong must be at least part animal in the first section, which ends with him licking Keng's hand before wandering off into the darkness. Even a simple shopping trip brings hints of disguise or transformation: Tong mooches around a shoe store wearing army fatigues from his days of military service. He isn't a soldier, he explains to the shop assistant, but he hopes the uniform will help him find work. It's a fake skin, in other words, useful for deterring predators, or camouflaging him as a productive member of society. In this way, there is magic in the film long before we encounter the swarming fireflies, the talking monkey or the bovine ghost rising from its own carcass and plodding casually away.

Even in his relationship with the medium itself, Apichatpong daydreams about the extinction of binaries. 'Film is a parallel life that keeps intersecting with real life,' he says. 'I wonder if it is possible to merge it with real life. Maybe in the future there will be a tool to facilitate this idea, to a point where you cannot differentiate the two.'

There was an age when queer subtext was by necessity a code to be cracked: the hints around Peter Lorre's character, say, which added up to the stench of lavender in *The Maltese Falcon*; the tension between Joan Crawford and Mercedes McCambridge, which could only be explained as repressed lesbian desire, in *Johnny Guitar*; the homoerotic shadings in *L'Air de Paris* in the mentorship between a retired boxer (Jean Gabin) and his young protégé, which prompted panic in that staunch, resolute actor: 'I don't want to look like a queer,' Gabin told his (gay) director, Marcel Carné. Or the joy of *Misery*, adapted from Stephen King's novel about an unhinged former nurse who holds her favourite novelist captive after rescuing him from a car wreck. Kathy Bates plays the queer-coded psycho-fan – a melodramatic misfit and Liberace nut – while James Caan is so smugly privileged and patriarchal as her incapacitated idol that he comes to symbolise every straight white man who ever merited his just deserts. Watched with the right raucous crowd, the film takes on meanings its makers couldn't have foreseen. Company loves *Misery*, you might say.

Today, there is less sport in identifying subtext when so little needs to be hidden. There are still exceptions where a queer audience has hijacked and claimed for itself material that might otherwise have been neutral. The most prominent early-twenty-first-century example is Jennifer Kent's remarkable horror film *The Babadook*, which is haunted by a monster that queer audiences took it upon themselves to adopt. Splay-fingered, frizz-haired and top-hatted, the creature enters a family home via a children's storybook, the pages of which contain a refrain that resonated with queer viewers accustomed to being demonised and legislated against: 'You can't get rid of The Babadook!' In no time at all, the creature became the ultimate meme queen, and the Pride costume du jour.

This is rare. Leaf through Jenni Olson's *The Queer Movie Poster Book*, which gathers examples of film advertising stretching back to the silent era, and you find a catalogue of discreet winks and salacious nudges. Olson admits that a follow-up covering the years from 2004 onwards wouldn't be half as scintillating. 'It would be less interesting culturally,' she says. 'I'm sure there are still examples of posters being coy or evasive, but it doesn't have to be that way now because we're generally more accepted. It was the tension that made it more interesting.'

Where treasures can be found now is in those films which address, surreptitiously or otherwise, the fluidity of identity. It is in this fertile realm that much of today's most rewarding queer cinema thrives, embraced by the trans, non-binary and gender non-conforming communities that are under attack. Think of Brandon Cronenberg's *Possessor*, Julia Ducournau's *Titane* or Jonathan Glazer's *Under the Skin*, with Scarlett Johansson as a predatory alien who assumes human female form to comb latter-day Glasgow for her quarry. 'For me, *Under the Skin* was a contemporary fairy-tale that spoke so much about trans embodiment, transition, the journey of going from perceived alien/monster to human, and the looming threat of death,' wrote the US trans critic Caden Mark Gardner.

The British trans stand-up Jen Ives argues in one of her meticulous video essays that the film-maker Charlie Kaufman is a trans woman who simply hasn't come out yet. Her initial evidence is drawn from *Being John Malkovich*, the surreal 1999 screwball comedy, written by Kaufman, about a puppeteer, Craig (John Cusack), who discovers a portal leading into the head of the actor John Malkovich. Ives identifies Craig as resembling a trans woman immediately pre-transition – 'The weak beard, the long hair, the scruffy clothes, the sort of "one last try at masculinity before the looming inevitable"' – and reminds us that Craig dreams of looking out from inside the body of Maxine (Catherine Keener), a colleague who mocks and tantalises him.

Maxine, though, is attracted to Craig's wife Lotte (Cameron Diaz) – but only when Lotte has entered the portal in Malkovich's head and is looking at Maxine through the actor's eyes. In other words, says Ives, Maxine gazes at Malkovich but sees through him into the woman within: this is 'two women having a lesbian relationship through a man'.

There is trans text, as well as subtext, in Kaufman's script. After her first stint inside Malkovich's head, Lotte is aroused by the idea that he has a portal: 'Sort of like he has a vagina . . . he has a penis *and* a vagina.' Later, she tells Craig: 'I've decided that I'm a transsexual. I know it's the craziest thing. But for the first time, everything just felt right.' When he dismisses this as a phase, she replies: 'Don't stand in the way of my actualisation as a man.' Carter Burwell's plangent score gives no indication that any of this is a joke.

Once Lotte is inside Malkovich and making love to Maxine, we can hear her thoughts. Because of this, says Ives, 'we get a pretty good representation of what it's like to be a pre-transition . . . trans woman. We see the body of a man – Malkovich – literally thinking in the voice of a woman.' Malkovich himself is perturbed that Maxine calls him 'Lotte' in the middle of sex, but his friend Charlie Sheen can only see the upside: 'Maybe she's using you to channel some dead lesbian lover . . . Hot lesbian witches! Think about it. It's fucking genius!'

The movie ends with Maxine and Lotte, now a couple, raising Emily, the child that Maxine conceived by Malkovich while Lotte was inside him. As the camera looks through Emily's eyes at her mothers, Craig's voice is heard: he is trapped inside this seven-year-old girl.

Ives concedes that Kaufman has yet to come out about his transness. But, she says, 'Trans people lie . . . Sometimes they'll keep it a secret their entire lives, and end up living with deep, deep regret inside a seemingly post-apocalyptic warehouse inside another seemingly post-apocalyptic warehouse inside another seemingly post-apocalyptic warehouse in a seemingly post-apocalyptic even-smaller warehouse' – a reference to the painstakingly constructed Russian-doll realities that make up *Synecdoche, New York*, Kaufman's 2008 debut as director, and his enduring (trans) masterpiece.

Where once queer audiences rifled through movies for evidence that gay characters were out there somewhere, even when governments, religious leaders and the Hays Code said otherwise, now the gender and biological freedoms which are subject to the same denials are finding new expression in cinema.

The division of a single role among multiple physically disparate actors is one way for fluid or non-binary identities to be articulated on film. The young female protagonist in Todd Solondz's *Palindromes* is played by seven female actors of varying size, age and race. Todd Haynes cast six performers to play different aspects of Bob Dylan in *I'm Not There*, including an androgynous, tumbleweed-haired Cate Blanchett. William Friedkin made it impossible to determine the identity of the killer in *Cruising* by alternating three different actors in a role intended for one and dubbing the voice of a fourth onto each of their scenes. This suggested, as Robin Wood put it, 'that there are at least two killers and could be several; that we don't have to feel we know who the killer is, because it could be anyone; and that the violence has to be blamed on the culture, not the individual'.

It's a tradition reaching back to Buñuel, who divided the role of one enigmatic woman between two actors (Carole Bouquet and Ángela Molina) in *That Obscure Object of Desire*. Perhaps even he couldn't have predicted that a single role – Virginia Woolf's Orlando – would be shared between twenty-six trans and non-binary actors in Paul C. Preciado's 2024 stylised drama-documentary *Orlando, My Political Biography*.

The expression of diverse gender identities stretches beyond the literal and into movies that cis audiences might never have recognised as trans were it not for clarification by the film-makers, or analysis by trans critics. Jane Schoenbrun's *We're All Going to the World's Fair* explores the destabilised identity of a teenage girl, Casey (Anna

Cobb), who submits to an internet horror game which requires her to log for an unseen online audience the changes she undergoes following her initiation. The film could play simply as a fright-night favourite, or as a commentary on the simultaneously nourishing and nullifying experience of growing up online. Its drift into body horror, though, signals an expression of dysphoria which has been described by Caden Mark Gardner and Willow Catelyn Maclay as 'a secret handshake of transness'. Schoenbrun's follow-up, *I Saw the TV Glow*, is an even richer allegory of identity in turmoil, this time charting the influence of a fictional supernatural TV show called *The Pink Opaque* on an adolescent (Justice Smith) with gender issues.

Asked which film they would show in a double bill with *We're All Going to the World's Fair*, Schoenbrun suggested a strange bedfellow: *Taste of Cherry*, Abbas Kiarostami's 1997 study of a suicidal man driving around Tehran in search of someone to bury his body in the grave he has dug. 'It's him almost, like, cruising,' Schoenbrun said. 'He's cruising around, picking various people up off the street and offering to pay them to do this job, and all of them want to know why he's doing this, and they wanna talk him out of this, and to understand what sadness could be in there so deeply that they would ask such a thing of him.'

Having watched it while making *We're All Going to the World's Fair*, Schoenbrun realised not only that they wanted screens in their film to be the sort of liminal spaces that cars are for Kiarostami, but also that both movies express an essential human unknowability. 'Kiarostami's work, I think, is reflecting on the medium,' they said. 'It's [asking] "what is realism?" in a medium that is, in essence, a dream, and this idea about the limits of what we can know about a person as another person is at the centre of *Taste of Cherry*.' It's a theme that can be applied also to Kiarostami's 2010 mystery *Certified Copy*, in which a couple (Juliette Binoche and William Shimell) who appear to be meeting for the first time are revealed gradually but without explanation to know one another intimately, rendering every aspect of the film slippery and provisional.

Some of the most encouraging signs of sophistication in queer cinema can be found in post-gender casting. One instance, in the superb 2022 horror film *Talk to Me*, prompted the Kuwaiti authorities to ban the movie: they objected to the presence on-screen of the non-binary and transmasculine actor Zoe Terakes, even though no reference is made in the movie to their gender. If the elliptical *Monos* got away with its own post-gender casting, that must be because this 2019 film is disorientating on every level. Set during an unspecified conflict in an unnamed Latin American country, it focuses on eight teenage soldiers guarding an adult female prisoner. One member of the adolescent platoon, Rambo, was written as male. After sifting through hundreds of audition tapes during the casting process, the director and co-writer, Alejandro Landes, seized on footage of a kid apparently named Matt, who was filmed playing basketball with friends. 'Matt ended up being Sofia Buenaventura,' said Landes, 'but a lot of her friends call her Matt.' Casting Buenaventura was a decision consistent with the film's idea of 'rejecting binary concepts of the world. Good or evil, adult or child, left or right, victim or victimiser, paradise or hell.'

The film's non-binary composer, Mica Levi (whose debut score was for *Under the Skin*), appreciated the ambiguity surrounding Rambo: 'It just felt like a relief,' they said. Responses varied. 'Half the audience has experienced Rambo as a boy and the other half as a girl,' said Landes. 'And yet, does it change the deeper impressions of the film? I think not.'

Monos was awarded a special prize at the San Sebastián Film Festival for reflecting 'the values and reality' of LGBTQ+ people. Among its most perceptive cheerleaders was the director Lyle Kash, who tweeted: 'Finally a film with a key character (Rambo) who can't be taken up as trans or cis. And the plot doesn't hinge on gender. *Monos* resists identity politics. The film is queer AF but doesn't announce itself. I loved this movie. Go see it.'

16

DEATH AND BOWLING

Lyle Kash was having a bad day. 'My friend was like, "We're going bowling,"' he recalls. 'There we are, sticking our fingers in the holes, and I realised something: "Hey, this ball has three holes. So do trans men!" That's when I knew I needed to go home and start writing the script.' The symbolism in his 2021 debut film *Death and Bowling* extends to the iconography of the bowling alley: the phallic pins, the ball return unit with its gaping abyss expressing both creation and extinction. It's literally a pregnant image. 'One hole or another, right?' he laughs.

Death and Bowling boasts the largest trans and non-binary cast and crew of any feature-length film made at that time, with the exception of *Maggots and Men*, Cary Cronenwett's 2009 reimagining of Russia's Kronstadt uprising (which used over a hundred trans performers). Kash's film stars Will Krisanda as X, a trans actor whose mentor Susan (Faith Eileen Bryan) commits suicide on her seventy-fifth birthday, leaving bereft him and fellow members of the Lavender League lesbian bowling team, of which Susan was the matriarch. At her funeral, X meets Alex (Tracy Kowalski), the trans son he never knew Susan had. Both are summoned to attend the reading of her will, which contains a treasure map showing where she wants her ashes scattered.

Despite what that précis might suggest, *Death and Bowling* is not a film which unpicks trans identity. Anything but. What Kash admired about *Monos* – its resistance to gender politics and representation – he has put into practice in his own film. 'There is play around the fact of having a trans cast without specifying whether everyone in the bowling league is trans,' he explains when we speak over video call. He has a black T-shirt with 'Carl's' emblazoned on it, a black beard and moustache, and shiny shoulder-length curls. 'But in no way is the journey of the characters about being trans.'

Try telling that to the audience. 'Even though I made the film I did, people sometimes come out of the theatre rewarding me for positive trans representation. Cis people continue to come up to me and say: "I learned so much about your community from watching that." Well, great. But I'm not quite sure *how*. Maybe they learned that trans people go to funerals. Or that they have kitchens. I don't know. I'm a little shocked. I don't think *Death and Bowling* is an educational piece. It's like they go in expecting to see something, and they come out convinced that they've seen it, even if that's not what the film is doing.'

An early hint that Kash's picture will turn expectations about trans stories on their head lies in X's idea of interior design. Hanging on one wall are portraits of a variety of cis actors who have played trans roles on-screen. Hilary Swank from *Boys Don't Cry* and Jared Leto in *Dallas Buyers Club*, both Oscar-winning performances, are there. John Lithgow, too, for *The World According to Garp*, and Eddie Redmayne for *The Danish Girl*. Chloë Sevigny is represented for playing a trans assassin in the series *Hit and Miss* by Paul Abbott, the British TV writer also responsible for *Mrs In-Betweeny*, starring Amelia Bullmore as a trans woman.

The other element connecting the pictures is that they are hanging upside down. 'The idea was that these actors would be reference points and possibly even heroes in his lexicon,' Kash explains. 'So X is compelled to have them on his wall. But it's an upside-down try, mis-orientated and uncomfortable. Look, I love *Boys Don't Cry*. I almost *nearly* don't have a problem with it. I thought Hilary Swank's performance was one of the greatest in trans cinema, period. And I hold the possibly controversial position that I don't think it's a problem when actors who aren't trans play trans roles. The issue is historically we've been so excluded. But acting involves taking on a subjectivity that isn't your own, so if we say, "You can't do that," then we're almost eliminating trans identity from one of the lived experiences of humans that can be portrayed on-screen.'

The film's trans and non-binary crew are visible during the opening shot, which shows X acting on the set of a trans-themed drama. After the director calls 'Cut!' the camera spins round to show everybody behind the scenes. In acknowledging its own construction and artifice in this manner, *Death and Bowling* takes its place in a tradition of queer cinema which foregrounds the process of queer world-building. Just as *Orlando, My Political Biography* would do a few years later, the film occasionally reveals its own cameras, studio lights, dolly tracks. The idea for Kash was to allude to, and seize control of, the impulse that says trans cinema must be educational or representative.

'In so much trans cinema, we're portrayed in documentaries, or else there's an impulse to show trans-ness in this real way, like we can't stray from teaching the audience or presenting our extremely misunderstood and under-represented community,' he says. 'I'd like to get away from that, so part of spinning the camera round at the start, like with the whole push–pull of the upside-down photos on the wall, is to engage in that feedback loop which says: "I'm participating in this and, if we insist it has to be seen, then let me show you on my terms."'

In other words: why do films made by trans people need to straightforwardly reflect trans experience? The trash-Americana aesthetic in *Death and Bowling* pays homage to John Waters, the ripe colours betray Kash's admiration for Almodóvar and the desert boxing sequences have a faintly surreal, spaced-out Lynchian quality. There is even an excerpt from Genet's *The Thief's Journal* read aloud at Susan's funeral. Knitted together with Kash's sensibility, the result is a film of defiance and playfulness which questions the priorities of all cinema, not only the trans variety.

'I really struggled with having a protagonist,' Kash admits. 'I just didn't want to show a fully fleshed-out trans character. I wanted to have an empty centre of the film's universe, and maybe that's why X doesn't really have a name.' After all, 'X' is what you sign in lieu of a name; spoken aloud, it also sounds like 'ex', as in an entity which once was but is no more. 'In the final version, I think he *is* fleshed out. But it's almost like I wanted to hide him and protect him from the eyes of the audience watching this trans character. It's because there is so much pressure to make a realistic, positive representation. I wanted a character who embodied avoidance and dissociation, but who could still be part of a community and feel grief and closeness and attraction. Instead of: "I can see everything in this character is trans and strong and fully actualised."'

Even after making *Death and Bowling*, he continues to wrestle with that. 'Something I'm still working on is: how do you have a protagonist who is not a hero and a role model? Maybe I'm not brave enough yet as a film-maker to be putting out films like this, but people like Almodóvar and Fassbinder have characters who are frequently detestable. I don't think we're in a place yet where you can have a detestable transsexual character per se, but could we just not give them so many *great* qualities? The role of film-makers shouldn't be to offer positive representation but to ask difficult questions. There are trans heroes now and coming-of-age stories and work being made for kids, and that is awesome. I definitely didn't see myself on-screen when I was out and queer and trans at eighteen. But where are the people making audiences walk out of the theatre in anger? Part of what that would do is to allow trans people to be fully human.'

Trans representation as it exists now, he argues, is largely placatory. 'If trans people have to be on their best behaviour all the time, the cinema is going to be horrible. We're missing an entire participation in what a story can be. Instead we get: "Trans people are great! They never kill themselves! Nobody has an addiction and they do good work!" I have the feeling of being not quite able to breathe.'

Only now is there starting to be pushback against the situation he describes. 'And that pushback is exciting to see,' he says. 'You've already interviewed some of these people for your book. When I saw Jessie Dunn Rovinelli's film *So Pretty*, I thought, "Thank fucking God!"' Why so? 'I didn't feel like I was watching a mandatory training video about trans sensitivity in the workplace. This should be first-line criteria for trans film programming. Instead, *So Pretty* is a work of art that doesn't play into identity politics as a substitute for point-of-view, and it isn't afraid of aesthetics.'

Converting his goals into directions for his actors, however, poses its own problems. 'I felt at the beginning Will and Tracy thought to themselves: "X and Alex are really good characters, and *you* as the director must tell us how good they are, and how we can portray these trans characters well in this momentous film." Whereas I wanted part of their romance to be right on the edge of horror, so there is something suspenseful and unresolved about it. A lot of my direction was maybe slightly confusing to them. Directing them to look away from each other at the end of a scene as though they've had an argument, that kind of thing. People on set were like, "Huh?"'

If the film is a frequently disquieting experience, that is partly because it diligently withholds prompts indicating how we should respond. Take the relationship between X, who is Susan's adoptive son, and Alex, the one she raised and then spurned. Doesn't that make them brothers of some kind? Isn't this incest?

'I feel like it's almost blasphemy that you're saying that out loud!' he cries. 'No one was fucking saying that and yet they're essentially brothers. If you believe in the framework of queer family and this

alternative kinship structure, then yes. On some level, Alex can understand that himself, having been replaced by this other brother.'

In trying to make a film which avoids being defined by its trans-
ness despite having a predominantly trans cast, there was always the
question of whether to include the t-word itself. An early cut of *Death
and Bowling* did not; in the final version, which Kash and his executive producer Rhys Ernst (director of *Adam*) worked on during the
delays caused by the Covid lockdowns, it is heard only once. 'I was
like, "Obviously, they're trans!" And nobody else felt like that. They
were saying, "You need to let your audience know. Offer them an olive
branch." Does he feel something was lost by including it? 'Not today.
But it was a struggle to decide how many of my hardline rules were
helping the film. There's no coming-out announcement, and I think
you can still watch the film and miss that Alex and X are trans. But if
you don't offer a few olive branches, you run the risk of none of the
aims of your film coming through – and that's a bit heartbreaking.'

There was one suggested olive branch, however, which felt more
like a stick to be beaten with – and which Kash adamantly refused
to offer. 'I'm not gonna throw anyone under the bus, but there were
things which people felt needed to happen to make the film legible
that were hard "no"s for me.' He is referring to one of the final scenes,
in which Alex removes his shirt to put on the bowling uniform.
'Tracy Kowalski and I have very similar-looking chests. We both got
top surgery. If you look closely enough, you can find some scars. But
no one at the beach is going, like, "A trans man!" No one is asking me:
"What motorcycle accident were you in?" Not any more. And some
trans people told me, "You need to increase the contrast so people
can see Tracy's chest scars, otherwise they'll get to the end of the film
and think that you lied about him being trans. Or that you cast someone who's not a trans actor to play a trans person." I refused to touch
the contrast. Those concerns for me are part of why trans adults are

not getting roles. It's that if you don't look trans to an audience who has an idea of what trans-ness is – as in "trans equals someone who doesn't pass" – then you can't play the trans role either!'

None of these battles have deterred Kash from soldiering on. When the Hollywood sign is glimpsed in the film, the first part of the word is obscured so that all we can see is 'wood' – which turns out to be a nod to his next project. *Wood* will be a version of *Pinocchio*, with a trans male in lederhosen yearning to be a 'real boy'. Kash's dream is to cast John Waters as Geppetto.

———————

After I hit 'end meeting for all' on our video call, it dawns on me that I forgot to ask two questions. I'll need the answers for when I write up our interview for my book, to lend it some extra colour on the page. First, what does the 'Carl's' logo on Kash's T-shirt refer to? And second, where was he speaking to me from today?

He emails back immediately:

Carl's is a butcher's shop in Kittery, Maine. And I am in Woodstock, NY, at the moment – my uncle passed away in this house almost two years ago, and while I was helping my mom clean the place out, we came upon:

1. a number of raccoons and squirrels alive and dead (very *Grey Gardens*), and

2. an incredible archive of 1970s gay porn.

Upon discovering that my uncle was gay, my mom gave me his falling-apart raccoon chalet in the woods (I think because I am also gay? hard to tell). In any case, if I ever shoot *Wood*, it will be here. I've removed the raccoons but not the porn.

17

ALL ABOUT MY MOTHER

Porn is a staple of queer life. I can say that with confidence now after being upbraided by William E. Jones for implying to him that it was a transgressive art form. 'I take exception to what I understand to be a conflation of porn and transgression,' he told me. 'Porn is integral to the lives of gay men and will continue to be so for as long as images circulate.' In Samuel R. Delany's analytical memoir *Times Square Red, Times Square Blue*, a young man in the balcony of the Variety Photoplays on Third Avenue allows punters to watch him jacking off from a few seats away but refuses to let them lay a finger on him. 'I'm gettin' off on her up there,' he tells Delany, gesturing to the straight porn flickering on the screen, 'and you guys are all gettin' off on *me* . . .? That's funny, huh?' The tension between Delany watching him, the kid eyeballing the screen while acknowledging that *he* is the main attraction, and then Delany reporting the whole spectacle back to us creates a multi-layered erotic charge.

A single, errant porn cinema trip is all it takes for the otherwise monogamous Andy (Tom Hanks) to become HIV+ in *Philadelphia* – but it's hard to consider that flashback scene as sinister when it represents one of the film's few engagements with authentic (rather than idealised) queer experience. In Ira Sachs's *The Delta*, a wealthy white Memphis native picks up a garrulous Vietnamese man at the porno booths in a movie arcade emblazoned with the slogan 'Giant Screens. Locking Doors. Long Lasting.' In Eloy de la Iglesia's *Hidden Pleasures*, a businessman snags a pretty young trick in the cinema toilets; after they take their seats, one goes down on the other just as the giant screen in front of them shows a beaming teenage boy brandishing a petrol pump's spurting nozzle.

In *Midnight Cowboy*, the movie on-screen also mirrors the action in the auditorium. Joe Buck (Jon Voight), tall and sweet as an ice-cream sundae, is picked up by a gawky college student (Bob Balaban) outside a Times Square grindhouse dive, the location having been switched by the screenwriter Waldo Salt from a tenement rooftop in James Leo Herlihy's original novel. Phallic rockets dominate the cinema screen as the kid dives head-first into Joe's lap in the balcony. Dustin Hoffman, who played Joe's compadre Ratso Rizzo, reported that 'people walked out in droves' during that scene at one of the film's preview screenings. 'We thought this could end everybody's career.'

In fact, the movie won the Best Picture Oscar and gave its director John Schlesinger even more confidence to tackle homosexuality again three years later in *Sunday Bloody Sunday*, this time without the mitigating gauze of his characters' homophobia and repression. Even as Joe and Ratso in *Midnight Cowboy* dismiss 'faggots' and 'faggot behaviour', Schlesinger scratches away at the inexpressible desires in their unspoken romance, and the anxiety it causes them. Ratso mocks Joe for the campness of his cowboy duds, but we know better, having been privy to his fantasies, in which he and Joe race shirtless on the beach.

There is an enthusiastic cinema blow job, too, in Wong Kar-Wai's *Happy Together*, while an intoxicating cruising vibe pervades the entirety of Tsai Ming-liang's spellbinding *Goodbye Dragon Inn*, set on the closing day of a cavernous Taipei cinema where the patrons move around the auditorium like chess pieces. The projectionist is played by Tsai's muse, the taciturn, alluringly blank Lee Kang-sheng, who has been the star of his films since *Rebels of the Neon God* in 1992. It's tempting to call the love between this heterosexual actor and queer director unrequited, except that their body of work, including the searingly intimate *Days*, represents a consummation as indelible as any physical equivalent.

For anyone who read *The Orton Diaries* before they had a sex life of their own to speak of, the expectations of what might happen in the average cinema could only have been raised to unrealistic heights. Joe Orton's first sexual experience was in his local Odeon in Leicester. 'Watched an old film on television called *My Favourite Blonde* with Bob Hope,' he wrote on 19 February 1967. 'This had sentimental overtones for me. It was at the companion picture, *My Favourite Brunette* (also with Bob Hope), some time in the early forties that I was first interfered with. A man took me into the lavatory of the Odeon and gave me a wank. I re-lived those happy moments as I sat watching the picture today. I remember coming down his mac. I must've been about fourteen.'

———

Britain never had a circuit of dedicated, above-board gay porn cinemas comparable to New York or San Francisco. They took the form instead of basements secreted beneath video shops, or upper rooms, some no better than fire-traps, accessible by narrow wooden staircases. Typical of London's haunts were venues like the Brutus, the fictional subterranean cinema imagined by Alan Hollinghurst in *The Swimming-Pool Library*, where men go 'to sit in a dark, anonymous place and do dark, anonymous things'.

Such unlicensed premises existed in the city as recently as 2013, when the Abcat Cine Club in King's Cross was shuttered after an Islington council official inspecting the premises was propositioned by a member of the audience. (He noted, too, the rows of men masturbating each other in the dark, which also did its bit to hasten the closure.) The Abcat's nearby sister cinema, Oscars, met the same fate when a staff member sold an undercover official an unrated DVD called *Meet the Barebackers II*, presumably without first bringing him up to speed on the events of *Meet the Barebackers*.

Many cinemas in central London had been known as cruising grounds since before the war: the Majestic, the Carlton, the Gaiety and the Super, all within spurting distance of each other. Most notorious was the one on Wilton Road in Victoria, south-west London, which opened as the Electric in 1909. It later became the Biograph, unofficially renamed the Bio-Grope once its reputation as a cruising spot had grown so notorious in the 1960s that the *News of the World* ran an exposé headlined 'Close Down This Cinema of Vice'.

Quentin Crisp alludes to the Biograph in his autobiography *The Naked Civil Servant*, noting that 'all the films shown have a "Q" certificate (no normal person may be admitted to any part of this programme unless accompanied by a homosexual)' and explaining the audience's preference for war movies ('their soundtracks help to conceal the noise of creaking seat springs') and aversion to shots of snowy landscapes ('these cast too much light back into the auditorium').

The erstwhile clientele seems to agree that the death knell for the place sounded when George Cooper, identical twin brother of the boxer Henry, came aboard as manager. He took it upon himself to eject anyone suspected of errant behaviour, and often kept the house lights partially on. The establishment was closed without notice in 1983, reportedly because the owners feared that it was liable to be listed and preserved; the land was too lucrative for that to be allowed to happen.

A Pathé news clip on YouTube from 1956 shows 'Mrs Griffith, "Britain's oldest cinemagoer",' visiting the Biograph, 'Britain's oldest cinema'. The comments posted below the video get straight to the point. 'She was brave going into the Biograph,' says one. 'I bet she had to have her coat dry cleaned,' offers markstephens36, who 'saw one of the *Thunderbirds* films there with a school friend. We did notice "activity" but didn't really think anything of it.' Another commenter doesn't mince their words: the cinema 'was a wankers' pit'.

———————————

At parties in the late 1990s, I used to bump into Howard Schuman, who wrote the coruscating 1970s TV hit *Rock Follies* and the 1995 AIDS drama *Nervous Energy*, starring Alfred Molina. It's more than twenty years since I last saw Howard, but while researching the porn circuit I come across an interview with him in which he admits to having once been thrown out of the Biograph for the crime of 'wilful hanky-panky'.

I drop by his sprawling basement flat behind Victoria Station, a short trot from where the Biograph once stood.

'How are you?' I ask him as I plod down the stairs into his living room.

'I'm eighty-three,' he croaks by way of explanation.

He has lived here ever since moving to London from New York in 1968 with his late husband, the director Robert Chetwyn. It was Chetwyn who helped make *There's a Girl in My Soup* one of the West End's longest-running comedies, and he later directed the first productions of both Martin Sherman's *Bent*, starring Ian McKellen, and Joe Orton's final play, *What the Butler Saw*, with Ralph Richardson. 'The one that was booed,' Howard points out, handing me a mug of corpse-reviving coffee as we sit across from one another, me on the sofa, him on a wooden chair.

'I'd arrived in London, and Bob was immediately rehearsing *What the Butler Saw*,' he recalls, breaking apart one of the raspberry doughnuts I've brought. 'While he was on tour with that, I was walking around Pimlico trying to get to know the city, and I noticed this cinema, the Biograph. I'd read that it was the oldest cinema in London.

The strange thing was that it only ever seemed to be men who were buying tickets. Then I realised what was going on.'

He soon became a regular. 'There was a guard, a strange limping guy, who would scuttle up and down the aisles breaking people up, putting the flashlight on you if you were having a wank. I spent some interesting hours there. It became a little bit of an addiction when Bob was away.'

Did he mind? 'We talked about it early on. I said, "When you're on the road or away, I would like to feel it's OK. You don't have to know the details but there are a lot of gay experiences I haven't had yet. If that's something you can't cope with, then I won't do it." He said, "What if you meet someone?" But I told him what we had was so strong that I could never imagine that happening.'

Being barred from the Biograph didn't have much effect on his habits. 'It certainly never kept me from coming back,' he chuckles. 'It was an extraordinary place. The prints were very good, by the way. They kept trying to encourage heterosexuals to go by getting rid of any gay activity, kicking out as many gay people as they could, but it never worked. Sunday was leather day, pretty much. Late Saturday nights, too. There was one guy who sat next to me a few times who brought with him not only a tube of KY to service you but a little vibrator to make the masturbation more exciting. *So* thoughtful! My final time there was when a super-sexy guy offered me the chance to be his toilet slave for the night. I turned that down, and that was the point where I said to myself: I think I'm done.'

Does he ever miss it? 'The SS *Libido* sailed a long time ago,' he smiles.

In the mid-1980s, he considered putting his Biograph experiences down on paper. The critic and short-story writer Adam Mars-Jones was editing *Mae West Is Dead*, a collection of gay and lesbian fiction, and asked Howard to contribute a story. 'He came here. I told him about the cinema idea and said I had a title: "Les Enfants du Biograph". Adam said he'd commission that. But when I sat down to write it, he was so terrifying – he didn't mean to be, but his *brain* was so terrifying – I just couldn't finish the story. We stayed friends but the idea of presenting him with it and receiving his critique . . . well, I was already insecure enough about my prose.'

We've been talking for hours by this point, the afternoon dwindling into evening, neither of us thinking to switch on the lamp as we melt into silhouettes, surrounded by shadow-theatre scenery: the fronds of the plants have turned into pointed black love-hearts; the framed photographs on the sideboard are now featureless dark oblongs. I stare into the grains at the bottom of my cup and mumble something to Howard about having always found Adam intimidating.

'You're not alone,' he says.

In the mid-1990s, I landed a job as the second-string film reviewer for the *Independent* newspaper, mopping up the bulk of the new releases each week while Adam lavished a few thousand words on the lead picture. I saw him for the first time at a press screening of John Greyson's agitprop musical *Zero Patience*, which features a Miss HIV+ glamour queen floating in a rubber ring amid blood cells seen through a microscope, as well as a duet between singing buttholes.

Adam was standing near the platter of breakfast pastries provided by the film's distributor, talking to a gaggle of other critics before the screening began. I hovered in the doorway, my eyes gobbling up every detail. He was stilt-walker tall, lean and elegant as a quill. His billowing white shirt, held in check by red braces under a black leather jacket, was tucked into his trousers, also black leather, which led in turn to motorcycle boots. His mouth was framed by a closely trimmed beard, as though it were a key word circled decisively in a book, and he gesticulated as he spoke, like a magician performing a conjuring trick. He was as poised in person as he was in prose. Most of all, he was gay, and I'd never felt straighter in my life.

He wasn't always in his biker gear. A few times, he turned up to screenings wearing furry brown chaps, as though a teddy bear had been slaughtered specially for his spring collection. It gave him the appearance of a mythical beast, a creature cleaved in two at the waist, the top part pale and human, chin-stroking and contemplative, the lower one shaggy and untamed. The mismatch was lightly comical, with echoes of a pantomime horse, but any element of the ridiculous was overruled by Adam's natural audacity.

I experienced my own mythical-beast moments whenever I found myself sandwiched in the front row between my girlfriend on my left and Adam on my right. Not knowing which incarnation of myself to be, straight or gay, it was as if I had been cobbled together from incompatible halves, ready to be torn down the middle by my competing allegiances to girlfriend and idol.

Adam and I covered the waterfront of the new releases with a minimum of coordination. He would ring me at home to ask if I had any reviewing preferences for the coming week, or to express his own. Sometimes he would call me at night, his unfazed, musical voice fluting down the receiver.

'I've just tuned into *Internal Affairs* on BBC2,' he said one evening. 'I take it you've seen the film?'

'Yeah! Mike Figgis. It's excellent.'

My girlfriend was getting ready for bed, mouthing: *Who is it?*

'Riddle me this,' Adam continued. 'Have we been given any indication that Laurie Metcalf's character is a lesbian prior to Andy Garcia noticing that they've both taken an interest in the same female passer-by?'

When I came off the phone, she said: '10.30 on a Sunday? It's like he's your bit on the side.'

'Don't be daft.'

She was right to feel suspicious, but for the wrong reasons. I didn't want to sleep with Adam. I wanted to *be* him. Partly it was his writing, forensic where mine was fuzzy. But it was also the ease with which he expressed and embodied his sexuality. He did it as effortlessly as breathing, whereas I was like a man with emphysema.

Four years after I started at the *Independent*, there was a round of budget cuts. Adam was esteemed but he was also expensive, which made him vulnerable. Andrew Marr, who had recently been appointed editor, summoned me to his office; the Docklands were spread out eighteen floors below like an architect's model. He informed me that I would be the paper's sole film critic from now on. I was elated until I realised what it meant.

Adam phoned me later that week.

'You've probably heard they're not renewing my contract,' he said.

'Yes,' I replied, trying to strike a suitable note of commiseration despite being the chief beneficiary of his sacking. I told him I had been asked to review everything from now on.

'It'll be a slog,' I said.

'Oh, you'll survive,' he purred. 'You're young.'

'I suppose so. Young and vibrant.'

There was a pause.

'I didn't say "vibrant",' he said.

The news was terrible for him, but it was bad for me, too, and not merely because I was stepping into his motorcycle boots when I was scarcely even ambulant. Had Andrew Marr spotted the fear in my eyes as he bestowed on me this new responsibility? 'You write freely over a range of genres rather than having one specialist area,' he reassured me. In fact, he couldn't have said anything more crushing. I would have been happier had he confessed the real reason for my promotion: *You're cheap*. What he meant by his apparent compliment, I realised, was that he felt my predecessor to be limited by his renown as a specifically gay writer, gay from the top of his head to the nib of his pen, and no one was likely to reach that conclusion about me.

In the niche area of closeted reviews expressing gay self-loathing, however, I had few equals. I railed against the queer coming-of-age film *C.R.A.Z.Y.*, accusing it of going 'to enormous lengths to disguise what it is that men do with one another in bed'. My friend Charles had a quiet word with me: 'This is *you* criticising a film for being in the closet?' he asked.

When I reviewed Pedro Almodóvar's *All About My Mother*, I took issue with the scene in which a nurse reconnects with her late child's father, who is now living as a woman called Lola. 'When it transpires that Lola has fathered a *second* child after a brief liaison with a nun named Sister Rosa (Penélope Cruz), it really is a contrivance too far,' I wrote. 'Perhaps my parents sheltered me from the harsh realities of life, but I was always led to believe that strapping, six-foot transsexuals in A-line skirts were way down a woman's list, only slightly above estate agents in fact, when it came to choosing a potential partner.'

Was I genuinely incredulous that women might find a trans woman to be attractive or reliable? A more likely explanation must be that I was expressing deep-seated doubts about myself. Like Lola, I had two children and two heterosexual relationships to my name. What's more, I was about to trump her record. Within a few months of writing that review, I found out I was going to become a father for the third time.

It's significant, too, that all the actors are credited by name in my review, except the one who plays Lola. Mocking the character wasn't enough: it was as if I needed also to erase the man who portrayed her. (For the record, he is Toni Cantó. *All About My Mother* was the high point of his acting career; he later became a politician with the centre-right Christian Democratic People's Party in Spain, which had initially opposed same-sex marriage before relenting in 2012.) When I began writing film criticism, I tended to think of the average reader as inherently disapproving: if not outright homophobic, then certainly homo-sceptical. They would surely prefer me to express distaste or embarrassment over any queer content.

I was happy to oblige. In my review of Bruce LaBruce's sex comedy *Hustler White*, I overlooked the movie's witty references to *Death in Venice*, *Sunset Boulevard* and *Whatever Happened to Baby Jane?*, as well as the clever subplot about a skinhead struggling to find a simple kiss among all the taboos and peccadilloes. (He fakes a collapse from auto-erotic asphyxiation in the hope that his lover might administer mouth-to-mouth: a skilful mix of the touching and the transgressive.) Instead, I primly suggested that the film's target audience would be more accustomed to receiving their entertainment in a brown paper bag.

18
VELVET GOLDMINE

There wasn't enough money to pay everyone at the end of making *Hustler White*, and that is how Wash Westmoreland met his husband.

It had been a seat-of-the-pants shoot: three weeks, sixteen-hour days, no permits, cops moving them on, LaBruce almost getting arrested. Real guerrilla stuff. Westmoreland was vegetarian: 'They ordered pepperoni pizza for everybody and gave me a banana for lunch,' he says.

He had arrived in Los Angeles at LaBruce's invitation, and with only one short to his name, to find himself appointed the film's AC, grip and gaffer. Born in Leeds, Yorkshire, Westmoreland had been in New Orleans since 1992. 'I was living in a shotgun shack with a woman called Squishy,' he tells me over video call from his home in Echo Park, LA. 'She worked as a stripper at Big Daddy's on Bourbon Street. One night, she came in at 3 a.m. and said, "I wanted to express myself sexually and freely but it's all going wrong." I liked the idea of a sex-industry worker who finds herself in that position and hits back.' Seeing LaBruce's zero-budget debut, *No Skin off My Ass*, inspired Westmoreland to get out there and make his first Super 8 short, *Squishy Does Porno*, starring his housemate. The film turned out to be 'an explosion of polymorphous perversity'.

The week LaBruce arrived in New Orleans with his second film, *Super 8½*, Westmoreland went to the local underground cinema to see it. 'I introduced myself to Bruce after the screening, and we clicked straight away. I had a bicycle that was yellow with black spots – everyone called it The Leopard – so he jumped on the back and we cycled round all the bars, having the best time and getting drunk all night long.'

Rumour has it they hooked up. 'We didn't,' he says. 'I think we were just excited to be around each other, and we didn't know what form that would take. We crashed in a hotel room, but when I woke up, Bruce had disappeared and stolen a few items of my clothing. That was a bit of a moment, let's say. Then we corresponded for a while, writing letters, and he told me he was going to shoot *Hustler White* in LA. I thought, "Ooh, I've never been to LA..." Santa Monica Boulevard was this Mecca for hustlers back then. Every corner had a different specialisation of sex work, and those stories formed the spine of the film.'

By the time *Hustler White* wrapped, several crew members were left without their final wages. Westmoreland had just $100 in his pocket, so he stayed on the couch of the assistant director, who was in the process of wriggling out of a relationship with a casual boyfriend. One night, the three of them went to a party, where Westmoreland ended up talking for four hours straight with his housemate's soon-to-be ex, the director Richard Glatzer. He and Glatzer spent the next twenty years together, co-parenting Westmoreland's daughter, getting married and co-directing a string of films, including *The Fluffer*, the award-winning *Quinceañera* (a kind of Echo Park *Taste of Honey*) and the Alzheimer's drama *Still Alice*, for which Julianne Moore's haul of prizes included the Best Actress Oscar in 2015.

Glatzer was diagnosed in 2011 with the progressive neurodegenerative disease ALS; he died a few weeks after the Oscars ceremony, at the age of sixty-three. He and Westmoreland watched the broadcast in the intensive care unit when Moore won. 'A few friends were there with us. We screamed so loud when Julie's name was announced that the nurses came running in thinking there was a medical emergency,' says Westmoreland. 'We were like, "No, no, our film just won an Oscar!" Richard had wanted to make movies since he was eight years old. And here was this supreme moment of happiness – right at the end of his life.'

Westmoreland got a husband out of *Hustler White*. 'You could say Bruce brought Richard and me together by not paying me what I was owed,' he says. And he got a career, too. One of the actors on *Hustler White* put him in touch with a porn producer, who invited Westmoreland to bring a VHS of *Squishy Does Porno* to his house. 'He watched it, then said: "That's very creative. Now suck my dick."' It's an exchange that would turn up later in *The Fluffer*. 'I was quite principled. I said, "I'm not into that. But if you give me the chance, I'll make you the best porno your company has ever seen."'

That was Tuesday. On Friday, he was in a warehouse on Hollywood Boulevard with ten naked men in front of him. The result was *Taking the Plunge*, which punctuated its sex scenes with playful interviews and kick-started a career that produced such delights as *Dr Jerkoff and Mr Hard*, about a nerdy academic who transforms into a sex god, and *The Hole*, a porn spin on the J-horror *The Ring*, but with a videotape that turns viewers gay instead of killing them. Westmoreland's porn masterpiece, though, is *Naked Highway*, a road-trip movie which incorporates scenes shot on Super 8 and set in five different states, dream sequences, flashbacks to past lives and excerpts from *Extra Topping*, a porn-within-a-porn about a pizza delivery guy. Strikingly, it doesn't stint on exposing the unfulfillable desires that the art form can engender in its viewers. 'Pornography presents a highly idealised view of sex between beautiful people,' says Westmoreland. 'But there's always a glass screen between you and them, and that's what fuels the need to purchase another experience or rent another video.'

Shortly before making *Naked Highway*, Westmoreland had been in London working on the set of Todd Haynes's *Velvet Goldmine*. (He and Glatzer were friends with Haynes and his boyfriend, James Lyons, and Haynes had rented Glatzer's house while shooting his previous film, *Safe*.) The influence of *Velvet Goldmine*, with its busy-bee collage of colliding styles, modes and textures, is apparent on *Naked Highway*. 'Watching Todd work was a formative experience for me,' he says. 'His creativity spills out and inspires everybody. I was the lighting stand-in for Christian Bale and Ewan McGregor, and I had a cameo in the film, too. The whole thing was a crash course in film-making.' His brother, Micko, was cast as Jack Fairy, the enigmatic glam god who swans wordlessly through the film, turning heads and bearing the emerald brooch first seen attached to the blanket of the infant Oscar Wilde. It's not a stork that delivers Wilde to his parents' Dublin doorstep in 1854 but a flying saucer.

The title of Haynes's film is borrowed from a David Bowie B-side, and the picture stars Jonathan Rhys-Meyers as a Bowie-esque chameleonic rock star. But whereas Bob Dylan would later put his complete back catalogue at the director's disposal for *I'm Not There*, Bowie refused permission for his songs to be used: 'At that time, I was seriously considering doing *Ziggy Stardust* as a project myself,' he said. Asked about *Velvet Goldmine* in 2002 by the comedian David Baddiel, Bowie's response was disappointingly literal-minded for someone who had done so much to advance the concept of queerness. 'The narrative was not there, and there was no character development, and it got lost about halfway through,' he said. 'I thought, "Where are we now? I'm lost" ... The sex scenes were good but I thought the rest of it was utter garbage.'

When Bowie conceded that Haynes 'understands gay stuff', Baddiel jumped in like a class swot keen to score points with teacher. 'Exactly! I just thought it was a gay film,' the comedian said. Then he reiterated his dismay: 'It was a gay film.'

'I made *Naked Highway* right after working on *Velvet Goldmine*,' says Westmoreland, 'and I really went to town stylistically.' It paid off. The film swept the board at the GVGuide awards and the AVN (Adult Video News) awards held in Las Vegas at Caesars Palace. At that time, the GayVN awards were a sidebar to the straight ones, rather than having their own ceremony.

'There were only three little tables for the gay companies, versus fifty or so for the straight ones,' he recalls. 'When the gay awards were announced, no one in the straight audience clapped – they were so homophobic. Going up to collect mine, I wanted to piss them off, so I said in my speech: "God bless anal penetration!" And this giant wave of laughter rolled through the whole auditorium. I realised I'd found some common ground.'

19
THEOREM

It is a spring morning in south London, and Kurtis Lincoln is holding his dick in his hand. He is wearing black leather trousers, black stack-heeled boots and a sleeveless white T-shirt with 'OH WOW' printed on it. He is pissing on the canvas. The canvas is lying on the stone floor of the white-walled gallery. The torrent of piss hits it at full pelt, making a noise like an endless drum roll. The canvas is covered with oxidised copper, which reacts with the piss to produce a Rorschach tangle of squiggles and blotches. The piss spatters the rug underneath, sending an acrid tang into the air.

Bruce LaBruce stands a few feet away, peering at the monitor. His eyes are hidden behind tinted Gucci shades, which he never removes. In the 1980s and 1990s, he looked like Puck: there he is hitch-hiking naked in *Super 8½*, his pert little behind, his leather boots. (He used to claim that Madonna stole the nude hitch-hiking idea from him for her coffee-table book *Sex*. These days, he freely admits that he thieved it from her.) Today, he is still short and compact, but, at fifty-nine, a twink no more; he has varnished skin and a chewy Burgess Meredith look about him. He carries himself like an ex-boxer, tough and springy, conserving his energy for when he might need it. His bare arms are blue with tattoos. He wears so many chunky gold rings that they could be mistaken for knuckledusters.

Hours seem to have elapsed but somehow Kurtis is still pissing. Life carries on outside. The beep of a truck reversing in the street is audible through the walls. A phone rings in an upstairs room.

'Ignore it,' says LaBruce, still watching intently.

233

The stream finally slows to a dribble, then dries up entirely. Kurtis shakes his dick and stuffs it back inside his trousers.

'Cut. Great shot. Very Rolling Stones, *Sticky Fingers*.'

He congratulates Kurtis on the strength of his flow.

'I used to have a bladder like that,' the director says.

'Ket, baby,' offers Kurtis in commiseration.

LaBruce inspects the rug. 'Could someone do a search on how to get piss stains out? I think it's, like, baking soda.'

A few crew members look up and laugh as they arrange the next shot.

'I'm serious though,' he says. 'Because that could really stain.'

I bound over to Kurtis to introduce myself. It was easy to fall in love with him a little as I watched him peeing. Now I see him up close: plump lips, black moustache, impish expression. His hair, normally a wild cascade of Louis XIV curls, hangs in two pigtails.

'In my mind, it's like Wednesday Addams if she was an eighties muscle boy,' he says.

We shake hands.

'Now you've got my piss on you.'

Victor Fraga, one of the producers, materialises alongside LaBruce to ask him to come and approve the sling.

'The sling?' says the director. 'We're not doing that scene today.'

'But the woman who has the sling is going on holiday in three hours.'

'That's three hours,' LaBruce shrugs, then walks off.

Victor turns to Kurtis and hands him a black rubber bulb.

'Can you use this now?'

'Sure,' Kurtis replies brightly, and heads for the bathroom.

On the way, he passes Bishop Black, star of Harvey Rabbit's *Captain Faggotron Saves the Universe*. Bishop, who is going to fuck Kurtis in today's big scene, has a shaved head that shines like a polished doorknob, tunnel earrings in their drooping lobes and drowsy, come-back-to-bed eyes; they are wearing a white towelling robe over silver trousers and a sequinned pink corset. The couple hug ('Hey babes!'), then Kurtis bops away, douche in hand, jiggling his shoulders and singing 'I Just Can't Wait to Be King'.

Bishop sinks into a chair in front of the mirror so that Laura Sessions, the make-up artist, can try out white contact lenses for the sex scene later. To give herself more elbow room as she works, Laura nudges aside a pair of lifelike silicon feet which are sitting on the table in front of her. Moulded into the sole of each foot is a vulva.

This is the set of *The Visitor*, the first film LaBruce has made in London since *Skin Flick*, his 1999 foray into skinhead porn. Originally titled *Gang of Four Skins*, *Skin Flick* features shots of skinheads fucking on a Union Jack, naked except for their DM bovver boots, and ejaculating on a copy of *Mein Kampf*. 'They were shooting in Brixton,' recalls Peter Strickland, who got his first industry job as a runner on the movie. 'Terry Richardson was there. It was the scene where the main guy's jerking off, and Richardson was taking non-stop photographs, all very close up. You could see the actor getting limper and limper. Finally, this crew member shouted at Richardson: "You've ruined his erection!" There was a big argument, and Bruce ordered everyone out. It was a very long, tense day.'

The Visitor is based on Pasolini's 1968 masterpiece *Theorem*. In the original film, Terence Stamp plays a nameless stranger (the role now taken by Bishop) who materialises almost magically in the home of a bourgeois Milanese family.

'Who is that boy?' someone asks at the party where he makes his entrance.

'A boy,' comes the reply.

With barely a word, he seduces each member of the family in turn – mother, father, teenage son and daughter, as well as the maid for good measure. Then he leaves. His imminent departure is announced one evening by telegram, just as his arrival had been a short while earlier. There are no explanations; he goes as casually as he arrived. He is on-screen for a vanishingly brief amount of time, but he permeates the movie. Once seen, Stamp's arctic blue peepers float in the memory forever.

The actor's serene carnality was glimpsed in one of his earliest roles, as the captivating sailor in the 1962 *Billy Budd*. Herman Melville's story was later filmed again by Claire Denis in even queerer form, the soundtrack laced with extracts from Benjamin Britten's opera, as *Beau Travail*. Denis shifted the action from a ship to the Djibouti outpost of the French Foreign Legion. 'The real Foreign Legion wanted to stop us,' she said. 'They thought we were shooting a gay porno movie.' You can appreciate the error.

When the stranger leaves the film and the family in *Theorem*, they – and we – are bereft. The father, an industrialist, ends up cruising a train station for sex and surrendering his entire factory to his workers. The mother picks up gigolos. The son starts making Warhol-style piss paintings. His sister becomes catatonic and is last seen being stretchered away in an ambulance. (The new version doesn't give her such a rum deal: now she falls pregnant.) The maid returns to her home village, cures a sick child and levitates above a rooftop. The film ends with the father wandering barefoot in the ashes of Mount Etna's slopes, screaming either in horror or liberation.

Theorem is an example of a narrative which has persisted almost since the beginning of cinema, in which a household is transformed, for good or ill, by an alien presence. It has a special kind of resonance for queer viewers, most of whom will have grown up suspecting themselves to be precisely that kind of corrupting or unwelcome presence in the family – and perhaps fantasising about the transformative and/or destructive effect they might have on their kin. Only a few will not have felt themselves to be the fly in the ointment, the viper in the nest.

It isn't hard to see why the narrative format of the seductive outsider is such a durable vehicle for queerness: it centres on the infiltration, subversion and pollution of the family. One important precursor to the stranger in *Theorem* is Boudu, the unhoused wanderer played by Michel Simon in Jean Renoir's 1932 *Boudu Saved from Drowning*. Seeing him about to hurl himself into the Seine, a bookseller takes Boudu into his immaculate family home and pays the price for his altruism. The grubby old soak wrecks the place, wiping his muddy shoes all over the satin sheets; he's a breath of foul air.

Paul Mazursky remade Renoir's film in 1986 as *Down and Out in Beverly Hills*, with Nick Nolte in the Simon role and, as the matriarch, Bette Midler. The son (played by Evan Richards) is reimagined there as an effeminate new-wave misfit of fluid gender and/or sexuality, who is persuaded by the tramp to come out to his parents. A colourful cameo from Little Richard adds an extra sparkle of queerness. The casting of Sandra Bernhard, the lesbian cabaret diva, has the same effect in *Dallas Doll*; she plays a golf pro who works her way systematically and sexually through an entire household, *Theorem*-style. Meanwhile, Steve Scott, a director at the US porn production company Hand in Hand, began his career in the early 1970s with *The Young Intruder*, his own explicit, extra-gay *Theorem*.

There are numerous other examples of the seductive stranger unlocking repressed desires: the soldier played by Robert Forster, who rides bareback (in both senses) in *Reflections in a Golden Eye*, sending Marlon Brando and Elizabeth Taylor into an erotic tizzy; or the 'angel of death' played by Richard Burton (opposite Taylor again) in *Boom!*, which Joseph Losey adapted from Tennessee Williams's *The Milk Train Doesn't Stop Here Anymore* six years after directing *The Servant*. (Posters for both *Boom!* and *Theorem* form part of the set decoration in John Waters' *Pink Flamingos*.) It's there, too, in Michael York's role in *Something for Everyone*, and Günther

Kaufmann as the maligned but sexually magnetic servant in *Whity*. Sting had two attempts at the archetype: first as the stranger who ingratiates his way into the drab home of a suburban couple and their disabled daughter in *Brimstone and Treacle*, then as a conniving butler in *The Grotesque*, a role indebted to Bogarde in *The Servant*. Barry Keoghan played a lower-middle-class infiltrator in the upper-class world of *Saltburn*, a film as gloatingly opportunistic and quasi-queer as its hero.

Joe Orton uses the plot device in his play *Entertaining Mr Sloane* – filmed in 1970, three years after his death – where a wily young interloper seduces a middle-aged brother and sister before murdering their elderly father. The seductive psychopath is played by Peter McEnery, seen nearly a decade earlier as the blackmailed 'Boy Barrett' caught in an affair with Dirk Bogarde in *Victim*. Barrett (a name he shares with Bogarde's character in *The Servant*) is reassured by his friend Frank, played by Alan Howard, who reflects on the scapegoat function that queers fulfil for the rest of society.

'Well, it used to be witches,' Frank tells him. 'At least they don't burn you.'

But they do. They burn you and worse.

––––––––––––

The penetrating stranger was a recurrent dramatic device in the plays of Harold Pinter, who adapted *The Servant* for Losey. James Fox, who plays the entitled young chancer corrupted by Barrett, took the infiltrator role himself a few years later as Chas, a gangster on the run, in *Performance*. Chas enters and disrupts a hermetic household – the Notting Hill basement home of a bohemian rock star, Turner (Mick Jagger) – but on that occasion the contamination flows both ways. The thug absorbs the rock star, the rock star bleeds into the thug, until the two are indivisible. Fred Halsted must have warmed to that idea: he is careful to include a lingering shot of the giant *Performance* billboard, with its doubled image of Jagger, looming over Santa Monica Boulevard in *LA Plays Itself*.

Halsted's lover Joey Yale might also be said to absorb Halsted, all the way up to the elbow, in fact, in that movie's infamous climactic fisting scene. Or rather, his stand-in did: though Yale was happy to be tortured and humiliated in the middle section of the film, the young actor, whose next job was playing Mowgli from *The Jungle Book* in a touring Disney stage show, drew the line at taking a fist on-screen.

In those days, Fox was part of the same foppish, dissolute breed as Stamp. When Peter O'Toole dropped out of the lead in Fellini's short *Toby Dammit* (one segment of the 1968 portmanteau feature *Spirits of the Dead*), the film-maker asked a London casting director to 'send me your most decadent actors'. It was Stamp and Fox who were summoned, and Stamp who got the role, which fed directly into his appearance in *Theorem*. 'Pasolini told me, "A stranger arrives, makes love to everybody, and leaves. This is your part,"' recalled Stamp. 'I said, "I can do that!"'

The actor claims that was the first and last conversation he had with Pasolini, though the director would sometimes offer instructions on set via Stamp's co-star, Laura Betti – 'Tell him to play this scene with his legs spread astride,' or 'Tell him to play this scene with an erection.' He filmed Stamp secretly with a hidden camera when he was lounging around on set. 'It didn't take me long to realise what he was doing. He just wanted me being, just being myself. Being present in the present. That was a new strata of performance for me.' Stamp saw how Pasolini's approach could inform his own perspective on the character. 'He was just somebody who was completely present . . . And he didn't look at anybody with any kind of judgement whatsoever. So it didn't make any difference to the guest whether it was a male, female, ugly, old, young, because the guest was just there, and he intuitively understood what they wanted.'

The picture is chaste and becalmed on the surface, nothing at all like the rambunctious bawdiness of Pasolini's 'Trilogy of Life', which began in 1971 with *The Decameron*, or his final picture, the laceratingly transgressive *Salò, or the 120 Days of Sodom*. At the Venice Film Festival in 1968, *Theorem* was awarded the special prize of the International Catholic Bureau of Cinema, which was rescinded after objections from the Vatican. A legal case of obscenity was brought against the picture. The prosecutor asked for six months' imprisonment for Pasolini and demanded the film's destruction. The court ruled that the artistic value of *Theorem* precluded any charges of obscenity.

What would they make of the Bruce LaBruce version? Upstairs in the gallery's open-plan kitchen, which takes up an entire floor, crew members are mixing enormous bowls of stringy, Joker-green lubricant, which will be used not only to make anal sex easier but to soak the actors in a glistening filmy skin as they fuck. The visitor played by Bishop is an alien in both senses: a refugee who emerges naked from a suitcase on a raft on the Thames, and an extraterrestrial. Hence the goo, which oozes from his unembarrassed pores.

The gallery is buzzing with pre-coital anticipation and activity. Today has been dominated by other scenes – Kurtis peeing, Kurtis painting – but now it's time. As the actors take their positions in the black-walled inner studio, which is bathed in electric blue light, LaBruce makes an announcement, calm but authoritative. 'We've got half an hour to shoot this, which is going to be kind of impossible,' he says. 'But let's see what we can do.'

The scene being shot now is recognisable initially from *Theorem*. The son, played by Kurtis, is sharing a bedroom with the stranger. They both get into their respective single beds. Then, once the stranger is asleep, the son in his checked pyjamas creeps round to the other side of the bed and peels back the sheet to reveal his roommate's taut naked body, before scurrying away to his own bed in fright.

LaBruce calls 'Cut', then turns to the room.

'That was kind of amazing. OK, let's goo Bishop up. Is there a goo wrangler?'

The actor stands naked on a plastic mat in the corner of the room, ready to be coated in the gloopy green liquid by two crew members.

'C'mon, goo, goo, goo!' calls LaBruce. 'Don't be timid, pour it on.' Bishop gasps, sucking the air through their teeth.

LaBruce turns to Jack Hamilton, the cinematographer. 'Kurtis and Bishop are gonna come at the end,' he tells him. 'Try and get the whole ejaculations and we'll get their faces later.' Then he realises the rest of the room is listening. 'Standard porn practice,' he says.

Once Bishop is fully slicked and back in bed, Laura inserts the white extraterrestrial contact lenses. When LaBruce calls 'Action' again, Kurtis returns to his kneeling position at Bishop's bedside. He pulls back the covers just as before and closes his lips around the dozing cock, which starts to fatten and stir. Bishop's alien eyes gaze coldly down at him. In an instant, Kurtis is clambering onto the bed and into Bishop's arms, the goo rubbing off on him in stringy threads. He almost whooshes off the edge of the bed, until Bishop applies a steadying hand, easing him onto his back. With Kurtis's thighs parted and his arse raised and spread, Bishop crouches to explore his hole, alternating little feline laps of the tongue with sudden daring stabs.

As I stand at the rear of the tiny studio, squinting through the grove of camera equipment, I realise how incongruous it is to be here in shirt and jeans and trainers while all this is going on under my nose. In any normal situation where one finds oneself in a room watching other people having sex, there is a reasonable expectation that one will participate at a moment that is mutually convenient for all parties. Right now, I want to turn to the crew members and say: 'This is madness! Are none of us going to join in?' Holding my notepad and pen seems to put me at an even greater remove, burdening me with an additional inhibiting layer to everyone else. I'm like the prissy dilettante played by LaBruce in *Hustler White*, who loiters at the back of a porn set and murmurs into his Dictaphone, 'I just hope my mere presence doesn't upset the delicate equilibrium' – right before he upsets the delicate equilibrium.

'Pussy light!' barks LaBruce now. 'Get the pussy light in there please.'

An anonymous arm extends out of the darkness, holding a strip light next to Bishop's mouth.

The actor glances up from between Kurtis's arse cheeks, the blank gleam of the alien eyeballs lending the scene a refrigerated chill. Then Bishop is upright, and all at once it's happening, it's really happening: Kurtis is wincing and moaning as Bishop's gluey cock vanishes inside him, his own half-awake hard-on lolling against his belly.

Gradually, I become aware of LaBruce beckoning me out of the shadows to stand next to him, where I can watch the action on the monitor instead. I presume at first that he is doing this so I can get a proper journalistic slant on the shoot and see how the camera is framing the scene. Then it occurs to me that perhaps he is rescuing me from the glare of the sex, the way a parent calls a child in out of the sun. Has he noticed my stupor and spotted that I've become porn-dazed? Does he want to remind me that it's only a movie?

'Pussy light again!' LaBruce demands. 'We need to see the dick going in. And we need more goo. Where's the goo? Can you keep the goo coming please? Just pour it on them, stay to the left out of shot. No, to the *left*. Bishop, can you kneel up more? And hold Kurtis's feet as you fuck him. That's it. Move back so we can see your dick. Turn to the right slightly. But also look up so we can still see your eyes. Oh, and can you do everything I ask you all at the same time?' He chuckles to himself. 'Just kidding.'

Kurtis is still on his back as Bishop grips his ankles, holding his legs apart in a V and pumping him diligently. The wet rhythmic squelch sounds like boots trudging through mud. Watching from the sidelines is the mousey, moustachioed actor Macklin Kowal, who plays Kurtis's father. On some unseen cue, he slips out of his robe, which drops noiselessly to the ground, and picks his way into the fray like a tardy guest at a New Year party. Within a few seconds, the three sets of tangled limbs are pretzeled together, the glossy faces forming a triptych of manufactured ecstasy.

At the end of the scene, Bishop and Kurtis try to ejaculate, but they can't quite get there, so Jack shoots close-ups of their expressions as they take turns pretending to come. Then LaBruce calls 'Cut!', the actors disappear to the shower and everyone else goes around the corner for lunch at the White Boar.

———————————

In the capacious, high-ceilinged pub, with its exposed brickwork and varnished beams, I sit with two young crew members, Josh and Ash, who have recently graduated from film school. The three of us fall into the usual movie chat; they ask me about my favourite Wes Anderson and Christopher Nolan films, and I dutifully give them my answers. But I'm still stunned from the past few hours.

'I can't believe I stood next to Bruce LaBruce while he shot a porn scene,' I tell them as we tuck into our burgers.

'Is he a big deal then?' says Josh.

'Fuck yeah! Have you heard of *No Skin off My Ass*? *Super 8½*? *Hustler White*? What about queercore? It was this Toronto queer punk movement invented by Bruce and the artist G. B. Jones in this zine called *J.D.s*, which stood for "juvenile delinquents". Except that there *was* no queercore. Bruce and G. B. Jones dreamt it up to annoy all the homophobic macho punks by pointing out the queerness of the mosh-pit. But because it was in their zine, it attracted international attention, and suddenly Toronto was the queercore centre of the world; they had created this non-existent movement by sheer force of will. Then Bruce, who studied under Robin Wood, directed *No Skin off My Ass*, where he played a hairdresser who brings home a skinhead to fuck. It was this grimy black-and-white punk film, based on Robert Altman's *That Cold Day in the Park*, that was only ever intended to be shown in art galleries or clubs. The soundtrack was on a cassette, and Bruce would press "play" at the same time the projector started, which meant it was always out of sync. But his producer had it blown up and sent it off to festivals, and it got shown and distributed. John Waters praised it, and Kurt Cobain named it as his favourite film. Then Bruce made *Super 8½*, which is about a director called Bruce LaBruce who has a big hit with his first movie and then suffers this creative crisis, hence the Fellini reference in the title. It contains the line "Pornography is the wave of the future", which has become a kind of battle cry for him. Even his horror-porn films *LA Zombie* and *Otto; or, Up with Dead People* have hardcore scenes, with zombies fucking each other in their wounds and gashes. He never sold out. He never diluted what he was doing.'

'Wow,' says Josh eventually.

He and Ash have cleared their plates while I've been talking. They say goodbye and head back to the set, leaving me to pick at my pale damp fries.

———————

LaBruce and I meet for lunch at the same pub a week later. As his order arrives – red wine, watercress soup, a hunk of battered haddock the size of an arm – we are in the middle of chatting about *The Visitor*. The shoot went well, he thinks, though there wasn't enough goo for his liking: 'There never is.'

He is wearing an Andy Warhol/*My Hustler* hoodie and those ever-present tinted shades, which make it impossible to know whether there are love hearts in his eyes or dollar signs, or both. When I saw him the previous night at a packed screening of *Theorem*, he was in a black Kenneth Anger/*Scorpio Rising* bomber jacket. As well as being formative influences on LaBruce, both those directors were the models for characters he played in his own movies: a Warhol-esque film-maker in *Super 8½*, then an imperious aesthete modelled on Anger in *Hustler White*. Though it was an affectionate portrait, Anger was furious. He let it be known that he planned to drive LaBruce into the desert, throw him on a cactus and leave him there under the sun for several days, before coming back to shoot him between the eyes.

Hustler White wasn't the only subject on which they differed. 'Pornography is boring!' Anger once said. 'I mean, so what? It's in, then it's out, then it's in again.' The eroticism in his films comes from clothes: the sailor suits in *Fireworks*, the gowns in *Puce Moment*, the motorcycle leathers against bare skin in *Scorpio Rising*. 'I always show people dressing. They are putting clothes on rather than taking them off . . . To me, that is how people really express themselves.'

But LaBruce stands by his claim that pornography is the wave of the future. 'It's like someone says in my film *The Misandrists*: "Pornography expresses an impulse that is oppositional to the governing order." It's an inherently subversive force.' Can this still be the case, now that perfectly respectable arthouse movies such as *Stranger by the Lake* feature unsimulated gay sex? 'In general, I have an issue with the way explicit sex is used in a lot of European art films,' he says. 'It's always portrayed as somewhat disturbing or perverse, and the characters generally are not allowed to take pleasure from it. It's more akin to compulsive behaviour, almost a disorder. People can have explicit sex in art films as long as they don't enjoy it and they don't look conventionally attractive. In my films, people have more fun having sex. And it's all shot in the porn idiom.'

There are one-off exceptions outside Europe, such as John Cameron Mitchell's *Shortbus*, but no one of LaBruce's status has displayed quite the same dogged loyalty to porn. 'I've always insisted on continuing to make pornographic films, even though everybody says, "Oh, why are you making another one? It's not gonna make it easier for you to get financing." You're meant to work with celebrities and bigger budgets, but I go back and forth between pure porn or indie features, between decent budgets and no budget. I'm kind of a misfit. I was always against the mainstream white gay male middle classes.'

He no longer stars in his own movies, but that's him you can see having sex on-screen in *No Skin off My Ass* and *Super 8½*, where he gets fucked and slapped around. 'It was my boyfriend in *No Skin off My Ass*, but we were so shy when we were making it that we wouldn't let anyone be in the room with us. We put the camera on the tripod and turned it on, and it's like this very awkward home-made porn. Then you jump to 500 people watching you have sex on-screen and it's a total mind-fuck. Moral judgements are made about you. People treat you differently, thinking that you're either sexually available or you have no boundaries.'

His attitude towards sex was formed by growing up on a farm. 'You learn pretty quickly about sex and nature. My father had a bull; he bred livestock, so I'd see them fucking all the time. It was quite aggressive. I'd castrate pigs. I watched kittens being drowned. I was a total sissy. I had orange ringlets and I was often mistaken for a girl, which mortified me. I wouldn't say I became inured to death, but I came to understand it was part of nature.'

He was queer as far back as he can remember. 'As a kid, there was this comic book I loved called *Turok, Son of Stone*, which had these muscular prehistoric Indians wearing these skimpy little things.' The corners of his mouth twitch into a smile. I can't see his eyes but I imagine they must be twinkling.

There is something of the pussycat about him in person, but he hasn't been shy in the past about flashing his claws. Even today, when he brings up Vito Russo's *The Celluloid Closet*, with its itinerary of occasions on which Hollywood has maligned LGBTQ+ characters, he refers to it as 'that horrible book'. For him, queerness in cinema can't be reduced to tallying up all the queer characters to see which ones are naughty or nice like some indignant Santa Claus, or else counting how many survive. 'Russo is always asking: Why does the lesbian or the fag have to die at the end? Well, because culturally they would have done because they were vulnerable. Look at Rod Steiger in *The Sergeant* as a closet case who ends up blowing his own brains out. That's probably what would have happened.' He purses his lips. 'I love that movie.'

He has long despised GLAAD (the Gay and Lesbian Alliance Against Defamation, which Russo co-founded) and has referred to it in his own writing as 'that dour, quasi-Stalinist organisation which attempts to police gay imagery in Hollywood movies'. And he has raged against the queer drift towards assimilation. 'What is this fight for the right to be as bland and boring as the heteronormative majority?' he scoffs now. I toy self-consciously with my wedding ring, then place my hands out of sight beneath the table.

Would marriage represent a betrayal of values to him, perhaps even a symbolic death? 'I actually *was* married,' he says, his tone softening. 'Just before I made *The Raspberry Reich*, I met a Cuban man and we were dating for a couple years but he had a fucked-up immigration status, and they tried to deport him. I didn't want that to happen, so we got married. We had a ceremony at City Hall. You had to make it seem like a real marriage – well, we *were* a real couple in love – and so my friends came and it was very emotional and ended up being kind of a real wedding and made our relationship stronger. Sometimes you have to do things that go completely against your nature. We were together for twelve years. And he taught me so much. People would say I was subversive and he'd laugh because he'd lived through a real revolution. He'd mockingly call me "Brucito Subversivo".'

Throughout our lunch, LaBruce has assumed I'm interviewing him for a magazine. No, I tell him as we push our plates aside: it's for a book about queer cinema. He brightens visibly at this news. 'You know, B. Ruby Rich never mentions me once in her New Queer Cinema book,' he says. 'Not even in the revised edition. I've run into her at festivals and I think she thinks I'm trash. A bad smell. Maybe this will be a corrective.'

20

CHOCOLATE BABIES

In the hallway of Prospect Cottage, Derek Jarman's bolt-hole amid the slapped-flat voidscape of Dungeness on the Kent coast, hangs a rendering by Gus Van Sant of an image from his woozy rent-boy road movie *My Own Private Idaho*. It shows a clapboard barn plunging from the sky towards a barren rural highway; a rubbery cactus looks on. In the film, Van Sant cuts to the barn crashing onto the tarmac just as Mike (River Phoenix) is climaxing from a blow job in a far-off hotel room. It is simultaneously an associative leap, a cinematic allusion to *The Wizard of Oz*, a naughty play on the phrase 'going down' – and, in its lyrical brashness, a defining image of the New Queer Cinema.

That Van Sant's gaily coloured painting should be found here of all places is fitting for several reasons. First, Prospect Cottage feels as if it, too, dropped from the heavens – 'flung out of space', as a woman says of her lover-to-be in Patricia Highsmith's *The Price of Salt* and Todd Haynes's 2015 adaptation, *Carol*. If it did plummet to Earth, Jarman's cottage has remained miraculously intact. Here it still stands, accessible by a doughty meandering bus from nearby Rye or Ashford. Built in the early 1900s, it is a monument to the potential that Jarman saw when he first set eyes on it in 1986: the year of his *Caravaggio*, and of his positive HIV diagnosis. And it is augmented by a garden cultivated implausibly in the shingle, just as Jarman's films were conjured from the unpromising terrain of the British film industry. 'Building a garden was Jarman's characteristically energetic, fruitful response to the despair of what was, pre-combination therapy, a near-certain death,' wrote Olivia Laing, who called the project 'a stake in the future'.

Van Sant's painting, which he gave to Jarman as a gift, seems to depict the origin story of the place in which it hangs, while aligning him with a director who, in films such as *Sebastiane* and *The Garden*, forged a space for queer defiance that was beautiful as well as confrontational. There is a certain symbolism, too, in this painting by the younger film-maker being 'housed' in the former home of one of his presiding influences – as though Jarman were a vessel containing or carrying the emergent Van Sant, much as a mother carries a baby.

The New Queer Cinema was the name given by B. Ruby Rich and her *Sight & Sound* editor Philip Dodd to a batch of gay-and-lesbian-themed features which emerged in the early 1990s, some of them informed by AIDS activism and directed by figures who had been instrumental in Gran Fury, the artists' collective that designed campaigns for ACT UP. The fight against AIDS, and the targeting of homophobic or obstructive political and public health bodies, lent new-found urgency, shape and focus to queer cinema. This was not a time for politeness or for imploring straight society to care, though that came a few years later with *Philadelphia*, the first studio picture about the disease.

Having just hit fifty, Jarman found himself the elder statesman of the crop: the anger and irreverence that had coursed through films like *Jubilee* and *The Last of England* resurfaced tenfold in his adaptation of *Edward II*, which featured his customary anachronisms (in this case, placard-waving OutRage! protestors and shield-wielding riot police), as well as a dyspeptic, Thatcher-like villain in the shape of Tilda Swinton as Queen Isabella. In the same year as *Edward II*, Van Sant, whose 1985 debut *Mala Noche* brought a scuzzy poetry to the problematic relationship between a white liquor-store clerk and a poor Mexican street kid, released *My Own Private Idaho*, with Phoenix as a narcoleptic hustler and Keanu Reeves his slumming rich-boy crush. Something integral to the New Queer Cinema was encapsulated when Phoenix quivered orgasmically in his seat and the barn hit the highway.

Van Sant, who laid the groundwork for the movement before becoming one of its figureheads, had been slow to admit to his own desires. In 1976, at the age of twenty-five, he picked up a hitchhiker. 'He'd made this little 8mm film and he invited me over to his house to watch it,' he said. 'It was the first time I'd seen or thought of making something like that. He told me he wanted to make the first authentic American gay film. He asked me, "Don't you want to make a gay film?" I said, "No, because I'm not gay." But in fact, I *was* gay. I was just in the closet. I think of that as a big missed-opportunity period in my life. I was dedicated to my film-making, but what your work should involve is saying something about your life. And I wasn't expressing myself. I think the guy was actually inviting me to have sex with him. And I was not getting it. I thought he just wanted to hang out.'

The objective in many of the New Queer Cinema works was to excavate the queerness of the past, proving that it had been there all along, hiding in plain sight. It could be found in the stylistic and narrative archetypes, and the moral panic, of *Poison*, and in the true-crime template of Tom Kalin's *Swoon*; it thrived in the social hierarchies of *Edward II*, the Shakespearean badinage of *My Own Private Idaho* and in the airbrushed, whitewashed histories challenged by *The Watermelon Woman* and *Nitrate Kisses*.

At the same time, there was the volatile present to contend with. The first movie about AIDS, Arthur Bressan Jr's *Buddies*, was released in 1985 and had its own special toughness signalled by the opening credits sequence, which plays over a seemingly relentless print-out of the names of people who had died from the disease. Others shoehorned the crisis into disease-of-the-week movie templates, such as

An Early Frost, shown on TV the same year *Buddies* was released. The well-intentioned *Longtime Companion* was better, even if it ended with a kitsch reunion-beyond-the-grave scene of fallen comrades.

Several years after *Philadelphia* had portrayed a gay relationship without so much as a kiss, the first West African film about homosexuality showed what bravery really looks like. *Dakan* (*Destiny*), shot in Guinea in 1996, begins with a scene of two high-school friends making out in a convertible. There is no coy build-up or timid flirtation: before we even know their names, the two men are already snogging with a ferocity that makes the face-huggers from *Alien* look diffident.

Philadelphia was a commercially risky enterprise, but for *Dakan*, any jeopardy was immediate and physical: homosexuality was (and is) illegal in Guinea. The director, Mohamed Camara, had such difficulty finding takers for the lead roles that he had to beg his own brother, Mamady, to star. Mamady and his eventual on-screen partner (Aboubacar Touré) kept their respective girlfriends nearby on set so that they could fall into the women's arms for a replenishing kiss between takes, like divers coming up for air.

Sanjay Sharma, who in 2008 directed the first gay Bollywood hit, *Dunno Y*, didn't permit *his* heterosexual leads (one of whom was his brother, who also wrote the script) even a quick pit-stop to pucker up and recharge their reserves of heterosexuality. Nor did he clear the set as his actors requested for one of their big love scenes. 'Many times, they got agitated,' he tells me. 'I tried to make them feel easier about it, but when they asked the crew to be less, I said no. I didn't want to make them even more self-conscious. My approach was: let them be lovers openly, no hide-and-seek, nothing. Let them be in love! And slowly things started happening.' But then *Dunno Y* is a film made up of what might be called acceptable compromises. One of the main characters dies at the end of the picture, as in *Brokeback Mountain* (the film was marketed as the Bollywood *Brokeback*), but the surviving one is warmly accepted into his late partner's family, as Ennis del Mar in Ang Lee's film explicitly was not.

Having girlfriends on set seems to have provided the required succour for the stars of *Dakan*: nothing about their indignant passion feels inhibited. And though gay sex isn't shown on-screen, Camara redirects the erotic voltage from heterosexual lovemaking by revealing that one of the men is visualising his male lover while sleeping with a woman.

Some audiences objected to the heterosexual Camara making a gay film, a charge for which he had little patience. 'How will there be progress if each person stays in his/her world?' he responded. Home-grown critics, on the other hand, took the opposite (and inherently homophobic) tack, accusing him of using his wife as a beard when he brought her to the film's Cannes premiere. 'The response was, "Camara does a film about homosexuality and then he brings his wife to hide his homosexuality. Does he think we are fools by showing up with a woman, when we know that he must be homosexual?"'

There were occasions, too, when it was necessary for Camara to make himself scarce after introducing screenings of *Dakan* to avoid butting heads with protestors. Those hazards persist today: Wanuri Kahiu's 2018 lesbian love story *Rafiki*, the first Kenyan film to screen at Cannes, was banned in its native country, save for a week-long run to allow it to qualify for the Oscars. But demand is there, too: by the end of that week, it was the second-highest-grossing Kenyan film of all time.

Djibril Diop Mambéty, the great Senegalese director of *Touki Bouki*, told Camara: 'You can be sure that your career is over, but in a hundred years, people will still talk about you.' It looks now as if the gloomy first half of Mambéty's prediction came true: Camara hasn't made another feature. Every so often, *Dakan* is still shown, its brazen passion intact, along with an ending in which Camara rejects what he perceived as pressure from Western voices for him and his compatriots to always show the 'real' Africa – to educate white audiences, in other words. His ending does nothing of the sort. An act of wish-fulfilment it may be, but it is not without agony. And no one who sees the film will easily forget the tender and still-shocking moment – one of the most scalding in all queer cinema, in fact – when Manga angrily tells Sory: 'If God were fair, he'd let me bear your child.'

Even progressive movements can conceal within them oversights or prejudice, like supposedly healthy foods harbouring undeclared carcinogenic content, and the New Queer Cinema was nothing if not predominantly white. That bias was evident from the start: 'Will queers of colour ever get equal time?' wondered B. Ruby Rich in her original 1992 *Village Voice* article. Included in her survey of emerging queer talent was a report from a lesbian pool party at the Amsterdam Film Festival where, according to the director Pratibha Parmar, 'there were more inflatables of colour in attendance than actual women of colour'. Rich did praise the early video work of Cheryl Dunye, four years before the release of *The Watermelon Woman*. One of Dunye's contemporaries, the film-maker Stephen Winter, remembers taking his own debut, *Chocolate Babies*, to festivals and screenings where he and Dunye 'were always walking around going, "Well, we're the only Black people here again."'

Winter is slyly handsome and beanstalk tall. 'I'm 6' 4",' he tells me over video call. 'I have tall privilege. People always ask me for directions on the street.' He arrived in New York from his native Chicago in 1992, a mere pup in his early twenties, all hopped up on AIDS activism and house music. 'They called it "night church" for a reason,' he says. It's fitting that today he is wearing a T-shirt on which the word 'Pleasure' is clearly visible. 'It was an exhilarating, transforming experience to hear music woven together like that, deconstructed and put back together. I got to experience Black queers of all different stripes and ages just having their life.'

He contributed photography to a Black queer zine called *Thing* (tagline: 'She knows who she is') and mucked in with the Chicago branch of ACT UP. 'I had an amazing time in terms of my political awakening and my queerness, but it was fraught. There was the experience of meeting Black queer elders such as Ortez Alderson, who was a gay Black Panther who had gone to jail for pouring pigs' blood on draft cards for Vietnam. He was one of the leaders of ACT UP Chicago but as a Black person he was relegated to what they called the Black caucus. ACT UP Chicago was dominated by gay white guys; women and people of colour and Black people were shunted into "special interest". I got to meet Ortez and learn from him, and then he passed away.' Alderson was thirty-eight when he died of an AIDS-related illness in December 1990; in October 1992, his partner, Arthur Gursch, scattered his ashes on the White House lawn during ACT UP's first Ashes Action protest.

At a meeting in 1991, Winter – who describes himself as 'slow to rile but quick to decide to do something' – left ACT UP, but not before delivering a speech decrying the Chicago branch as racist. Though he quit in high dudgeon, his time there strongly informed the script for his first film, which he hammered out on a typewriter in the space of two or three weeks. 'I got to experience Frankie Knuckles and be part of that history as a little kid, and to make my first acquaintances who were trans, and I took all that with me to NYU, along with the idea of Black people in ACT UP having to do things on their own, blood being poured on draft cards, my love of Humphrey Bogart movies – and that is how *Chocolate Babies* came about.'

The cast of *Chocolate Babies* was cherry-picked mainly from *House of Lear*, a queer Black production of *King Lear* staged at the time in a New York ballroom. The movie was shot on Fuji 16mm stock because 'it was well known among Black filmmakers that Kodak film at the time sucked for shooting Black skin'. Its elevator pitch was simple and provocative: a gang of HIV-positive Black and Asian drag queens become political terrorists, striking out against anyone who is stymieing access to drugs, funding and research. 'Everyone always asked, "Oh, is it a documentary?" "No, I made it up!"' On a point of fact, there are no drag queens in the movie. 'The catch-all of "drag queen" back then made the most sense, but what I appreciate about my younger self in conceiving *Chocolate Babies* is that while I used "drag queen" to get people on board, the distinctions of who those people were didn't matter because it was part of the queer continuum.'

I assume that the success of Jennie Livingston's 1990 documentary *Paris Is Burning* in making drag mainstream was also a factor in Winter's use of that art form to sell *Chocolate Babies*, but he sets me straight on that. 'Remember, *Paris Is Burning* did *not* bring drag into the mainstream,' he points out. 'It brought drag into the *video store*. Drag did not become mainstream until the aughts, and arguably not until RuPaul jumped to VH1. Throughout the 1990s, drag was still an outlaw thing to do. A gay thing to do. Bordering on illegal.'

Chocolate Babies is focused in its rage, wide-ranging in its insights into internal clashes among activists (over race, abortion, promiscuity and politics) and savagely funny from the get-go. 'I'm a fat Black faggot and I'm gonna kick your fucking ass!' cries the orange-wigged Larva (Dudley Findlay Jr) during one blood-hurling street-corner stunt. It is Larva, too, who issues a memorable warning during one of the film's cabaret-style interludes: 'I'm the only infected person in the history of AIDS who hasn't lost weight. You'd better be scared.'

For all the scrappy, early-Godardian energy, there is panache in the film-making, and delicacy in the portrayal of the group's emotional fractures, notably between the HIV-positive Max (claude e. sloan) and his younger, HIV-negative partner Sam (Jon Kit Lee). 'Max, you'd better take better care of yourself,' says Sam, who is holding out for a medical breakthrough, while Max (older, less hopeful or conciliatory) dangles a tiny skeleton keyring from his finger as he talks. Sequins dot the hairline on his shorn scalp. During his rooftop deathbed scene, he peels them from his own skin and presses them onto Sam's cheek to create a string of tears.

The idealistic Sam is the director's on-screen surrogate. 'Not only is the naive young one and jaded older one in a relationship a great movie trope, it was also the experience I had going into those worlds,' Winter says. 'Going into ACT UP Chicago, I was HIV-negative. The majority of people I met there were either HIV-positive or their world had been decimated by the plague. I was a hair too young to have had all my friends die. I did not have that experience. Instead, I had the experience of coming into that world and seeing all these holes in the atmosphere. The folks who were left were fighting and determined and cold-hearted – that is, *warm-blooded* but cold-hearted about how things were going. It was very much like a World War II movie of the young idealistic kid coming in, only to meet the hardened veteran.'

Within that is the danger surrounding any intimacy between Sam and Max. '*Chocolate Babies* was made when being HIV-positive was essentially a death sentence. You were advised to get your affairs in order when you got that. This is before the cocktail that came out in 1996, before the retroviral drugs kicked in; this is the time when people were trying to do miracle cures. The pressure for an HIV-discordant couple to keep the negative one negative puts a tremendous stress on the relationship. Not just on intimacy but friendship. How could I understand what they were going through? I couldn't, so I took that experience and put it into that on-screen relationship.'

Like Dunye, Winter's confidence had been boosted in his twenties after crossing paths with Marlon Riggs, director of *Tongues Untied*. 'He watched my work at a masterclass back in Chicago and gave me feedback, encouragement and wisdom,' Winter recalls. 'The vibe was: "I see you – and keep going." I didn't have a lot of people who directly understood me, so knowing he had liked what I was up to was great. Though I was still too young to know what I was up against.'

That included thinly veiled homophobia from an established director who provided feedback on the *Chocolate Babies* script at NYU, where it was Winter's thesis project. 'That well-known film-maker has evolved quite a bit when it comes to queerness,' he says. 'So I credit myself for helping him come to that place, because he was very uptight when he was critiquing me. But I held my ground. And now he's *all* about it!'

A prominent indie producer dangled the possibility of raising the money for the film, on the proviso that Sam, the HIV-negative boyfriend of the HIV-positive Max, could be changed from Asian American to white. 'That would've destroyed the whole thing,' the director says. 'That intra-community experience of being the only Asian in a Black group is crucially important.' Max's racist outburst against Sam would have been deprived of its cruelty and vitriol. 'There's nothing a Black man could say to his white boyfriend that would have the same sting. Racism does not have equal opportunity offence, so when Max lashes out in that very ugly way, it is important for that experience to be felt. ACT UP in Chicago, like the gay community itself, was very racially divided, and it was really important that *Chocolate Babies* reflected this world: there are no white characters that they're bouncing up against, no white villain.'

One of the numerous inspiring aspects of *Chocolate Babies* is that it bucked the trend for queer films to be placatory to straight (and/or white) audiences. That's also why it lost out commercially, though, never acquiring the distribution deal afforded to its white New Queer Cinema stablemates, nor winning any approbation higher than 'special mentions' at film festivals.

Winter believed the film would follow the same route as *Go Fish* and its director, Rose Troche: Sundance buzz, distribution deal, happy ever after. 'Rose was and is a friend of mine, and I expected what happened to her would happen to me. And it did not. Everywhere we went on the circuit, they kept saying, "You're gonna win the big award!" And they kept giving the awards to a Canadian film that was as white as could be.' He is referring to Thom Fitzgerald's *The Hanging Garden*, much lauded at the time and little seen today. 'There was a point where we kept not winning, and I thought, "Well, the fix is in. They're not allowing it to move forward."' With the internet in its infancy, and online distribution a good two decades away, *Chocolate Babies* had effectively been smothered in its crib.

'For every title from that era that is beloved and remembered, there are dozens of stinkers that took up a lot of oxygen,' says Winter. 'One thing uniting them is whiteness. And I don't just mean who was in front of and behind the camera; I mean in their value system. That Generation X thing of ennui is really bullshit. Whenever people talk about Gen X they go: "It's Ethan Hawke and these slacker white guys." Which is fine but hey, it's also Queen Latifah. It's also me. People who are Black and/or queer were not looking at the world through the lens of ennui 'cos there was still so much left to do. Now we're seeing how easy it is to include Black queer voices in the conversation. It was just as easy to do it back then in 1990-something. Except they wouldn't.' He flashes a joyless smile. 'They would make it a *point* not to.'

Though there was solidarity between the few film-makers of colour who were permitted access to the festival merry-go-round, there was only so much Winter could do without an audience turning out for him. 'The pink dollar, as it were, the thing that was selling gay maga-zines or gay bar rags – they would never consider featuring brown and Black people, and that is a well-documented fact that goes way beyond *Chocolate Babies*. Someone like Todd Haynes had access to the pink dollar, and to academia. I did not have that kind of support, nor could I gain it, and that's just what the score was back then.'

He spent 'some dark days' working in reality television, then ran MIX NYC, the queer experimental film festival. It was there that he came across three hours of material by the young queer film-maker Jonathan Caouette. Spread across two VHS tapes and using a tapes-try of home movie footage, it told the story of Caouette's turbulent youth, his devoted relationship with his mother, and her mental health struggles, as well as his own. 'I was, like, "Oh, *this* is special,"' Winter says. With his stewardship, *Tarnation* was eventually released to enormous acclaim in 2004.

As producer, he put a team together to support Caouette in making his rough cut accessible to a wide audience. John Cameron Mitchell, creator and star of the trans-punk musical *Hedwig and the Angry Inch* (which Mitchell filmed in 2001), came on board as an executive pro-ducer, along with Van Sant.

'I knew the film would work, not only because it was brilliant, but because it was very white,' says Winter. 'And I don't say that to be derogatory; it was just the fact of the matter. All the gatekeepers who could not see what *Chocolate Babies* was would be able to see what Jonathan was. Because when the smoke clears, he is an ador-able working-class white twink for half the movie, with a handsome Colombian boyfriend and a mother who was movie-star glam and had that "Why do birds suddenly appear...?" delicacy about her. I was like, "Oh yeah, they're gonna live for this! They're gonna *live*!" And they did. Then there was the stone-cold fact of the genius of the work and the pragmatic aspect, in terms of which queer things had the potential to go worldwide. This had the elements in an era which could do that, predicated on the eroticisation of the white working-class gay boy. That was very much part of the 1990s and the aughts.'

Pale, wan, unformed boys, foetus-like and drug-addled, were the embodiment of white queer culture at that time in the films of Larry Clark (*Kids*) and Gregg Araki (especially his 2004 adaptation of Scott Heim's rent-boy/alien abduction novel *Mysterious Skin*); the scabby, transgressive writing of Dennis Cooper (notably *Frisk*, filmed by Todd Verow in 1995); and, of course, *My Own Private Idaho*, the height of queer breadline hotness, namechecked on-screen in *Tarnation*.

Writing as his alter ego Libby Gelman-Waxner, the gay screen-writer Paul Rudnick (*Addams Family Values, In & Out, Sister Act*) lamented this trend, calling it

> paedophile chic, for people who like androgynous, slack-faced teens who seem to have been born stoned and angelic, like the creatures who come out of the spaceship at the end of *Close Encounters* . . . the boys' ultra-baggy pants barely stay on, and everyone in this movement is really sad about the death of River Phoenix. Larry Clark, Michael Stipe and Gus Van Sant are the most fixated dirty old masterminds, and Stephen Dorff, Leonardo DiCaprio and Keanu Reeves are their dream-weeds . . . Paedophile chic doesn't really seem dangerous; *Kids* is like *Home Alone* if Macaulay Culkin didn't want to find his family and his parents never missed him. It's John Hughes with unprotected sex and many meaningful shots of homeless people who are upsetting because of their bad hair.

It was Mitchell and Van Sant, says Winter, who convinced people to give *Tarnation* the time of day. But their presence also overshad-owed his. 'I was expecting that I could be taken seriously, and I found that this was exactly not the case. What people thought was, "Gus and John produced this!" In fact, a Black queer person was the one who saw it first and saw what it could be.'

Part of the reason he was able to bring that insight, he says, was that Caouette was 'a working-class queer film-maker. He wasn't part of academia or any elite system, never went to film school. He was a self-made genius with no money or connections. As a Black queer film-maker, I understood where he was coming from and could envisage what the film could become in the wider world. I was the one who was the engine throughout its entire lifespan. This is not taking away anything from what Gus and John did, but I got overlooked. I had a producing credit but what I did not get was the career opportunities that would have come to the white producer of a unique and profitable worldwide hit. Because I was Black, no one was interested.'

He took a few years off, travelled the world, came back to the US and joined the team behind *Precious*, written and directed by his friend Lee Daniels. He played a part in many of Daniels's subsequent projects, including *The Paperboy*, adapted from the clammy novel by Pete Dexter, which Pedro Almodóvar spent a decade trying unsuccessfully to bring to the screen. This overheated Southern thriller is best remembered for the scene in which Nicole Kidman urinates on Zac Efron after he is stung by jellyfish. 'If anyone's gonna piss on him, it's gonna be me!' she rages as nearby sunbathers offer to help. 'He don't like strangers peeing on him!' Winter also helped in assorted capacities on other people's films. He was story editor on the Oscar-nominated AIDS documentary *How to Survive a Plague*. On *Kill Your Darlings*, he coached Daniel Radcliffe, as Allen Ginsberg, in how to be a power bottom.

Nearly twenty years after *Chocolate Babies*, Winter finally made another film: *Jason and Shirley*, which imagines and dramatises what went on behind the scenes of Shirley Clarke's 1967 documentary *Portrait of Jason*. James Lyons, one of Winter's allies from back in the day, had first introduced him to Clarke's movie. Lyons, an actor, editor and screenwriter who was a key figure in the New Queer Cinema, edited in the same building; he would use the facilities by day, Winter by night. 'He was very gruff with me at first,' says Winter. 'Very Lou Reed, "Walk on the Wild Side". Gradually we became friends.' Lyons's advice to Winter after viewing a cut of *Chocolate Babies* was simple. 'Take out all the bad acting,' he said. 'Leave in all the good acting.' Winter immediately shelved the pages of dialogue he had shot for Max's rooftop deathbed scene, arriving at the distilled gesture with the sequinned tears.

Lyons, who was in a relationship with Todd Haynes, had edited all Haynes's films beginning with *Poison* (in which he also starred), and would continue to do so up to *Far from Heaven* in 2002. He can also be glimpsed in Jim Hubbard's 2012 documentary *United in Anger: A History of ACT UP* being hauled off in handcuffs from a 'Storm the NIH' protest in 1990. He died in 2007 of cancer, after more than a decade of treatment for HIV; his is one of the vacated abodes featured in Ira Sachs's Akerman-esque 2010 short *Last Address*, which comprises static shots of the exteriors of New York residences that were formerly home to artists who died of AIDS. Among them is the photographer David Wojnarowicz, whom Lyons played a version of in *Postcards from America*, based on Wojnarowicz's writings.

One afternoon in the mid-1990s, Lyons took Winter to Film Forum in Manhattan to see *Portrait of Jason*. Shirley Clarke's movie, made two and a half years before Stonewall, was regarded as a monument to its Black queer star, Jason Holliday, and an example of its director's skill and audacity.

Does Winter remember how he felt about it when he left the cinema that day with Lyons?

'Oh yeah,' he grins. 'I hated it.'

21

PORTRAIT OF JASON

'Shirley Clarke. *Portrait of Jason*. Roll one, sound one.'

The opening image in Clarke's film is a grey-and-white blur which rearranges itself gradually to become a monochrome close-up of Jason Holliday, a loquacious thirty-three-year-old Black man with a cigarette cocked between his fingers and spectacles that call to mind the wobbly little wheels on a drinks trolley.

'My name is Jason Holliday,' he says, pushing the smoke out of his nostrils. Then he repeats the line, a subtly different reading now, a tinge of irony. He seems to tease us for taking him at face value the first time.

'My name is Jason Holliday.'

His eyebrows rise as he says his surname, as if to enclose it in parentheses or inverted commas.

Having twice introduced himself, he then laughs, closes his eyes momentarily and stares straight down the lens.

'My name is Aaron Payne,' he says.

Only ten seconds into the film, he has already planted the first seeds of doubt. Perhaps we shouldn't have expected anything else from Clarke. Her 1961 debut, *The Connection*, concerns a documentary film-maker hanging out with the jazz musicians and heroin addicts he has chosen as his subjects, his journalistic distance gradually melting away like ice in a tumbler of whisky.

The tension between art and life is distilled to its essence in *Portrait of Jason*; even the first word in the title establishes a frame around the film's star. Clarke is giving notice that this isn't necessarily the real deal (as if such a thing could exist), but merely a rendering.

For the next hundred minutes, Holliday recounts fragments of his life story, name-drops as casually as he flicks ash from his cigarette, impersonates Mae West and Butterfly McQueen and generally floods the screen with charisma and camp. As the film progresses, though, there is a taunting quality to Clarke's attention. 'The whole thing is like watching him audition to play himself,' says Stephen Winter. 'And then he doesn't get the part.' The cruelty reaches its apogee when another off-camera voice is heard in the final reel. It belongs to Carl Lee, a brooding, seductive presence from *The Connection*, whose father, Orson Welles's collaborator Canada Lee, was blacklisted during the McCarthy witch-hunts.

'Carl was a Black actor, addicted to drugs, a bit of a criminal, and Shirley Clarke's main love interest and collaborator,' explains Winter. 'She met Jason through Carl. He and Jason had a relationship – a friendship with sex, a brother-on-brother love. The reason Shirley brings Carl in is because she knows that the only way Jason's going to give the climactic emotional response she wants is if Carl gets it from him. Only a Black man could look at another Black man and know exactly who they are. In *Portrait of Jason*, it's portrayed as a nasty kind of thing, but Carl is also being antagonistic out of love; he wants Jason to get to this point artistically so Jason can have the satisfaction of having given a climactic performance. It's wicked but it's to an end.'

Clarke had been toying with the idea of making a film of this kind for some time: 'I was very curious about the whole discussion of documentary and dramatic films and what was truly true.' What she lacked was a suitable subject; any potential candidates she liked either too much or not enough. She had known Holliday for a while: he would sometimes clean her house, and she would give him $40 towards costumes or music for his nightclub act. 'There were times when he was very funny, and times when he was very cruel and dangerous,' she said. 'We would be sitting around, and he'd suddenly take amyl nitrate and pop it under your nose. I thought I was having a heart attack. I could have killed him.' Seeing Holliday in the street one day, she suddenly thought: 'Yes, that's who I could make the film with.'

She pitched it to him as a project that could be shot in a day, showing 'you doing what you do, telling those stories you tell and talking about your life'. It was filmed at the Chelsea Hotel on 3 December 1966 over a period of twelve hours, and the footage was boiled down from that.

Clarke, who defined her role as 'white lady director', asked Lee to join them because (as Winter suspected) she sensed he alone could break through the carapace and provoke a strong reaction from Holliday while the camera was rolling. 'I knew that I would have to get Jason to face the truth at some point. But I wasn't positive how. In other words, I was going to let Jason do whatever he wanted for as long as I could, and then I was going to challenge him to come clean, to tell the truth.'

In the last twenty minutes, Holliday seems to disintegrate, dissolving into tears and pleas, before rallying unexpectedly, asking, 'Is this what you want?' in a way that calls into question even his ostensible breakdown. Clarke can be heard repeatedly trying to draw the film to a close by announcing 'the end' as Holliday keeps on rolling – the final example of these titans wrestling for control of the movie.

Clarke's assertion that she wanted him to 'tell the truth' suggests that there is only one such truth to be told. And that's where *Portrait of Jason* runs into all sorts of problems. 'An interesting and important fact is that I started the evening with hatred, and there was a part of me that was out to do him in, get back at him, kill him,' Clarke admitted in 1983. 'But as the evening progressed, I went through a change of not wanting to kill him but wanting him to be wonderful. Show him off.' So is this the truth of the 'white lady director', or the Black performer she wanted to 'kill'? It can't easily be both.

Winter didn't come across that interview until after he had shot *Jason and Shirley* in 2014. 'But when I read it, I went: "A-ha! I *knew* it!" We were right. She was doing it to get him. She says she didn't fall in love with him until the editing room, and I was like, "Yeah. *That's* clear enough!" It's one of the reasons that *Portrait of Jason* stands outside of the cinema canon in a way. The documentarians don't want it because it has this grime of exploitation. Black film people don't want it for the same reasons, and because of respectability politics. LGBTQ film doesn't want it because it's not glamorous, unlike other queer documentaries from that era like *The Queen*, and because it centres a Black gay man. As a result, Jason Holliday as a historic figure has fallen through the cracks of history. One of the things we do in *Jason and Shirley* is to reclaim him and give him his own voice.'

―――――――

Two years into running MIX NYC, Jim Hubbard and Sarah Schulman set out to programme films by and about Black gay men. 'There were very few at the time,' says Schulman. 'We decided to include *Portrait of Jason* but when we looked at it, we realised this was not necessarily a supportive film. In the second reel, it turned into something that maybe wasn't appropriate for our festival. We weren't sure how to deal with it exactly, so we made the very strange decision to only show the first reel. So we didn't really treat it with respect as a film, we looked at it more as documentary material. Film people got very upset with what we did, and later we realised we'd made a mistake. But that was the first time I'd seen it.'

In the same strand, they also programmed *Tongues Untied* and Isaac Julien's *Looking for Langston*. 'Isaac's film had been censored by the Langston Hughes estate. There was a big hunk of it which had no sound. So some of the films we showed were mangled. We were trying to create something that didn't yet fully exist.' The situation didn't greatly improve with time. 'Marlon died of AIDS, and Isaac Julien became an installation artist, so there was no one making Black gay features, apart from a few like *Brother to Brother*.' Having talked for years about *Portrait of Jason*, Schulman and her friend, the artist and activist Jack Waters, decided to make 'an answer film' and approached Winter with the idea.

'It was all about facilitating features with Black gay men,' she says. 'There were a handful – Stephen had made *Chocolate Babies* – but what we wanted wasn't just to reply to *Portrait of Jason*, but to address the larger problem of the lack of features.'

Waters was a natural fit to play Holliday in *Jason and Shirley*, while Schulman, who had acted before in Cheryl Dunye's work, as well as appearing in several films by Rosa von Praunheim, took the role of Clarke. Winter claims the two actors each wrote their own dialogue, though Schulman puts it differently. 'I would say "wrote" is in quotes,' she says. What Winter did was stage the whole shoot as an unbroken twelve-hour improvisation, reflecting the production of Clarke's film, and then edit the footage down to 90 minutes.

Sparks fly, as they will in any clash of opposing sensibilities. 'Stephen is against Shirley, and I'm not,' says Schulman. 'This whole "white woman who isn't accepted by the white establishment and works with Black artists" thing also happens to be my story. I've collaborated with Cheryl, Stephen, Jack, as well as the theatre director Marion McClinton and the composer Anthony Davis. There's a lot there that I'm sympathetic to.' Winter insists that 'it's not about demonising Shirley Clarke. It's about giving the Devil his due.'

Conversations about whether *Portrait of Jason* was Clarke's story to tell were thin on the ground in the late 1960s. 'That discourse didn't exist yet,' Schulman says. 'Don't forget, she had made four films about Black men, so she thought she was part of this move towards social progress. The problem is, she didn't have a modern racial analysis. It's like the question Vito Russo asks in *The Celluloid Closet*: is a flawed, stereotyped or biased representation better than none? And he decides it is, because even if you're seeing the gay person on the screen as a coward, or however we used to be represented, at least you know you're not alone. Is a flawed, racist, objectified representation of a Black gay man better than none? In this case I would say yes, because Jason conveys a lot about what it means to be a Black gay man despite Shirley's limitations. It's the first film of a Black gay man in the history of cinema, and we learn a lot. The problem is that Shirley Clarke seizes control in the edit.'

It was Clarke's contention that she never meant for *Portrait of Jason* to be an assassination attempt. 'I didn't take somebody who was easy to destroy,' she said. 'I picked somebody who was going to win. Jason ends up winning in that film.'

But at what cost?

22

BLUE JEAN

'Each letter of LGBT+ is having a separate experience right now,' says Sarah Schulman. 'But lesbian content is different because it has never been allowed to be seen, so we have no idea what authentic lesbian content really is. People are too prejudiced to universalise to a lesbian protagonist who's authentic. If the protagonist is fitted into a derivative model, *then* they can. But not if it's someone with a different kind of perspective.'

How different is the perspective of Céline Sciamma, the most revered lesbian film-maker since Chantal Akerman? If she can't yet claim credit for any equivalent formalist innovations, she has still mapped out her own emotional and textural landscape and tested the viability of a cinema largely free of men. That project is exemplified by *Portrait of a Lady on Fire*, set on a remote island in eighteenth-century Brittany, where Marianne (Noémie Merlant) is hired to secretly paint Héloïse (Adèle Haenel), a young woman bereft after her sister's suicide; the portrait is for the benefit of the Milanese nobleman whom she is to marry but has yet to meet.

Two women stuck on an island, one in a traumatised state, the other trying to tease from her an intimacy she is reluctant to surrender – what is this, if not a description of Bergman's *Persona*? No wonder Sciamma repeats that film's most recognisable image, in which two faces, one seen in profile, the other head-on, form halves of a single unit. For good measure, Haenel also gets to stare reproachfully down the lens at us, just as Harriet Andersson did in Bergman's *Summer with Monika*.

One difference from *Persona* is that the women in Sciamma's movie are not at loggerheads; any conflict arises from external forces. The film is also a partial response to Todd Haynes's *Carol*, starring Cate Blanchett as a wealthy, urbane but unhappily married mother in 1950s Manhattan who sets her sights on a young shop assistant (Rooney Mara). Haynes has talked of the 'excitement of the idea that you're inventing this language for this love. In a way that's how everybody who falls in love feels. They feel like they're inventing it themselves, but in this case there really wasn't a language. There was even less a language or a depiction of lesbian love than there was of gay love.'

Now listen to what Héloïse asks Marianne after they have slept together for the first time: 'Do all lovers feel they're inventing something?'

Sciamma observed that *Carol* is 'not a narrative about two women meeting and then, "Oh what's happening to us?" Cate Blanchett is a pickup artist. She sees her, she wants her.' Though the desire itself may be natural and simple, there is a power imbalance, which is mostly weighted in Carol's favour. In contrast, Sciamma paints Marianne and Héloïse as equals. 'There's all this surprise that lies within equality, that's the new tension,' she said in 2020. 'You don't know what's going to happen if it's not about the social hierarchy, gender domination or intellection domination.'

Men exert an unreasonable pressure on women's lives in *Portrait of a Lady on Fire*, as they do in *Carol*, but Sciamma largely denies them the luxury of visibility. She is not the first director to keep men more or less out of the picture. Sally Potter's 1983 feminist musical *The Gold Diggers*, starring Julie Christie, has a female-led narrative and was made with a women-only crew, including Akerman's former cinematographer Babette Mangolte; George Cukor's 1939 comedy *The Women* features no male performers, though it ends with Norma Shearer's capitulation to her off-screen husband. In Sciamma's film,

Héloïse's Milanese suitor is never shown, and nor is the father of the child that the maid is carrying. When a man appears near the end of the movie, it is as if a wondrous spell has been broken.

———————

Among the rest of the early-2020s crop of lesbian cinema, Schulman is contemptuous of *Tár*, which she describes as 'a fake lesbian film that has nothing to do with lesbian life'. But she singles out *Blue Jean* for praise. '*Blue Jean* is fantastic. It really gets across how high the stakes were for everyone at that time.' That time was 1988, when the UK's Conservative government brought in the homophobic Section 28 (originally known as Clause 28). Exploiting the hysteria surrounding AIDS, the legislation was teed up by Margaret Thatcher during the previous year's Conservative Party conference speech, when she inveighed against teaching children 'that they have an inalienable right to be gay'.

'Do you remember in *Blue Jean* they talk about the women who jumped into parliament on those ropes?' Schulman asks.

Of course: she is referring to the Lesbian Avengers, the direct-action group who abseiled into the House of Lords using ropes and a washing line bought from a market in Clapham, south London.

Wasn't Schulman part of the Lesbian Avengers, so named because of their fondness for Diana Rigg in the 1960s TV series *The Avengers*?

'I co-founded the Lesbian Avengers in New York,' she explains. 'This was the London one. I wasn't involved but I knew about them, and I had a friend who was in them . . .'

———————

Three women gay rights protestors caused pandemonium in the House of Lords when they abseiled from the public gallery onto the floor of the chamber. Black Rod and his staff quickly seized the demonstrators and escorted them out. The women were protesting that the Lords had approved a clause banning local councils from promoting homosexuality.

BBC Nine O'Clock News, 2 February 1988

Ahead of the implementation of Section 28, the Rio cinema in east London hosted a week-long run of *Maurice*, and warned its patrons: 'As a "positive" portrait of homosexuality, *Maurice* is the kind of film which the Rio (as a local authority funded project) will be banned from showing if the Local Government Bill and its Clause 28 become law . . . Catch *Maurice* quick before Clause 28 reaches what's left of your civil liberties.' Though no prosecutions occurred under Section 28, the climate of fear and stigmatisation was often deterrent enough. Performances of the Glyndebourne Touring Opera production of Benjamin Britten's *Death in Venice* were pulled from the Kent and Sussex schools festival by the local education authority, which deemed it unsuitable for pupils aged eleven to fifteen. Section 28 was never cited as the reason, though it's worth noting that when the law was finally repealed in 2003, Kent was the one council to hold on to it for another seven years. There was also the case of Calderdale Library Services in West Yorkshire, which refused to stock copies of the *Pink Paper* for fear of being prosecuted; that decision was reversed only following intervention by the civil rights organisation Liberty.

Section 28 had already been on the statute books for nearly six months when Georgia Oakley was born. A little over three decades later, in 2022, she made *Blue Jean*, the first great film about what it meant to be a queer person living in those oppressive conditions. 'I grew up during Section 28 and felt I had been robbed of the opportunity to learn about queer history,' she says. 'Now it was up to me to teach myself.'

It is mid-morning, and she is speaking from a cool, shaded room in Mallorca. A wasp drones into view, and she shushes it away. 'When I read this first-hand account of a lesbian PE teacher who was working at the time, I saw a correlation between the things she was talking about – living a double life, with the internalisation of shame and how that manifests itself – and the way I'd been thinking about my own experiences. I'd unconsciously internalised a lot of the damaging messaging that I had grown up with.'

She hit upon the idea of exploring that through the character of Jean, a PE teacher who is out to friends, even has a girlfriend, but who hides her sexuality at work and in front of her family. 'At the beginning, a few people said, "Are you sure you want to make a film about a lesbian PE teacher? Isn't that a nasty stereotype we should do away with?" But my intention was to sit with this character for ninety minutes and allow her to tell her own story. It was about unravelling a stereotype rather than reinforcing one. I knew she had to be a PE teacher because her job needed to be primarily concerned with bodies.'

Jean also had to be situated in a city without a prominent queer scene that might have assuaged her sense of isolation, so Oakley chose Newcastle, where she went to university. Jean lives on the other side of town to where she teaches – a strategic choice to ensure that the disparate sides of her life don't overlap. Except one night they do: she bumps into one of her students, Lois, in the local lesbian bar. She can't be supportive of Lois's sexuality when Section 28 expressly forbids it, so she withdraws from the girl, failing to defend her when she is the victim of homophobic bullying.

Oakley interviewed fifty people with experience of the culture at that time and drew Jean's story from extensive accounts by two lesbian former PE teachers, Catherine Lee and Sarah Squires. 'They both had this strange feeling when they read the script,' she says. 'They wanted to confront their younger selves, to grab them and shake them. After they watched the film, they wept because of this duality: they're looking at a version of themselves on-screen that didn't know the world would change as it has done. Catherine had told me she'd had an experience much like Jean has with Lois in the bar. Even three decades later, she couldn't stop thinking about how she had responded to that girl; there was still guilt and shame in her voice, and not a day had gone by when she didn't think about that student. It was what made me think this would be an interesting story to tell: it's about the forces that conspire to push someone who is a great teacher and a loving person to behave in a way they regret deeply.'

Sitting with those failures of nerve is part of the experience of watching the film, she says. 'That's why Sarah's initial reaction was not liking Jean and wanting her to be better.' Rosy McEwen, who presents as guarded while making Jean's internal maelstrom magically legible to the camera, draws on this conflict in her haunted work in the role. 'Catherine told Rosy, "I wish I could have been braver," and Rosy really clung to that in her performance.'

Jean's inability to do the right thing when cornered, or to comfort Lois (Lucy Halliday), was a stumbling block for some readers of the script. 'The fact that she is morally ambiguous or makes choices that are questionable became a problem,' Oakley says. 'My feeling was that you could make a film about a straight white guy who was morally ambiguous, but it became complicated as soon as it was about a lesbian. It was partly a response to this feeling I was having that, as a queer film-maker, I was being expected to make a film that would sugarcoat the gay experience and make everyone lovely and happy. Those stories do exist, but so do ones about people who are struggling. It shouldn't be one or the other.'

It isn't as simple as putting more LGBTQ+ people in positions of power. 'My experience was that if it happens to be a queer person who reads your script, often they will expect that story to mirror their own experiences, and if it doesn't, then it's not valid. The most vocal people who couldn't get on board with *Blue Jean* were all queer women who felt I should have made the film about a different thing that clicked with their experience. It's just down to the fact that not enough queer films are being made. And when they are, they're expected to tell everybody's story.'

She saw that response, too, during audience Q&A sessions. 'I didn't realise the scale of it until then,' she says, still sounding bruised. 'There was one person who was in tears at a Q&A after a screening in Newcastle. They asked why I hadn't made it about lesbians in the army, because that was illegal at the time. They were so impassioned. I said, "Hang on, that's a whole different film." It's not the kind of feedback or question that any straight film-maker would ever receive.'

The novelist and former hustler John Rechy made the same point in 1980, after the furore over *Cruising*: 'Why does every homosexual film or book – unlike a heterosexual film or book – have to represent our entire world, each and every one of us, when we have so many diverse and rich voices?'

Oakley has found her own kind of solace in queer cinema. 'When I was coming out, things like Céline Sciamma's *Tomboy* helped me look at my childhood in a different way. Not having seen that kind of experience before, I felt an affinity. I was talking to my wife's step-daughter about this – she's eighteen – and we were saying how complicated it is; everything's constantly evolving, and it's more common now to meet teenagers who are non-binary. But when I was a teen, that language wasn't available. Maybe if it had been, I would have identified as non-binary.'

The term 'micro-aggressions' hadn't been coined then either, but Oakley is adept at identifying these in the film: the sniping comments of Jean's family and colleagues, the sites and spaces actively disavowing queerness. When Jean is in the bar with her friends, or hanging out at the lesbian co-op, the colour palette is diverse, the camera level with the actors. Elsewhere, the visual language hints at surveillance. The billboards that Jean jogs past ('Are your children being taught traditional moral values?' asks one) comment sneeringly on her life and choices. The TV, which only ever seems to be showing the prime-time dating show *Blind Date*, badgers her with hetero-aggressive propaganda. Even when she is alone at home, the camera spies on her from above or peers at her through doorways to suggest she is being monitored.

'I wanted to get inside what it feels like to be constantly assessing how other people might be viewing you,' says Oakley. 'It's a feeling that can be with you even in your own home. Even when Jean is alone with her nephew, other people's perceptions have wormed their way into her head.' The neighbour across the street, who might be a miniature Margaret Thatcher, personifies the air of prying disapproval. 'In one draft, the neighbour had a dog called Maggie,' laughs Oakley. 'Maggie was always barking: this ever-present threat.'

When Jean accepts an invitation to attend after-work drinks with her colleagues after repeatedly declining, it proves to be an unedifying night. Red predominates here: the theatrical curtains, pulled back from the window where Jean and her party are sitting, seem to underline the element of performance in their social interactions. And there is a red neon arrow in the window, too, which appears to point from Jean to her male colleague, who has vague romantic designs on her. It is he who delivers a line that doubles as the film's mission statement: 'One day I'll crack you, Jean Newman.'

When I mention that neon arrow, Oakley smiles. 'I was sent a load of options, and none of them were quite right for the shot. But when I saw the arrow, I thought: "That's it. It's like a one-way ticket to hell." The lowest point in the whole film is Jean having to go out for the evening with a load of straight people.'

23

ALL OF US STRANGERS

The barren brick plazas and pebbledash walkways of the Barbican Estate give off a dismal gleam in the early-morning drizzle. London feels desolate, emptied out in a way that suggests its inhabitants have fled under the wail of air-raid sirens. I am here to meet Andrew Haigh, and today this is unmistakably the London of his 2023 film *All of Us Strangers*. I cross hurriedly in front of the dormant fountains on the way to the Barbican café, feeling as if I'm the last person on Earth. Or the first: an Adam in an Adidas windcheater.

There's an Adam, too, in *All of Us Strangers*. Played by Andrew Scott, he is a screenwriter – or, as Adam puts it, 'not a proper writer'. He has a habit of apologising for his backstory, to use a screenplay word. During a getting-to-know-you chat with the younger Harry (Paul Mescal), who appears to be the only other resident in Adam's high-tech high-rise, he reveals that his parents perished in a car crash when he was a child. 'Not the most original death,' he says, wielding an invisible blue pencil over the manuscript of his life. The script he is working on is autobiographical, set partly in his childhood home in Croydon, in London's weak outer ring, during the second half of the 1980s. (The scenes shot there were filmed in the house where Haigh grew up, adding grist to the autobiographical mill.)

Though Adam is shown typing feverishly, the only glimpse we see of his work reveals a single slug line: EXT. SUBURBAN HOUSE. 1987. Just as it is not out of the question that Julie in *Je tu il elle* is writing the film itself, so we are invited to assume that Adam is drafting *All of Us Strangers*. The movie could well be depicting its own creation.

As a screenwriter, names will be important to Adam, so he would appreciate the biblical connotation of his own, as well as its suggestion of the anonymous or unremarkable ('wouldn't know him from Adam'). Then again, he probably has enough on his mind, what with visiting his childhood home for research purposes and finding his late parents (played by Claire Foy and Jamie Bell) still living there, right as rain, and keen to catch up on all his news. They are now visibly younger than Adam, an effect which illustrates the tendency of queer kids to become parents to their parents, doing all they can to cushion the shock of the secret that sets them apart.

Adam has much in common with Russell (Tom Cullen) in *Weekend*, the 2011 film that established Haigh as one of the most searching voices in modern cinema. Like Adam, Russell lives high up in a tower block (though his is in Nottingham), with only a laptop for company. Also like him, he fills the empty space in his life with the written word: he has a diary devoted exclusively to cataloguing the men he has slept with. The latest notch on his bedpost is short, sharp Glen (Chris New), brought home by soft, lanky Russell from a nightclub in town. The pick-up itself isn't shown – an elision characteristic of the film's sleepy, even elegiac, editing. Russell is standing in the foreground of the near-empty dancefloor, while Glen is slouched in the snug in the background. The cinematographer, Ula Pontikos, racks focus so that Russell is reduced to a blur, while Glen zings sharply into view in the distance. Cut to morning, interior, bedroom, coffee, Dictaphone.

Dictaphone? It turns out Glen has his own sex-related project on the go, though his is artistic rather than diaristic in nature. He records morning-after interviews with the men he fucks, encouraging them to analyse what went down once the heat of passion has a skin on it.

We don't get to see the couple's first kiss or to eavesdrop on the first words they exchange. But Glen's project means that we do get to *hear* about the sex, blow by literal blow, the eroticism of the act itself displaced onto language, which has the effect of italicising gestures that might have been overlooked. Perhaps among the drunkenly thrashing limbs and jabbing tongues, we would not have noticed Russell demurely kissing Glen's hand as if to say '*enchanté*'. But when Glen instead recounts the act in a kind of amazed afterglow ('. . . And then you kissed my *hand*'), it keeps the moment alive and lingering. His recollection co-opts the audience into completing the act: Russell delivered the kiss, Glen put it into words the next morning, but it is the audience which is left to visualise it, and to hold the image in our heads.

A similar effect is achieved in the film's final seconds, once Glen has flown off to the US to study art for two years – the plan which lends the movie its plot-based imperative, its ticking clock. Before he goes, he entrusts the cassette of that post-coital post-mortem to Russell. The final image is a wide shot of Russell's apartment block at night, as we hear the tape's opening words; because we have already heard those words earlier in the film, when the tape was being recorded, it is once again left to us to imagine, recall, conjure up what it was that happened between Russell and Glen. As with the previous example of sex described rather than shown, Haigh leaves part of the scene unfinished and invites us to do the rest.

When Glen nags Russell to record his thoughts, we feel the annoyance that Russell is politely concealing – as well as his curiosity about this strange creature in his bed. Who precisely is going to see this installation? he wonders. 'No one's going to come to see it because it's about gay sex,' sniffs Glen. 'The straights won't come because it's nothing to do with them.' He could be expressing fears about the prospects of *Weekend*, long before anyone knew that this modestly scaled picture, shot for £100,000, would rake in nearly ten times its budget worldwide.

'Even trying to raise that was so difficult,' says Haigh as we carry our coffees past rows of booths and benches in the Barbican canteen, to a table near the back where only the houseplants by the window can hear us. 'I kept being told that no one wants to listen to gay people talking: "It's *boring*." But *Weekend* came out of my frustration at not feeling an experience as I understood it was being represented. I'm not on some agenda to speak to all queerness. That's sometimes where confusion creeps in: "Why is he making a film about *this*?" Well, because it's my experience.'

One of the magical elements of *Weekend* is that the characters seem to be willing the film into existence before our eyes. Glen craves visibility because he's tired of the straights getting all the books and movies and billboards. He argues that gay people must make their own narratives, while heterosexuals inherit theirs fully formed. In *Weekend*, then, he has got the movie he wished for: it's a rejoinder to precisely these criticisms. A not dissimilar trick was pulled off by *Go Fish*, with its lesbian movie characters complaining about pathetic lesbian movie characters, and the tradition continues in *The Summer with Carmen*, a gay Greek film about making a gay Greek film called *The Summer with Carmen*.

Any echoes of *Weekend* in *All of Us Strangers* are intentional. 'When I started writing it, I knew it would be connected to *Weekend*,' says Haigh. 'It's been twelve years since I wrote that film, and I hadn't done a movie with gay characters since then. And because *All of Us Strangers* is about someone who essentially can't escape how he feels about the past, I knew it would be interesting to relate it to the earlier film. When I made *Weekend*, I thought: "I'll do this, and all my feelings about queerness will be worked through by the time I move on." But it's all there. You still have to enter a room and go, "Like me, everybody!"' That impulse manifests itself in *All of Us Strangers* in Andrew Scott's quietly tormented performance as a man still lugging the hurt from an intolerant world into the more inclusive modern one.

His induction into the ghostly limbo where his parents reside looks at first glance like cruising. He is standing in a field, the wind caressing the trees, when he turns to see a figure in the distance on the periphery where overgrown grass meets manicured park. With an unmistakably seductive tilt of the head, the man indicates that Adam should follow him. This is a pick-up.

It is only once they have arrived back at Adam's childhood home, and the man – handsome, a bit ferrety, leather-jacketed and moustachioed – invites him in that we twig this is his father. Not for the first time, Haigh has fudged the boundaries between lover and parent. On their final morning together in *Weekend*, Russell admits to Glen that he wishes he had got the chance to come out to his dad. To act as a balm, Glen asks Russell to forget for a moment that the two of them have just had sex and adopts the character of Russell's father to facilitate the coming-out conversation he never had.

'For me, it's about how closely related parental love and romantic love are,' Haigh explains. 'It's all the same feeling wrapped up in this confusing ideal of what love is. You learn about love through your relationship with your parents, and that echoes into your romantic life. Somehow sex becomes part of that.'

Not having had the chance to come out to his parents before they died, Adam in *All of Us Strangers* finds himself cornered into doing it now. Aren't people nasty to him in the street? asks his mum. And what about that terrible disease? She alludes to the adverts with tombstones and icebergs: a reference to the portentous public information films directed by Nicolas Roeg and narrated by John Hurt, which scared many and enlightened few.

'What I love about that scene is how he's trying to make his mum feel OK,' says Haigh. 'That's what a lot of gay people experience when they come out, rather than the parent being there for them. Talk to queer people of a certain age, and you'll find their parents have never asked them, "What was it like for you growing up? How did you feel?" We just ignore those conversations. Once they've accepted us, that's it: don't rock the boat. It's unlikely you or I have had a real conversation with our parents about how we felt before we came out: you know, "This is how you made me feel, and this is how desperately unhappy I was for all those years." We don't want to tell them. I felt horrendous as a teenager; I'm sure you did, too. It was *awful*. I thought: "I do not know how I'm going to get through this. I'll have to marry a woman, live a lie, not have sex with men. Or, if I do, I'm going to die or my family are going to reject me."'

After Haigh's own mother saw *All of Us Strangers*, she quizzed him about the scene in which Adam confesses to his father that he was bullied horribly at primary school. 'She wanted to know if that had happened to me,' he sighs. 'And I realised I'd never told my parents that I was picked on at nine years old, essentially for being gay. Even with my mum asking me now, I was, like, "Oh no, I'm fine."' He laughs mirthlessly. 'I made a film about someone doing it and I *still* can't face doing it in real life.'

What's the worst-case scenario? 'She'd feel really upset that she wasn't there for me. And I know lots of reasons why she wasn't. But we try to spare our parents from the pain of realising they could have done more to help us. I don't know why we take it all on as our own. I think there's still some sense that all this is our fault – that we made a mess of family life, which is, of course, not true. Inside we feel we're to blame for fracturing something within the family.'

What are older LGBTQ+ people supposed to do with the anger they're still carrying with them from back then? 'I feel a certain amount of rage about all that,' says Haigh. 'It wasn't that long ago, and everyone's decided we can't be bothered about it any more. I do feel it's very close to grief. Part of me does want to remind people. Nobody admits to being homophobic now, but they were. You turned on the news and there were people in the House of Commons calling us evil and sinful.' Now the same opprobrium is repackaged and dished out to trans people, with the intensifying amplification, unavailable to bigots of earlier eras, provided by social media and the internet.

———————

Haigh, who has a track record in US television after co-writing and co-directing the gay, San Francisco-set HBO series *Looking*, tried in 2023 to pitch a limited series adapted from *Let the Record Show*, Sarah Schulman's scrupulous oral history of the ACT UP movement and the early days of the fight against AIDS. 'Of course, it's about horror and tragedy,' he concedes. 'But it's also about love, passion, politics, queerness and fighting the system. The epitome of good drama. When I read the book, I thought: "Who's *not* going to want to make this?"' The answer, it transpired, was everybody. 'We pitched it to Amazon and Netflix, and to smaller places. No one would fucking touch it. Too scary, too angry. Queer anger terrifies people, I think because the straight world knows it is the cause. The finger points at them. They didn't want a show that asks: "Why weren't you supportive? Why weren't you out on the streets?"'

He thinks the key to the future of queer cinema may lie in fully expressing these unpalatable emotions. 'I'm trying to work out now what the next step is. We don't need another historical drama about it being tough for two people and how their love is pure and true. We've had quite a lot of them. If you're gonna tell another queer story, what might it be? I think it's about how we are told now that we can live a life like everybody else, get married, have kids – but do we want this thing that we've fought for, this heteronormative ideal?'

Many parts of the world *are* broadly less hostile; others have got better at concealing it. But Haigh felt antipathy close to home at an advance test screening of *All of Us Strangers* for which the studio invited 300 members of the public. 'During the first sex scene, ten people – all couples – got up and left. It reactivated that feeling for me: they are *so* unhappy and disgusted about seeing intimacy between two men on-screen that they have to leave the cinema. I remember the meeting with all the execs afterwards and feeling upset and a little bit annoyed that they couldn't understand why I was hurt. They probably could, but I felt they didn't know what it was like to sit in a room and have people leave because who you are is so offensive to them.'

Though *All of Us Strangers* has been a critical and commercial hit, responses have tended to be delineated by age. 'Some younger queer people don't like it, don't get it, don't want it to be their thing, it's not their life. Something has gone wrong in the culture, I think, when everything needs to relate to you in a very specific sense or else it doesn't mean anything. It shows a basic lack of empathy. People really don't need to like what I do. I get that. But when it comes from the queer community, it feels personal – like I'm doing something wrong.'

Doing queerness wrong? 'Yeah. "*You're* telling me I'm doing it wrong?" We grew up when straight people were telling us we were wrong, and now younger queer people are saying the same? *Fuck* off. I'm doing it the only way I know how.'

This is said – almost *spat* – with palpable bitterness. That's when it occurs to me that people have got Haigh slightly wrong. The affable manner, the beard, the twinkly eyes: I've heard him described as a teddy bear, and perhaps he has styled himself that way, like many queer people who know they must be disarming or unthreatening to be heard. But there is also a knotty, unresolved anger in him.

Even this turns out to be nuanced. 'In another sense, I'm sort of happy there are people saying: "Fuck *All of Us Strangers*. I want a big happy ending!" It means they don't have the same burden we've had. The question of "queer joy" comes up a lot. It's a younger-generation thing: "Why can't we have stories that end in an outpouring of happiness?" You hear that a lot in Q&As, and it's never from older people. And I'm, like, "Because life's not like that." I'm all for queer joy but you can't *only* have that.'

On the other hand, he never sets out to make films for a wide audience. 'Why does it have to be for everyone? I feel there's an obsession now that you have to join the middle. Why? I'm alright out here. I'm fine on the edge.'

In that light, his 2008 debut *Greek Pete*, a no-budget documentary about male escorts, looks now like a mission statement. In the opening scene, the film's main subject, Pete, begins disrobing for the camera as he asks Haigh: 'Who is this for?' and 'Why do you wanna make this film?' It's telling that the novice director began his career by interrogating his own motives. 'That's interesting,' he says. 'The first real thing I'd made, and *that's* what I was asking myself. I never have the answer before I go into making a film. I think it's why my endings are always a bit open. I don't necessarily have the answer to what I'm trying to say.'

Weekend leaves Russell on the cusp, seemingly ready to make important changes in his life, while Glen is also suspended, literally so, somewhere over the Atlantic. *All of Us Strangers*, too, looks to the heavens in its final moments: as the camera zooms out from Adam and Harry spooning together on a bed, they are transformed into pinpricks of light, then dazzling stars in a constellation. Even *Greek Pete* ends with its hero dangling. Having won the Escort of the Year award in Los Angeles, he returns to London, where he phones his regular clients, alerting them to his triumph. The film confronts him, and us, with a lingering question: what was it all for?

'Maybe my whole psyche and my whole career is all in that film!' Haigh gasps. 'Part of me is Pete as well. Being a film-maker is not dissimilar to being an escort: you're trying to make the thing that works for people and makes them feel something. You win a prize and you're like, "I dunno. What does this mean?"'

Prizes don't solve everything, right? 'Prizes don't solve *anything*.'

Had he seen a film like *All of Us Strangers* when he was fifteen, he thinks it would have made a big difference to his life. 'It comes back to that question you asked: how do we deal with that stuff? Where does it go? When you're going through that as a kid, you want someone to say, "You know what? It's shit. And it's OK. And there is a way to get through it." I always wanted the film to feel like a hug.'

24

BEAUTY

There were no queer films that felt like a hug when I was fifteen. Whereas *Beauty* was a shove, and no mistake: it helped push me out of the closet at the age of forty-one. Directed by Oliver Hermanus in South Africa in 2011, the film opens with the sound of rippling conversation. We are at a wedding reception in Bloemfontein where the guests are mingling, drinking, laughing. The camera pans around the room, taking everything in, before gradually beginning its slow, stately zoom, burrowing deeper into the crowd. Eventually, a face stands out in the hubbub as the focus of our attention – a blithely handsome man in his early twenties. A tentative piano makes itself heard, bestowing on this figure an air of wistful romantic idealism. We are enchanted.

So, too, is François (Deon Lotz), who turns out to be the beast in *Beauty*. A cutaway reveals that it is through his eyes that we have been watching this young man, Christian (Charlie Keegan), the son of one of his oldest friends. François, a closeted middle-aged Afrikaner businessman with anger management issues, dominates the film. The camera gives us no respite from his corrosive perspective, making us complicit in the plans he hatches to get what he wants. And what he wants is Christian. The young man is courteous, deferential and eager to please. He can't see that the older man's feelings towards him are tainted by a desire that is both resentful and ravenous.

Beauty (the original title, *Skoonheid*, has connotations of purity) is a commentary on a specific type of Afrikaner male hostile to change. This manifests itself most obviously in François' racism and homophobia: he and a group of similarly middle-aged white men

288

meet to have sex at a remote farmhouse, but they react angrily when one of their group brings along a younger companion who is Black and obviously gay. Beyond those details, though, there is a generality to the repression which is broadly chilling regardless of nationality or socio-political context. Within minutes of the film beginning, I recognised myself in François. I saw what I could become, or already was. I had looked through his eyes so many times they felt like mine.

One weekend at Borough market in south London, I had noticed two men a few years my junior holding hands and nuzzling as they strolled among the stalls. It was a crunchy autumn afternoon, and they were both wearing scarves and cosy coats. You could practically smell the morning sex they'd had in their stylishly rumpled apartment, the breakfast pastries they'd warmed up after showering off, the fresh ink on the newspapers spread out on their kitchen table.

Every time they paused at a new stall, they would nudge one another, leaning in to share a joke or plant a kiss. It wasn't only their queerness that gnawed away at me; it was how at ease they were with themselves, and with their affection. There was a defiance about them that I wanted to crush under the heel of my boot. I seethed with envy, indignant that they enjoyed the honest liberty I was denying myself.

One of them noticed me staring. He glanced away, then looked back again a few seconds later to see if I was still watching him. I didn't care. All I could think was: 'I want what you've got.'

Everything in *Beauty* feeds into this central thesis of the malignancy of repression, right down to the score by Ben Ludik, an ebbing wave of musical calm that never gives way to a storm. There's no crescendo, no release, just as there is none in François' pursuit of Christian. He gets his paws on the lad eventually in a harrowing scene, his lust transmuted fully into violence. But resolution evades him, and the film. As it ends, the cycle begins all over again, with François watching someone else.

Hermanus credited *Death in Venice* – the novella, rather than the film – as one of the influences on *Beauty*. The poignancy of Thomas Mann's writing had already been preserved without its attendant creepiness in *Love and Death on Long Island*. And the insistence with which *Death in Venice* has weighed on cinematic renderings of queer love was alluded to in Eloy de la Iglesia's late-1970s films *Hidden Pleasures* and *Confessions of a Congressman*. In the latter, a politician introduces his wife to the rent boy with whom he has become obsessed. 'You imagined him different, didn't you?' he asks her. 'I assume you expected a more fragile person, a Visconti character, lying on the beach in Venice listening to music by Mahler . . .'

It is *Beauty*, though, which coaxes out the true cruelty of Mann's novella, and strips away the bogus romanticism of the screen adaptation, to expose the cancerous rot within. Visconti made the film, but it was Hermanus who performed the autopsy.

No movie had ever rattled me like *Beauty*, though the films of François Ozon came close.

'Didn't you and Ozon have a thing?' asked Catherine, one of my editors at the *Guardian*, before she sent me to interview him in 2012. 'That's what I heard.'

She was right. We did. Though only one of us knew about it.

It wasn't Ozon I was in love with, not really, but his films. *Under the Sand*, his fourth feature, would qualify him as a master even if he had directed nothing else. (Ingmar Bergman thought so, too.) Made in 2000, it is a tightly controlled study of a middle-aged woman, played by Charlotte Rampling, whose husband wades into the sea while she is sunbathing on the beach and never comes back. In the weeks and months that follow, her sanity crumbles like a sandcastle.

Ozon has been drawn repeatedly to the beach. It forms an important backdrop to *Regarde la mer, 5×2, Time to Leave, Le Refuge* and
Summer of 85, as well as the setting for the short film that first attracted
me to him – or to his cinema, at least, with its breezy freedoms. In *A
Summer Dress*, a teenager who is irritated by his boyfriend while on
holiday takes off for an afternoon alone. After going skinny-dipping
in the sea, he is picked up on the deserted beach by a young woman.
While they are having sex in the woods, an unidentified passer-by
notices them through the bracken – a minor detail that is not pur-
sued and doesn't need to be for its destabilising voyeuristic effect to
ripple through the rest of the film.

When the two of them return to the beach, they find the boy's
clothes have been stolen. The only option for him is to wear the red-
and-blue dress that the woman has in her bag. Ozon filmed his actor
reluctantly squeezing himself into it. 'I thought the shot of him putting the dress on was so sexy,' he said. But the veteran editor Claudine
Bouché, who had worked with Truffaut, persuaded the director
instead to cut straight from the boy's initial protestations about wearing the garment to the shot of him trudging sullenly along the beach
already with it on. The result is euphorically comic: a purely cinematic
joke conjured in the edit.

The dress has an unspoken, totemistic power. It is this garment,
rather than any of the bodies on display, that is the erotic focus of
the film. It revives the teenager, rejuvenating his sex life with his boyfriend. When he turns up wearing it at their holiday apartment, they
fuck hungrily – getting it on before he has had a chance to take it
off. Red and blue are first shown as separate colours hanging on the
lovers' washing line, but in the pattern of the dress they are intermin-
gled, just as different desires co-exist happily within the boy. Ozon
specialises in the cinema of fluidity. From *A Summer Dress* onwards,
he has been visualising sexuality as an empty beach where our desires

could be scrawled in the sand. The tide would erase these impermanent yearnings, leaving us free to start all over again the next day.

The feeling that an unsayable truth about myself was being expressed in Ozon's films sometimes blinded me to their flaws. My girlfriend, on the other hand, identified instantly the misogyny in Ozon's second feature, *Criminal Lovers*, a *Hansel and Gretel* update in which the boy rejects the girl in favour of the woodcutter who imprisons them both in his cellar. Perhaps she saw it as a warning. At the end of the movie, the boy weeps as he is dragged away from the woodcutter by police. The girl is shot dead, then savaged by dogs.

I had interviewed Ozon for various newspapers and magazines five times in the years since his 1998 debut *Sitcom*. At the end of our second meeting, in 2001, I asked him to sign my DVD of his Fassbinder adaptation, *Water Drops on Burning Rocks*. He wrote: '*Jamais deux sans trois*' – 'Never two without three' – which I convinced myself was a come-on.

Now it was the end of 2012, and I was being dispatched to talk to him about *In the House*, his clever thriller about a teacher (Fabrice Luchini) who is so spellbound by a talented pupil (Ernst Umhauer) that he urges him to continue writing a story about his obsession with a classmate's family. He must encourage the boy's talent without endorsing his voyeurism, and yet he wants to know how the tale ends. Like any reader or viewer, he is a sucker for a juicy yarn. In the most self-reflexive scenes, the teacher analyses his story, which has been dramatised for our benefit: 'Are you writing what you see, or transforming it?' As the boy's attention shifts between different members of the coveted clan, the ghost of *Theorem* makes itself felt. 'The father, the mother, the son,' says the teacher. 'Is this Pasolini?'

It was six months after *Beauty* had upended me, but I still hadn't come out. I decided I would make a pass at Ozon. Catherine already thought we'd dated, so we were practically an item.

My interview with him was at 11 a.m. in a hotel overlooking the Thames. I took with me a postcard of Diana Dors lying on a bed in *Yield to the Night*. Tragedy coupled with camp glamour: he would dig that. On the back, I scribbled my phone number and email address. At the end of our time together, I would slip it into his possession somehow.

With his boyish looks stiffening subtly with age, Ozon was beginning to resemble Dirk Bogarde, only with an important difference: he was glowing rather than glowering. Our conversation went swimmingly. He was, as ever, an engaging talker. Reflecting on the way his work and his life had run together, he said: 'When you make a film, what you are shooting becomes as important as the events in your private life, because you are so close to the characters. I think when I become old, I will also become mad. I will say, "I have done all these things."' At that, he waved his hand expansively, taking in the whole suite. 'But they will only be the things I have shot.'

Once the hour was up, he hurried out of the room to make a phone call, nearly crashing into the next journalist, who was waiting in the corridor. I glanced down at the postcard of Diana Dors. She stared back at me reproachfully through the bars of her bed.

The PR assistant poked her head round the door.

'Time to leave,' she said.

25

APPROPRIATE BEHAVIOUR

Even though I spent twenty-two years of my life in two relationships with women, I've never identified as bisexual. 'Why would you?' says Desiree Akhavan. 'I mean, who wants to be with a bisexual? The PR is not good. It's the worst. It sounds terrible. It's like: "Hi, I'm disingenuous. I have no loyalty to anyone." It really sucks.'

Akhavan is the Iranian American actor–writer–director responsible for *The Slope*, a 2010 web series in which she plays a bisexual in a lesbian relationship; *Appropriate Behaviour*, a 2014 movie in which she plays a bisexual getting over a lesbian relationship; and *The Bisexual*, a 2018 Channel 4 series in which she plays a bisexual who leaves a lesbian relationship and takes up briefly with a man, causing her ex-girlfriend to go ballistic.

For a while, then, Akhavan made a point of interrogating bisexuality every four years, until she went and ruined the pattern by directing and co-writing *The Miseducation of Cameron Post*, also in 2018, starring Chloë Grace Moretz as a queer teenager dispatched to a conversion-therapy camp. 'You always end up working through something,' Akhavan reflects. 'I wrote *The Bisexual* when I was in a relationship with somebody who was older than me. She was settled, and ready to have a home and a wife, and I was jonesing for adventure. I remember showing what I'd written to my girlfriend, and she was like, "This is not a good sign." She knew before I did.'

We are sitting opposite one another in a covered booth in the garden of a north London pub. It is late afternoon, and we are the only customers. Akhavan, who has erratically curly black hair and enormous eyes that are part sceptical and part playful, is wearing a blue windcheater; Elvis Presley's giant face stares out forlornly from her T-shirt. Around her neck is a string of coloured plastic beads, so tight it could be a choker. She is in town to work with her London-based co-writer, Cecilia Frugiuele, on a new script about a family torn apart during the Islamic Revolution. On the back burner is a project she describes as 'a lesbian *When Harry Met Sally*'.

Did she foresee when she made *Appropriate Behaviour* the extent to which she would become cinema's ambassador for bisexuality? 'Wait, am I?' she says, glancing around the pub garden as though some of her rivals for the title might be lurking behind the bins. There's nobody else in the movie world, I tell her. Even Tricia Cooke, who made *Drive-Away Dolls* with her husband Ethan Coen, identifies as lesbian and queer. That film diverts some of the swagger of *Appropriate Behaviour* into a crime caper and begins, as Akhavan's film does, with a lesbian break-up in which a dildo given as a gift in happier, hornier times becomes a cause of consternation. Cooke and Coen are reportedly hatching more comedies to follow in the wake of that bawdy, brassy vehicle, originally titled *Drive-Away Dykes* and described by a lesbian friend of mine as 'canny fanny fun'.

So Akhavan would appear to be the uncontested champion of bisexual cinema. 'Maybe by default, then,' she says.

For all her comic badmouthing of bisexuals, she continues to identify as one. Did she ever think of coming out as a lesbian instead? 'That would have been easier. But it would also have been a lie. I am so *not* a lesbian. That's what sucks. And I have such respect for lesbians. I love lesbians. I'm in love with a lesbian right now. I feel if I were to call myself a lesbian, I'd be disrespecting the truth of someone who knows they could never be with the opposite gender. That's a certain experience of life that is just not mine. And never was. But I also knew I was queer. It's not like, "I'm straight except for that one time." I do live a gay life.'

She came out as bisexual in her early twenties – an unprecedented move, as far as she was concerned, since she had never met or heard of another gay or bisexual Iranian. But she found comfort in Lisa Cholodenko's acutely observed 1998 drama *High Art*, in which an up-and-coming magazine editor, Syd (Radha Mitchell), advances from business to pleasure with Lucy (Ally Sheedy), the reclusive photographer whose career she helps to resuscitate. In the process, Syd inadvertently exploits Lucy and damages the photographer's relationship with her girlfriend, Greta (Patricia Clarkson), a faded German actor given to reminiscing dreamily about her time in Fassbinder's inner circle.

'*High Art* is so good and sexy and honest and raw,' says Akhavan. 'I felt understood by that film, and there are so many other amazing queer films that don't speak my language in the same way.' Such as? 'Well, I always felt alienated by camp. There's so much camp out there. John Waters or *RuPaul's Drag Race*. I love it but I'm not a camp person. And when I saw *High Art*, I gasped. Sometimes, you watch a film and it's like, "*This* is a conversation I can get into." It's the camera, the dialogue, what they're communicating on-screen; that love story made sense to me and felt real and sexy. It's rare that I saw gay couples on-screen that I felt had agency and that I wanted to see fuck. I was invested in it. *High Art* is one of the very few films that engaged both my heart and my loins.'

Before *High Art*, sex she'd seen on-screen was 'pornographic or farcical. But this found that sweet spot where it felt like a real relationship with high stakes.' Her thoughts turn to Ira Sachs's movie *Passages*. 'It's like in Ira's film, you could feel the physical tie between those two men.' She is referring to Tomas, a director played by Franz Rogowski, and his husband Martin (Ben Whishaw), who is blindsided when Tomas has an affair with Agathe (Adèle Exarchopoulos). The film includes several bracing sex scenes, including one, shot from behind, in which Martin fucks Tomas, who reaches around to insert a finger into his husband's butt.

'It was toxic, but they couldn't let go of each other,' Akhavan sighs. 'That intense ownership of each other's body. You're thinking, "I wonder how often Ben Whishaw's character has topped." To me, it read like the first time he's topping. He's really going for it. You can read that shift in them.'

Sachs was one of Akhavan's tutors during her third year at New York University. She met him in 2010, a few months after coming out, and it was one of his class assignments that led her to make *The Slope*, in which she and her then-partner Ingrid Jungermann play exaggerated versions of themselves: a lesbian and her bisexual girlfriend, sniping and sneering at the queers around them. 'One day, Ingrid and I were talking about how much we hated all gay things. We were like, "Why does the flag have to be a rainbow? It's ugly and it doesn't go with anything!" And she said, "This should be your film for Ira's class – two self-hating homophobic narcissists!"' Out of that, *The Slope* was born.

In the first episode, Ingrid chastises Desiree for using 'gay' as a pejorative; Desiree protests that she can't be homophobic because she's hanging out with her 'super-dykey' girlfriend. 'People who aren't homophobic don't call their girlfriend "super-dykey",' Ingrid points out. Semantic territory is constantly being disputed, gained and lost, sexuality and gender identity weaponised. Later in the series, Desiree shames Ingrid for wanting to stay at home instead of going to an underground rave at the back of a textile mill in Little Cambodia. 'This is what it is to be bisexual,' she crows. 'I'm here, I'm there, I'm everywhere! One day I'm with men, then I'm with women, you can't pin me down. I'm an enigma. The only people cooler than bisexuals are transgender.'

This achingly funny study in cooler-than-thou self-regard was later channelled by Akhavan into Shirin, her character in *Appropriate Behaviour*, who first meets her girlfriend Maxine (Rebecca Henderson) in a similarly bristling bout of semantic swordplay, this time on a stoop on New Year's Eve, where they bicker over who has dibs on the word 'dyke'. Shirin is informed that the word is 'incredibly offensive', to which she replies: 'Oh I'm bisexual, so it's OK.' No, Maxine tells her, it's still offensive, however you mean it. 'Tomay-toe, tom-art-oh,' Shirin grins. Trying to smooth things over, she tells Maxine: 'I like girls like you. You know – manly but also a little bit like a lady.'

'That persona I created is this psychotic delusional princess,' Akhavan explains. 'I don't know why she became my alter ego, but she's not that dissimilar to me. There is a crazy psycho princess that I saw in myself that I thought would be the comedic foil to Ingrid's very serious lesbian. In *Appropriate Behaviour*, she's kind of psychotic but not quite as bad. And she's there in *The Bisexual*, too. I think it's just my vibe. My worst features exaggerated.'

The Slope, she says, was about 'just trying to make each other laugh. But I was also clearly chewing on the question of "What is it to be gay?" Every episode is, like, "I'm not the right *kind* of gay." I was obsessed with that idea, and it caused me a lot of anxiety. I wasn't a lipstick femme, I wasn't a butch.'

She grew up in New York City, only wore black, only did cynicism. She went to Smith: 'A very gay college, but the hierarchy was the same as high school, only instead of the jock at the top of the pyramid it was the stone butch with a mullet, gauged ears and a sleeve of stick-and-poke tattoos. There was a slight aesthetic shift from high school but for the most part it was just as exclusionary. You know this – just because it's gay doesn't mean it's any kinder. It was not inclusive, and I was such an outsider. I went looking for comfort in films. I came into my own watching *Muriel's Wedding* and *Welcome to the Dollhouse*. That's where I saw myself.'

Appropriate Behaviour traffics in the same queer self-deprecation, bordering on self-loathing, as *The Slope*, with the addition of the racial and religious complications of being a bisexual Iranian woman hiding your girlfriend from your traditionally minded family. It is structured, though, on the *Annie Hall* model, looking back at a broken relationship and encouraging the audience to invest in a romance which we know from the outset won't last.

'Cecilia and I made the film thinking no one would watch it,' she says. 'Then when we were editing it, I thought: "It's insane and intense that I cast myself. What kind of a sick fuck does that?" It's where my princess persona comes in. But if you're doing it, you've also got to take a magnifying glass to some of your ugliest qualities. It's hard to feel exposed, though, when you're so in control.'

With one exception: the scene in which Shirin has a threesome with a male/female couple she meets in a bar. As the passion intensifies back at their apartment, the balance of power keeps shifting unpredictably between them, until it is the two women who forge a connection and the man who becomes the gooseberry. 'I watched playback on the first take, then locked myself in the bathroom and wouldn't come out,' says Akhavan. 'It looked pornographic and disgusting to me. There was a knock at the door, and it was Cecilia saying, "Trust me, it's good." She was right. The one thing that never changed from the first cut was that threesome. It's my only example of something I've shot that is better than I could have hoped. Originally, I thought it was just "she's lonely, she has sex". But when you watch it, you see it flipping from "everyone's on the same journey" to "oh no they're not". I love how it's all in the same frame. That's happened for me so many times: you're not at the wheel, or you are and then it slips through your fingers.'

In subsequent work like *The Bisexual*, Akhavan has confronted other subjects through the prism of her queerness – such as the yawning disparity between herself and the generation immediately behind her. 'You're happy for what is happening, but you also know that a part of the gay experience is dying. Every first date used to be, "Tell me your coming-out story!" It was like this instant intimacy. We all had these war wounds. My life was before I came out and after I came out – and I'm not even a lesbian. I also think it's a privilege that I got to come out. It was always a hard thing to articulate to a straight person, and now it's a hard thing to articulate to a young queer person. I both feel sorry for that generation and happy for them. It's wonderful not to have to fight so much, because we're all wounded; I still have so much homophobia against myself, and I see it constantly. So I'm grateful that many of the younger generation may not be feeling that internalised hate. But at the same time, it was such a unifier. It made us so tough and indestructible.'

When it comes to bisexuality, Akhavan will always fly the flag, though preferably not a rainbow one if other options are available. Does anyone even identify as bisexual any more? 'It's been rebranded as pansexual,' she sighs. 'Bisexuality is seen as binary, which is unfortunate because I never saw it that way. I can't tell if it's language evolving or if people are just desperate to drop the baggage associated with such a cringe label. It's probably a bit of both. I'm still very protective of it, perhaps because I fought so hard to claim that space, despite how deeply uncool it was. I guess someone has to carry that torch, and it might as well be me.'

I tell her she has almost persuaded me.

'Come on,' she says. 'Stand up for the losers!'

———

Akhavan walks me to the bus stop, and we say our goodbyes.

'Can we hug?' she asks. We can.

As she heads off to Whole Foods, I watch her getting smaller and smaller, a shrinking speck of blue under the baleful sky.

Something twangs in my chest, like a string breaking. I had this far-fetched idea that my book could end with the two of us sparking romantically, perhaps even ending up together. What a satisfying structural device that could have been. It would ratify the state of impermanence and instability to which I want the book to aspire, proving that maybe I'm not wholly gay after all, and that nothing is as simple as I'd thought. Perhaps there is still time for a last-minute, rom-com-style dash to the supermarket, to suggest that we give it a go for the sake of my book. With Akhavan's taste for romantic cringe, she would surely appreciate such a flourish, such a big swing. When the 476 arrives, I clamber on, taking a window seat on the left side of the bus so I can peer into Whole Foods as we trundle past. But I can't see her in there, and I'm not sure what I would do if I could.

The bus lurches on, rain slashing the windows. Passing shopfronts fade into coloured smudges behind the fogged-up glass. I realise it is getting to that time of year when I'll need to decide whether I am returning to Venice in February or not. It's only four months away now. I'm reluctant to give over all those weeks to preparing lectures and finding new film clips, especially as I should be devoting that time to my book instead. But there is another, less rational reason for not wanting to go: I feel I ought to put some distance between myself and Aschenbach. Right now, the prospect of lurking around Venice, following in his shuffling footsteps, makes me feel like I'm stuck in a role that I need to escape.

The ghost of *Death in Venice* hangs over queer cinema. Or perhaps it is only me that it haunts. Either way, I want out. I draft an email letting the organisers know I won't be available to teach there the next semester. I have a book to write; Venice can wait. Once the email is sent, I scroll through my contacts looking for Ramon.

26
END OF THE CENTURY

'Hi Ryan, I am sending you this voice message because it will be better for English as it's easier for me. Yes, I still live in Barcelona. 28 and 29 February is OK for me. I leave my son at kindergarten around 10 and I have to be back at 2.30, 3 at most. You want to walk through the areas where we were shooting the movie, is that possible? We shot a bit in Montjuïc, a bit in Barceloneta, some in Horta, too. I'm going to send you right now the – I don't know the word for it – *ubicación*. Sorry, I feel I haven't been very concrete. *Concrete?* Concrete is not a word. Well, it is a word but for a material, I think. If you need more clarity, let me know. We could start on the platform at Vall d'Hebron Metro station and go forward together on the green line. Then we can walk up to Montjuïc, where we shot the long scene you mentioned. I send you big hug and take care.'

End of the Century begins with Ocho arriving at the train station in Barcelona. He checks into his Airbnb apartment, mooches around the city, scrolls through Grindr, masturbates, goes to sleep, gets up the next day, sees someone he likes the look of from his balcony, spies him again at the beach and fails to make contact but spots him a third time from the balcony later that day. The stranger is wearing a black Kiss T-shirt, so Ocho calls out 'Kiss!' to him and beckons him upstairs. The opening twelve minutes of the film have passed without dialogue, which makes 'Kiss' the first word we hear.

The Kisser is Javi. He appears at the apartment door. The two men talk, share a beer, have sex, then part. Later, they meet up for cheese and wine, which they take to one of the stone terraces high up in Parc Montjuïc, beneath the Museu Nacional d'Art de Catalunya, which overlooks the city. The day is dying. As they rake over their lives, and the light fades, Ocho confesses to the strangest feeling: it's as though they've met before.

'We *have* met before,' Javi replies.

Without fuss or fanfare, the film then cuts to the same city twenty years earlier. Ocho arrives off the train, goes to stay with his friend Sonia and ventures out alone to Parc Montjuïc, where a stranger gives him a blow job. He rushes back to the apartment in a panic, fretting that he now has AIDS. As he is hunched over the toilet, the key turns in the apartment door and Sonia's boyfriend comes in to find him vomiting – and this is how Javi first meets Ocho. Later, the Kiss T-shirt will drop from the heavens and into their lives.

End of the Century is a plangent love story with hints of the yearning of *Weekend* but also the alienation of Antonioni. The elisions in time recall *Come Back to the 5 & Dime, Jimmy Dean, Jimmy Dean*, which also went to no special effort to delineate between present-tense action and flashbacks. The dominant mood, though, is elliptical and disorientating: a kind of *Last Hook-Up at Marienbad*. 'There should be something a bit off about the film,' said its writer–director, Lucio Castro. 'I want the audience to doubt what it sees.'

Ramon Pujol is not wearing the Kiss T-shirt this morning as he sits opposite me on the stone balcony at Parc Montjuïc, exactly where he sat six years earlier, when he starred as Javi opposite Juan Barberini as Ocho. 'What happened with that T-shirt?' he asks himself now.

'I'm amazed I don't have it. I know I took some white socks that Javi wears. I wore them until they broke.' He is short and slim, with thick, sculptural red hair: a handsome Pan. His stubbly beard has grown dense around his chin, where there are white strands swirling among the ginger in a way that suggests a whorl of ice-cream flavours. His ears have an adorably crumpled look, as though he fell asleep on them and they haven't yet regained their original shape.

That vital scene between Ocho and Javi, the moment on which the rest of the movie hinges, was shot in one ten-minute take at dusk; the sky behind them was streaked with darkening blues, except for one horizontal seam of gold like the last crack of light beneath a closing door. Today, the sun is insistent, its heat pricked only by an erratic breeze. To reach our elevated vantage point, we have climbed here from Plaça d'Espanya below, borne ever closer by a series of outdoor escalators that could be zips set into the landscape. Now the city is laid out before us like a picnic, the sea a ribbon of distant dancing sparkles.

Ramon peers over the edge of the stone balcony. 'I feel there's something different,' he says. 'Maybe all this was more grown when we made the film.' He indicates the plants and shrubs reaching up to us from below like outstretched hands. Then he points to a building not far away, just below the park. 'I used to study there at the drama school. Then I would come cruising here in my free hours. Ah, I was so young.'

Shooting that scene on the balcony was a race against the clock. There was a problem with the memory card in the camera, which meant the producer had to rush down the hill to upload it, and then scramble back up for another take before they lost the light. 'Then we did the last take and it just happened,' says Ramon. 'We got it. There are beautiful things in it, like the bird crossing the sky at exactly the right time. One of the reasons the film works is because there are elements about it that you can't explain. Lucio is a super-intelligent guy, so maybe these were all planned, or maybe they happened and he knew how to catch them.' Given the nature of the narrative, I wonder if Ocho's name was deliberately chosen to suggest a never-ending loop. 'Ah wow, yeah,' he says, his eyes glinting. 'Then you put it on its side, and it's *infinito*.'

It is one of the masterstrokes of *End of the Century* that in slipping back and forth across time, it resists the usual signifiers of cinematic transitions, such as ageing make-up or pronounced changes in hairstyle. If anything, the film foregrounds its resistance to those rules: in one of the first close-ups of Ocho during the long flashback sequence in the middle of the movie, grey threads are clearly visible in his beetle-black hair and beard. 'If you think about how you were twenty years ago, it's not as if you imagine yourself younger,' says Ramon. 'You just see yourself as this unchanging fact.'

There are already plenty of natural disparities between the two periods in the film, without needing to resort to make-up or de-ageing technology. Mobile phones are conspicuous by their absence from the late-twentieth-century scenes. During Ocho's earlier visit, he cadges a room from Sonia, a pal's ex-girlfriend, whereas now he stays in a characterless Airbnb. Back then, he was so terrified of AIDS that he became physically sick. Fast-forward to now and he is blasé about taking PrEP. Javi has to positively badger him into wearing a condom.

The performances are also fuelled by contrasting energies: the idealism of youth versus the diminished opportunities and calcified guardedness of middle age. Ocho seems physically looser as a younger man, and quicker to smile, while Javi in his early twenties has a perkiness that has hardened two decades later into something more sceptical, even wary. 'In the past, he is playful but less clear. In the present, he is clearer but closed, more focused on who he is and what he wants.' Javi explains to Ocho that he is now married with a daughter. He and his husband don't have sex with each other any more, and their relationship is open, but they have one rule: no staying overnight with other people. Ramon describes the scene: 'There is that moment where Ocho and Javi say goodbye in the present day, and he says to me, "So we can't see each other?" And I make like: "*C'mon...*" He gives a little tilt of the head and a shrug that says: obviously not. It's a devastating gesture. The past is gone.

Ramon reaches under his grey hoodie and produces a roll-up from the pouch around his waist. 'Do you mind if I smoke?' he asks. Then he turns back to the subject in hand. He seems incredulous on Javi's behalf that Ocho didn't remember him twenty years on. 'For me – I mean, Ramon – I remember perfectly the first guy I kissed. It was in a club. We kissed, then we talked a little. And when I met him on the street, maybe ten years later, it was like: "Gerald, it is so good to see you!" He is important. I still remember him, and it's been another ten years now since I saw him. Maybe I'll never see him again, but he has a place in my emotional and sexual life forever.'

If Ocho hadn't confessed to his uncanny feeling that they'd met before, would Javi have said anything? 'Wow, that's a good question. I don't know.' He studies me and looks suddenly protective. 'Do you want to get out of the sun? Come on. You're like me, we burn so easily.'

Jumping down from the balcony, we head to a shaded bench and sit facing the road that snakes down the hill. It's quiet, except for the occasional car purring past or a skateboarder rattling around the bend. A saxophonist playing on the terrace below sends muted plangent notes wafting up to us like perfume.

How it ended twenty years earlier was with Javi and Ocho making love after dancing drunkenly in Sonia's apartment to A Flock of Seagulls. The next morning, Javi discovers in Ocho's vacated bedroom a copy of David Wojnarowicz's *Close to the Knives: A Memoir of Disintegration*. His eyes scan the page, the text flowing across the screen as a silent horizontal ticker-tape: 'Destination means death to me. If I could figure out a way to remain forever in transition, in the disconnected and unfamiliar, I could remain in a state of perpetual freedom.' It's vital that Castro chose not to scroll the text from the bottom of the screen, or to have anyone read it in voiceover. The effect of the lines moving across the frame, from right to left, is akin to watching a train leaving the station. A train you were meant to be on. But you were too late. It left without you, and it's not coming back.

Ramon drags intently on his tiny roll-up and says he believes the film found its way to him for a reason. 'It's a bit magical, but my acting teacher says that every time a project comes to you, it's because you need to learn something from it. Not as an actor – as a person.' What did he learn from *End of the Century*, then? 'At that point, I was not trusting in love. I had split from a long-term relationship. It wasn't working, I wasn't feeling seen. But after making the film, my point of view changed. I was like, "No. Love is important."'

There is something else, something even more significant. During the scene on the balcony at sunset, Javi talks about bringing up his daughter with his husband, and how having a child gave him a sense of relief: now he has someone else to care for. That scene was shot in June 2018. Five months later, Ramon began the registration process to adopt his own child.

'The film moved things inside me,' he says. 'It changed me.'

At that moment, a clump of pigeons swoop low above our heads in an unruly formation, like a handful of seeds thrown down at us from the hills. We both duck instinctively, then laugh at each other to hide our embarrassment. The birds are already heading for the city, nothing more now than fading pencil marks in the sky. I think about what Ramon just said, and how it applies to me: how this book fell into my life when I didn't know I needed it, and how all my research into queer cinema has begun to teach me how to be queer myself. Or rather, it has revealed that the options are infinite: I can choose any of them, or none, or I can invent my own. I need to channel that sensation into the book somehow.

———————

We trudge into the park below, past the fountain where Ocho writes a postcard to his girlfriend in the flashback scenes. The water isn't flowing today: a drought emergency was recently declared in the region. Birds screech above us as we stroll through the vine-tangled pink stone arches, watched over by the parasol pines. As we pass the statue of a woman bathing, her body seems to bend deferentially, welcoming us onto the dusty pathways that weave in and out of the shade. This is the sheltered area where Ocho had the gay encounter that sent him into a panic. And it's where Ramon came as a teenager to get his kicks.

As we exit the park and descend the hill, I notice a figure standing sentry at one of the concealed entrances to the undergrowth. He's wearing a tight T-shirt, black jeans and sunglasses. His arms are folded, his head turning slowly like a CCTV camera to scan us as we walk by. We both glance back at him.

'I guess the cruising area is still in use,' says Ramon.

Then: 'I need to pee.'

Once we reach his old drama school, the Institut del Teatre de Barcelona, he darts inside to use the toilet, while I wait on a bench in the sun. I leaf through my A4 notepad to make sure there aren't any questions left that I need to ask him for the last chapter.

When he reappears, he takes me by surprise.

'Ah, what is this?' he asks.

He points to the cover of the pad, which I've pasted with images to make the book feel real, and to urge me along as I write: Essex

Hemphill standing behind Marlon Riggs, both men shirtless, Hemphill's arm forming a diagonal seat belt across Riggs's chest, in *Tongues Untied*; Susannah York and Beryl Reid in Laurel-and-Hardy fancy dress in *The Killing of Sister George*; Pepper LaBeija cocking her head and gazing defiantly in *Paris Is Burning*; the soldier camouflaged by the foliage in *Tropical Malady*; and Bugs Bunny dolled up in lipstick, lashes, blonde wig and boob tube. Slap-bang in the middle is Gene Anthony Ray, boogieing in his too-short shorts in the electrifying audition scene in *Fame*, and Harris Dickinson, with his grave frown and his spiralling seashell belly button, in *Beach Rats*. Watching over it all from the corner like a chaperone at a school disco is Dirk Bogarde in *Victim*, his brow corrugated with concern. Bogarde seems to be seething quietly at the freedoms unfurling across the rest of my pad.

The picture that grabs Ramon's attention, though, is one of Mowgli in *The Jungle Book*: the cartoon man-cub is covering his face, a single eye visible as he plays peek-a-boo from behind his hands.

'Ah, Mowgli was sexy!' he cries, then amends his observation: 'When I was a child, I mean.'

Was it the orange pants?

'Yeah, and the movement.'

As we walk off together, he snaps his fingers in a swaggering little Mowgli-esque dance. 'He's, like, cool and strong, but not aggressive. Wow, I never thought about that until I saw him on your book. He was sexy when we didn't know what sexy meant. Before him, I only liked the princesses.'

That's pretty gay, too.

'Exactly. But you don't understand that until later.'

We pick our way through the neighbourhood, past yapping dogs caught up in a cat's cradle of leads. Pavement café parasols throw watery shadows across our path.

I ask Ramon if he has always been out as an actor. 'At drama school, yes. When I started working professionally, people said, "Be careful." I had a boyfriend who played lots of "Latin lover" parts, and he was super-scared of being outed. An agent told me not to be open about my sexuality, but it got to the point where I was like, "Fuck off." I want to be who I am and have a free life. I've paid a price for that in my career. I haven't been considered for certain parts. But maybe I prefer fewer opportunities if it opens the way for other actors coming, to show them not to be scared, not to hide. For a long time when I was younger, I thought being gay drives you straight to a place of suffering and complication. But it doesn't have to.'

———

After Ramon leaves, I zig-zag through the wedge-shaped streets towards Plaça de Jean Genet, and on to La Rambla. It was here that Genet scratched out his lice-ridden existence for a few months in 1933. The roads along the seafront are being dug up today, and the area surrounding the Mirador de Colom is cordoned off by mesh barriers and wire fences, the air furious with drilling and digging. There is no hint of the squalid adventures that formed part of *The Thief's Journal* for Genet and his fellow beggars. They were peered at and patronised by the milling tourists who poured off the boats, and who saw their poverty as a terrible yet noble spectacle. Under the blameless blue sky today, there are only rows of luxury yachts with racehorse names: *Starburst III*, *Heartbeat of Life*. Lined up along the marina, blindingly white, they look like new sneakers in a teenage bedroom.

I think about Genet again on my flight home the next evening. The plane has already surged into the dusk, the discarded runway quickly forgotten. The horizon blushes purple, bringing to mind the passage from *The Thief's Journal* that is quoted in *Death and Bowling*:

the part about how 'an apparition of this kind would disturb us less' if it occurred at noon 'when nothing is happening in the sky . . . the wonder is that it occurs in the evening, at the most poignant time of the day, when the sun *sets*, when it disappears to pursue a mysterious destiny, when perhaps it dies'.

It is exactly that poignant time. Now it feels as if the plane is hanging in the air, perfectly static as the world shifts around it: a state of suspension and flux, neither here nor there. A Wojnarowicz moment, forever in transition. Lana Wachowski, co-director of the *Matrix* series, said in 2012 that the notion of transition itself is 'a very complicated subject . . . because of its complicity in a binary gender narrative . . .' A transition implies a place to start from, and a definitive destination at which to conclude. As Harry Dodge said: 'I'm not on my way anywhere.' And, as Wojnarowicz pointed out, destination means death.

The most profound queer films often occupy naturally this state of impermanence. I think of the trans-coded hero in the queer animated fantasy *Nimona*, who morphs from punky teenage girl to whale to ostrich to whatever takes their fancy. When asked what it feels like, they say: 'Honestly, I feel worse when I *don't* do it. Like my insides are itchy. You know like that second right before you sneeze? That's close to it. Then I shape-shift – then I'm free.' They joke that if they didn't shape-shift, they would die, before rephrasing the sentiment: 'I wouldn't *die*-die. I just sure wouldn't be living.'

Turbulence again. The seat-belt sign pings on. To take my mind off the lurching and trembling, I clamp my headphones over my ears and listen back to yesterday's recording. It ends with me and Ramon ambling down the hill to the Metro station at Poble Sec, leaving the park with its cruising ground and its parched fountains floating behind us, and above us, like an island in the sky.

It was nearly two in the afternoon, time for Ramon to collect his son from kindergarten. Maybe it was because we were about to part ways, but we found ourselves drifting onto the subject of farewells. *End of the Century* closes with the most extraordinary goodbye. After Javi leaves for good, Ocho imagines an alternate reality where they are not in fact two people on a hook-up at all, but a couple with a daughter of their own and two unbroken decades of history together – another life. This is only one in an infinite number of possible realities, but it plays out here in the film's final minutes, offering a glimpse of what might have been. Then the action reverts bluntly, jarringly, to the prevailing narrative: Ocho watching from the balcony as Javi walks out of his life. The dream is over.

'When I leave the apartment at the end of the film, he sees me in the street from the balcony,' said Ramon. 'But I don't know if I look back at him.'

'You do,' I told him as we reached the Metro. 'You linger for a moment, and you glance up, but you don't wave.'

'That's it,' he said. 'I look up, and then I continue walking. In that shot, there are these little bats that fly across the sky. It's a bit phantasmagorical, a bit creepy. It's like: the life you could have had is leaving.'

I felt as if he were addressing me directly. That maybe he wasn't talking about *End of the Century* any more. *The life you could have had is leaving.* I've always felt it, even as a child somehow, and it was an ache that I associated with my sexuality. Perhaps I even clung to that ache, reproducing it across other areas of my life, because it was what I knew. But now I don't need it any more.

'Think of all the people you meet,' said Ramon, glancing around at the oblivious strangers streaming past us, weaving in and out of one another with their mumbled complaints and apologies. 'Over there is a completely different life that could have happened, and it hasn't. But you can't live all the possible lives you could've had. You just can't. You don't have time.'

Except, that is, in films.

PERMISSIONS

pp. 105–6: lyric excerpts from 'Glad to Be Gay' used by permission of BMG Publishing (UK) Ltd.

pp. 144–5: excerpt from *Night Voltage* used by permission of Peter Strickland, Tristan Goligher, Christine Vachon and Film4.

pp. 168, 171, 172: excerpts from Paul Hallam and Ron Peck archives used by permission of the Bishopsgate Institute, London.

ACKNOWLEDGEMENTS

Thank you to everyone who generously gave their time to be interviewed for this book: Desiree Akhavan, Babatunde Apalowo, Cheryl Dunye, Sam H. Freeman, Andrew Haigh, Harriet Harper-Jones, William E. Jones, Lyle Kash, Justin Kelly, Bruce LaBruce, Sebastian Meise, Ng Choon Ping, Georgia Oakley, Jenni Olson, Ramon Pujol, Elizabeth Purchell, Harvey Rabbit, Tom Robinson, Jessica Dunn Rovinelli, Isabel Sandoval, Sarah Schulman, Howard Schuman, Sanjay Sharma, Nathan Stewart-Jarrett, Peter Strickland, Wash Westmoreland, Stephen Winter and Campbell X.

I am indebted to Cathy James and Joanna Nadin, my oldest friends, whose faith in this book from the very start was invaluable, and to Mick McAloon, Tim Robey and Ben Walters, who each gave it the sort of close reading that would flatter and possibly terrify any writer; their criticisms and suggestions improved it immeasurably. My first agent, the late Cat Ledger, read early versions of some of the material here, as did Leo Robson. I am grateful to both for urging me on.

Behind-the-scenes help also came from Arifa Akbar, Sophie Dent, Hannah Farr, Charles Gant, Jane Giles, Sarah Harvey, Jen Ives, Matt Johnstone, Charlotte O'Sullivan, Sam Ritzenberg and John Waters, as well as Alex Babboni at Doesn't Exist, Harvey Brown and Karina Gechtman at Anton, Ian Cuthbert and Alex Davidson at the Barbican, Victor Fraga at DMovies, Becky Haghpanah-Shirwan at a/political, John and Charlie Hall at the John Hall Venice Course, Mehelli Modi and Chris Barwick at Second Run and Sala Shaker at Scott & Co.

Hats off to the staff at the Bishopsgate Institute, the Reuben Library at BFI Southbank and Close-Up film centre, all in London, and to Creative Folkestone, Kent.

I wish to thank my superb editors at the *Guardian* – Catherine Shoard, Alex Needham, Andrew Pulver, Chris Wiegand, Robert White, Diana Gower and Kate Abbott – whose commissions have fostered, overlapped with and seeped into parts of this book. Thanks also to Antonia Quirke, whose invitation to pitch a remake of my choosing on *The Film Programme* on BBC Radio 4 in 2020 led me down the *Withnail and I* rabbit hole described in Chapter 9; and to Rosie Gilbey, whose photography collections *E8 Transformatives* and *Beyond the Cellar Door* inspired some of the structural choices in the book.

Thanks to Anne Owen, Hannah Knowles, Phoebe Colley, Henry Petrides, Rosie Catcheside, Mollie Stewart and everyone at Faber who worked on the book. The mightiest of thank yous are due to my editor Walter Donohue, whose encouragement has lasted the quarter-century we have known one another, and to my agent Matthew Marland, who has crammed his own tireless support into a fifth of that time.

Thank you to my parents and my children. And thank you most of all to Chris Butler, who simply cannot help but make every day blissful.

NOTES

1 Death in Venice

3 'two-people-sitting-on-a-sofa', 2006 interview with Jack Hazan on *A Bigger Splash* DVD (BFI).

4 'there was something dreadful', Matthew Sweet, *Shepperton Babylon* (London: Faber & Faber, 2005).

4 'backed away like rearing horses', John Coldstream, *Victim* (London: BFI Palgrave, 2011).

4 'That *Victim* helped', ibid.

5 'implicit approval of homosexuality' and 'thematically objectionable', *Time*, 23 February 1962.

5 'You could have heard a feather drop', *Daily Telegraph*, 21 April 2007.

5 'you never asked me to do it', John Coldstream (ed.), *Ever, Dirk: The Bogarde Letters* (London: Weidenfeld & Nicolson, 2008).

6 'two in a row', David Caute, *Joseph Losey: A Revenge on Life* (London: Faber & Faber, 1994).

6 'I'm certainly in the shell', *Dirk Bogarde – Above the Title. A Conversation with Russell Harty*, 1986. https://www.youtube.com/watch?v=QfeDhkJ-w_8&t=1056s.

6 'simply a study of a little homosexual affair', Caute, *Joseph Losey*.

10 'to turn every gay person straight', *The Times*, 10 January 2004.

10 'Listen to white straight millennial news pundits', author interview with Stephen Winter, 21 February 2023.

11 'hate crimes against trans people': all figures from https://www.stonewall.org.uk/about-us/news/new-data-rise-hate-crime-against-lgbtq-people-continues-stonewall-slams-uk-gov-, 5 October 2023.

13 'HOMOSEXUAL DIALOGUE', *Guardian*, 1 August 2009.

18 'As Visconti portrays the boy', *New York Times*, 15 August 1971.

19 'the love in my film', Brendan Hennessey, *Luchino Visconti and the Alchemy of Adaptation* (New York: State University of New York Press, 2021).

19 'a fifty-two-year-old Jewish Genius', Coldstream (ed.), *Ever, Dirk*.

19 'the agonies', ibid.

19 'Granny glasses', ibid.

19 'until seven every morning', ibid.

19 'The last thing', Dirk Bogarde, *An Orderly Man* (London: Chatto & Windus, 1983).

20 'Luchino was the sort of cultural predator' and 'Fuck off', *Guardian*, 16 July 2021.

21 'the time when queer people were outcasts', *Guardian*, 26 May 2023.

23 'hands down', https://aframe-stg.oscars.org/news/post/jane-schoenbrun-i-saw-the-tv-glow-interview, 16 May 2024.

24 'The greater my guilt', Jean Genet, *The Thief's Journal* (London: Faber & Faber, 1949).

24 'When people start seeing representation', https://www.youtube.com/watch?v=UPQG6AHU6rU, 11 June 2022.

25 'posit the lesbian', Barbara Hammer, *Hammer! Making Movies Out of Sex and Life* (New York: The Feminist Press at CUNY, 2010).

25 'The thing I dug', *New Yorker*, 4 November 2019.

26 'being a lesbian *is* experimental', 2000 interview on *History Lessons* DVD (Barbara Hammer).

2 Femme

27 'In the US, we're totally past that', and all quotes from Jessica Dunn Rovinelli from author interview, 13 March 2023.

28 'a video of the director kissing', https://www.kickstarter.com/projects/1865556054/empathy-a-performative-documentary-on-sexual-socia, September 2015.

31 'please share with me', https://x.com/CampbellX/status/1641419621868744704, 30 March 2023.

31 'Make your gay characters complex', https://x.com/strawhousefilms/status/1642430761700831232?lang=en, 2 April 2023.

32 'Our desires are shaped', and all quotes from Ng Choon Ping from author interview, 27 May 2024.

32 'No one we saw', and all quotes from Sam H. Freeman from author interview, 30 April 2024.

33 'I was crying', and all quotes from Nathan Stewart-Jarrett from author interview, 19 September 2024.

34 'Before we proceed', and all quotes from Harvey Rabbit from author interview, 9 May 2024.

36 'Why are we all so addicted', https://letterboxd.com/ilikeweirdfilns/film/
femme-2023/, 6 March 2023.

36 'haven't seen', https://letterboxd.com/bruceclarklois/film/femme-2023/, 22
April 2024.

37 '5 billion Xs', *Sight & Sound*, November 1998.

37 '*Cruising* is a picture', Peter Kramer, Gary Needham, Yannis Tzioumakis and
Tino Balio (eds), *United Artists* (Abingdon-on-Thames: Routledge, 2020).

38 'the worst possible nightmare', *Village Voice*, 16 July 1979.

38 'There was pushback', and all quotes from Harriet Harper-Jones from author
interview, 21 February 2024.

40 'a fucking breath of fresh air', *Interview*, 5 April 2024.

40 'I absolutely love this film', https://x.com/meganeellison/status/
1774120795616452968, 30 March 2024.

42 'Fassbinder, heavily into abusable substances', *Financial Times*, 25 June 1992.

43 'a version of homosexuality that degrades us all', Robert Katz and Peter Berling,
Love Is Colder Than Death: The Life and Times of Rainer Werner Fassbinder
(London: Jonathan Cape, 1987).

43 'sour determinism', *Film Comment*, January/February 1978.

44 'Homosexuals have always been very self-pitying' and 'All in all', Katz and
Berling, *Love Is Colder Than Death*.

44 'a recurring theme of "things getting cut off"', *The Gateway*, vol. 3, no. 2, August
1980.

44 'will do little for the predicament of the transsexual', *Les Girls*, vol. 1, no. 3,
November 1980–January 1981.

45 'Trans Representation Validity Marginalisation', Twitter, 26 July 2023, accessed
26 July 2023.

3 Ask Any Buddy

46 'Oh cool', and all quotes from Elizabeth Purchell from author interview, 21 July
2023.

48 'I was interested in gay porn from the 1970s', from author interview with Wash
Westmoreland, 21 November 2023.

52 'I searched for lesbian images', Hammer, *Hammer! Making Movies Out of Sex
and Life*.

4 Call Me by Your Name

57 'Its worldwide gross of $43 million', all box-office figures taken from Box-Office

Mojo, https://www.boxofficemojo.com/, accessed 8 October 2024.

57 'I wish he was gay', Matthew Hays, *The View from Here: Conversations with Lesbian and Gay Filmmakers* (Vancouver: Arsenal Pulp Press, 2007).

58 'One of the ideas', ibid.

58 'animalistic', https://www.vulture.com/2019/10/pedro-almodvar-interview-pain-and-glory-director-opens-up.html, 8 October 2019.

58 'I think the shot that truly did it', *Guardian*, 14 May 2021.

59 'For some reason, we never got around to casting it', *Fantastic Man*, Autumn/Winter 2008.

59 'I'd like to be wrong', from email to author, 10 January 2019.

60 'two obviously gay people', *The Advocate*, 13 January 2006.

60 'I have no gay agenda', *Guardian*, 9 May 2023.

60 'Of course, it's about two men', ibid.

60 'never saw this as a gay film', *Guardian*, 20 October 1988.

60 'It's not a film about being gay', *The Face*, no. 95, March 1988.

60 '*Cruising* is not about homosexuality', Vito Russo, *The Celluloid Closet: Homosexuality in the Movies*, revd edn (New York: Harper Collins, 1987).

60 'There's no such thing as a "gay film"', *Gay News*, no. 231, 1982.

61 'It's not a gay story', *Sunday Times*, 17 January 2010.

63 'There's something in you', Lillian Hellman, *The Children's Hour* (Acting Edition for Theatre Productions) (London: Josef Weinberger Plays, 1934).

63 'I confess', email to author, 30 May 2023.

64 'this absolute picture-perfect household', *Saturday Review*, BBC Radio 4, 28 October 2017.

64 'It didn't matter to me', *Guardian*, 27 March 2018.

64 'Ismail wasn't as driven', *Guardian*, 12 March 2024.

65 'He did not marry', *Guardian*, 26 May 2005.

65 'And then I was dropped', James Ivory, *Solid Ivory* (New York: Farrar, Straus and Giroux, 2021).

65 'When people are wandering around', *Guardian*, 27 March 2018.

66 'Old age doesn't bring wisdom', *Sight & Sound*, Winter 2024–5.

66 'I was in the theatre', author interview with Elizabeth Purchell.

68 'The shit-on-the-dick scene!' author interview with Ryan O'Connell, 10 May 2021.

69 'He doesn't react', *Guardian*, 25 May 2021.

72 'the subproletariat of homosexuality', https://4columns.org/anderson-melissa/the-wounded-man, 19 May 2023.

72 'too literary' and 'the basic idea', Robert Payne, *L'Homme blessé: Queer Film Classics* (Montreal and Kingston: McGill-Queen's University Press, 2022).

72 'he evolved in a very marginal world', from Blu-ray booklet essay by Hedi el Kholti, *L'Homme blessé* (Altered Innocence, 1983; Blu-ray released 2023).

73 'had done some other film together first', *Bay Area Reporter*, 3 November 1983.

73 'When one invests', Payne, *L'Homme blessé*.

74 'One year later', ibid.

74 'made it possible', from Blu-ray booklet essay by Hedi el Kholti, *L'Homme blessé*.

74 'the passion' and 'I was drunk', *Bay Area Reporter*, 3 November 1983.

74 'The only reference which encouraged me', from Blu-ray booklet essay by Hedi el Kholti, *L'Homme blessé*.

75 'I'm not sure it's beautiful', *Bay Area Reporter*, 3 November 1983.

76 'In all love stories', *New York Times*, 13 January 1985.

76 'Mainstream films about homosexuals', *Film Comment*, March–April 1986.

76 'When you're dealing with a sliver', https://www.youtube.com/watch?v= wJ6As_HaoT8, 21 April 2023.

77 'an infantile leftist viewpoint', Russo, *The Celluloid Closet*.

78 'They ignore the very essence', Danny Lee Wynter, *Black Superhero* (London: Nick Hern Books, 2023).

78 'My mother was dating him', *Sunday Times*, 8 January 2017.

79 'does the impossible', https://www.bfi.org.uk/sight-and-sound/greatest-films-all-time/all-voters/grace-barber-plentie, accessed 11 October 2024.

79 '*Moonlight* wasn't Black queer love', and all quotes from Campbell X in Chapters 4 and 5 from author interview, 15 September 2023.

5 Stud Life

80 'I found that out from my lesbian friends', author interview with Wash Westmoreland, 21 November 2023.

84 'These are films made for us', https://www.criterion.com/current/posts/8193-a-rich-counterhistory-of-masculinities-on-screen, 10 July 2023.

84 'the easier language', *Sight & Sound*, December 2015.

6 The Watermelon Woman

89 'Little Cheryl', and all quotes from Cheryl Dunye from author interview, 12 January 2024.

92 'perverse' and 'denigrating', *Los Angeles Times*, 3 April 1991.

92 'the hottest dyke sex scene', *Philadelphia City Paper*, 3 March 1996.

93 'multi-vocal queer aesthetic', *Guardian*, 17 February 2018.

94 '*The Owls* was a sixty-page script', and all quotes from Sarah Schulman from author interview, 19 December 2023.

7 Un Chant d'amour

98 'like tattooed skin', Jane Giles, *Criminal Desires: Jean Genet and Cinema* (London: Creation Books, 2002).

99 'The cinema can open a fly', ibid.

99 'It touches the quick of the soul', ibid.

99 'too bucolic', Edmund White, *Genet* (London: Chatto & Windus, 1993).

99 'That's a wonderful illusion', Bill Landis, *The Unauthorised Biography of Kenneth Anger* (New York: Harper Collins, 1995).

100 'I believe I saw something about it', White, *Genet*.

8 The Secret Policeman's Ball

114 'Thanks for your kind words', from email to author, 28 September 2022.

115 'I wrote it when I was with my previous band', and all quotes from Tom Robinson from author interview, 29 September 2022.

117 'Could this be Dorothy's Revenge', *Time Out*, no. 942, 7–14 September 1988.

9 Trash

120 'Joan Hart noticed a young boy', Joseph Howard, *Damien: Omen II*, from the screenplay by Stanley Mann and Michael Hodges (London: Futura, 1978).

120 'his was the name oftenest', Thomas Mann, *Death in Venice* (London: Penguin, 1912, translation 1928).

121 'Now what I really wanted', Cameron Crowe, *Conversations with Wilder* (London: Faber & Faber, 1999).

122 'grateful' and 'died of Scottish dancing', *Guardian*, 17 June 2023.

123 'There was certainly some intentional subtext', Roman Chimienti and Tyler Jensen (dir.), *Scream, Queen! My Nightmare on Elm Street* (Virgil Films, 2019).

124 'It wasn't in the script', *Fantastic Man*, Autumn/Winter 2008.

124 'On the issue of the gayness', *Entertainment Weekly*, 17 November 2000.

125 'fear of being outed', https://www.thepinknews.com/2009/04/27/robert-carlyle-my-trainspotting-character-was-gay/, 27 April 2009.

125 'There was no role there', Alan McKenzie, *The Harrison Ford Story* (New York: Arbor House Publishing, 1984).

125 'I wish that they'd let the steam', Russo, *The Celluloid Closet*.

126 'I think homosexuals probably wouldn't like it', *Evening Standard*, 11 February 1988.

126 'anti-Black', https://www.richard-e-grant.com/archives/withnail-and-i-ten-years-on-2/, February 1996.

126 'about as funny as lung cancer' and 'I'm most certainly not homophobic . . .', https://www.youtube.com/watch?v=WxcGoEz0IOk, 22 September 2017.

127 'superficial and never knocking the real issues', Russell Davies (ed.), *The Kenneth Williams Diaries* (London: Harper Collins, 1994).

127 'I fail to see why not', *Daily Telegraph*, 17 February 2007.

128 'dangerous to other men' and 'human dregs', Peter Parker (ed.), *Some Men in London. Volume One: Queer Life, 1945–1959* (London: Penguin, 2024).

128 'He was a complicated protagonist', *Guardian*, 15 June 2021.

129 'Sometimes you see a movie', https://www.youtube.com/watch?v=UPQG6AHU6rU, 11 June 2022.

130 'two queer lads', *Guardian*, 23 March 2021.

130 'a hint of ambiguous sexuality', https://www.criterion.com/current/posts/2781-life-is-sweet-life-is-bittersweet, 28 May 2013.

130 'an upper-working-class, slightly pretentious', Michael Coveney, *The World According to Mike Leigh* (London: Harper Collins, 1996).

131 'Nobody else knew', ibid.

133 'It was nothing new', https://www.firstpost.com/entertainment/indias-first-gay-film-badnam-basti-resurfaces-after-nearly-half-a-centurys-hibernation-in-berlin-archive-8419921.html, 25 June 2020.

133 'It was a very critical film' and 'His philosophy', Sam Ashby (ed.), *Little Joe* (London: SPBH Editions, 2024).

135 'so that he can be dramatically murdered', Russo, *The Celluloid Closet*.

135 'the Krays and the police', Hugo Greenhalgh, *The Diaries of Mr Lucas* (London: Atlantic Books, 2024).

136 'rag dolls a bored child', David Ernest Roessel and Nicholas Rand Moschovakis (eds), *The Collected Poems of Tennessee Williams* (New York: New Directions, 2002).

136 'hellbent on survival', Holly Woodlawn with Jeffrey Copeland, *A Low Life in High Heels: The Holly Woodlawn Story* (New York: Harper Perennial, 1991).

136 'volcano-like', ibid.

137 'like a live-action version', https://www.screenslate.com/articles/scarecrow-garden-cucumbers, 26 August 2024.

137 'a rabbit born in a human world', Robert McKimson (dir.), *What's Up, Doc?* (Warner Bros, 1950).

137 'We hit it off famously!' Woodlawn with Copeland, *A Low Life in High Heels.*

10 Night Voltage

138 'That whole junkyard aesthetic', and all Peter Strickland quotes from author interview, 5 December 2023.

146 'butchery on a scale', *Sight & Sound*, November 1998.

147 'Maybe I'm just gay', *Entertainment Weekly*, 5 January 2011.

148 'a timid and artless policy', *New York Times*, 22 June 2024.

149 'cold feet', *Variety*, https://variety.com/2024/film/news/joaquin-phoenix-drops-out-todd-haynes-gay-romance-movie-1236101595/, 9 August 2024.

149 '[I]f you are tempted to finger wag', *People*, https://people.com/joaquin-phoenix-drops-out-of-gay-romance-5-days-before-production-8693573, 10 August 2024.

149 'I never saw James's performances', and all Justin Kelly quotes from author interview, 13 May 2024.

150 'stop hiring non LGBTQIA+ actors', https://x.com/rightwingedgoob/status/1534955737943711745, 9 June 2022.

150 'u don't know my alphabet', https://x.com/lukasgage/status/1534960946287980544, 9 June 2022.

150 'Let me [come out] when I'm ready', *New York Times*, 9 March 2023.

11 All the Colours of the World Are Between Black and White

156 'I'd never heard of the Teddy Award before', and all Babatunde Apalowo quotes from author interview, 14 December 2023.

12 Nighthawks

164 'Child Porn Row Looms on Gay Film', *Sun*, 3 July 1978.

164 'Our *Nighthawks*', from Paul Hallam's archive, held by the Bishopsgate Institute, London.

166 'AIDS: THE VICTIMS', *Time Out*, 28 February–6 March 1985.

168 'the male looking at the male', *New Statesman*, 29 April 2019.

168 'Don't be above (or below) plot', *Sight & Sound*, vol. 2, no. 6, October 1992.

168 'There was a real confusion in my mind', Ron Peck (dir.), *Strip Jack Naked: Nighthawks II* (BFI and Channel 4, 1991).

168 'You see me shit in the morning', *Gay Times*, no. 231, 1982.

169 'disseminated [himself] inappropriately', from *Taxi Zum Klo* press notes, 1981, reproduced in Ashby (ed.), *Little Joe*.

169 'in real life when I escaped' and 'Because it's not a "problem" film', from *Gay Times*, no. 231, 1982.

171 'An additional visit', from Ron Peck's archive.

171 'After some encouraging video tests', ibid.

171 'foolhardy', https://movingimage.org/event/je-tu-il-elle/Akerman.

13 Je tu il elle

172 'There it is . . . the mattress', from Ron Peck's archive.

176 'what brought me out as a lesbian', Smithsonian Archives of American Art, https://www.aaa.si.edu/download_pdf_transcript/ajax?record_id=edanmdm-AAADCD_oh_393526, 15–17 March 2018.

176 'witches' land', and all Barbara Hammer quotes in this paragraph from https://www.youtube.com/watch?v=ILzUvPnsDUI, 28 April 2017.

177 'I won't be ghettoized', https://forward.com/culture/322320/our-lives-with-and-without-chantal-akerman/, 10 October 2015.

177 'We always programmed her films', and all quotes from Sarah Schulman from author interview, 19 December 2023.

178 'the city of dreams' and 'all sorts of adventures', http://www.lolajournal.com/2/pajama.html, June 2012.

178 'I walked out of the theatre thinking', https://www.youtube.com/watch?v=vCxr2x1-M3g, 2009.

179 'the conspiracy of homosexuality', *Film Culture*, no. 3, 1955, quoted in the *New Yorker*, 6 January 1973.

180 'I wrote Mekas a letter', Hammer, *Hammer! Making Movies Out of Sex and Life*.

180 'When we met', email to author from William E. Jones, 30 May 2023.

180 'When do we shoot?' *Guardian*, 8 October 2015.

181 'I was very scared that the police would come', Marianne Lambert (dir.), *I Don't Belong Anywhere: The Cinema of Chantal Akerman* (Icarus Films, 2015).

183 'At one point', Jones, email to author.

14 Tearoom

184 'No one who has not seen the film', William E. Jones, *Tearoom* (Los Angeles: 2nd Cannons Publications, 2008).

185 'as illiterate and hateful', ibid.

185 'the growth of homosexual cults', ibid.

186 'disco Fassbinder', https://www.billboard.com/music/pop/george-michael-outside-video-20-years-later-8458161/, 29 May 2018.

187 'if *every* sexual encounter', Samuel R. Delany, *Times Square Red, Times Square Blue* (New York: New York University Press, 1999).

187 'The work divided audiences', Jones, email to author.

188 'We were trying to find a form', all quotes from Sebastian Meise in this chapter from the *Guardian*, 14 March 2022, and from email to author, 23 May 2023.

190 'The format was a matter', Jones, email to author.

191 'I had made one short video', and all quotes from Jenni Olson in this chapter from author interviews, 11 June 2021 and 23 April 2023.

191 'embodying, living and creating queer culture', https://blog.teddyaward.tv/en/2021/05/28/special-teddy-award-goes-to-jenni-olson/, 28 May 2021.

193 'the first time gays rose up', Russo, *The Celluloid Closet*.

193 'many of [them] look irrepressibly happy', Robin Wood, *Hollywood from Vietnam to Reagan . . . and Beyond* (New York: Columbia University Press, 1986; expanded and revd edition 2003).

193 'lasting legacy', *Village Voice*, 28 August 2007.

193 'That's a *ballsy* film', author interview with Andrew Haigh, 13 February 2024.

193 'People were in full gear', *New York Times*, 9 June 2022.

15 Lingua Franca

197 '*Lingua Franca* is my third film', and all quotes from Isabel Sandoval from author interview, 28 April 2023.

201 'The two territories are linked', from interview on *Tropical Malady* DVD (Second Run, 2008).

202 'Film is a parallel life', ibid.

203 'I don't want to look like a queer', Richard Dyer, *The Culture of Queers* (London: Routledge, 2002).

203 'It would be less interesting culturally', Olson, author interview, 11 June 2021.

204 'For me, *Under the Skin* was a contemporary fairy-tale', looneytunesindrag. substack.com, 19 October 2023.

204 'The weak beard', and all Jen Ives quotes from *Charlie Kaufman Is Trans: A Queer Reading of Being John Malkovich – Extended Edition*, https://www.youtube.com/watch?v=_7e50yClqEo, 24 March 2024.

206 'that there are at least two killers', Wood, *Hollywood from Vietnam to Reagan . . . and Beyond.*

207 'a secret handshake of transness', Caden Mark Gardner and Willow Catelyn Maclay, *Corpses, Fools and Monsters: The History and Future of Transness in Cinema* (London: Repeater Books, 2024).

207 'It's him almost, like, cruising', *'We're All Going to the World's Fair' Director Jane Schoenbrun Talks Trans Horror Cinema*, https://www.youtube.com/watch?v=g-W3os156r4, 20 April 2022.

208 'Matt ended up being Sofia Buenaventura', https://iffr.com/en/blog-alejandro-landes-over-monos, 2 September 2019.

208 'It just felt like a relief', https://www.dazeddigital.com/film-tv/article/46512/1/monos-alejandro-landes-mica-levi-interview, 25 October 2019.

208 'Half the audience', *Monos* press notes, https://le-pacte.com/storage/uploads/415e7fc9-b91e-429d-a454-4d6a5ff6a1e9/MONOS-Press-Notes-(Press-Kit).pdf, accessed 10 October 2024.

209 'Finally a film', https://x.com/lylekashtweets/status/1175464901537484800, 21 September 2019.

16 Death and Bowling

210 'My friend was like', and all Lyle Kash quotes unless otherwise stated from author interview, 11 September 2023.

214 'I didn't feel like I was watching a mandatory training video', Kash, email to author, 26 August 2024.

216 'Carl's is a butcher's shop', Kash, email to author, 11 September 2023.

17 All About My Mother

217 'I take exception to what I understand', Jones, email to author.

217 'I'm gettin' off on her', Delany, *Times Square Red, Times Square Blue.*

218 'people walked out in droves', *Independent*, 25 May 2019.

219 'Watched an old film', John Lahr (ed.), *The Orton Diaries* (London: Methuen, 1986).

219 'to sit in a dark, anonymous place', Alan Hollinghurst, *The Swimming-Pool Library* (London: Chatto & Windus, 1988).

220 'Close Down This Cinema of Vice', David McGillivray, *Little Did You Know: The Confessions of David McGillivray* (London: FAB Press, 2019).

220 'all the films shown have a "Q" certificate', Quentin Crisp, *The Naked Civil Servant* (London: Jonathan Cape, 1968).

220 'She was brave', and all other comments, *Rare Film of the Biograph Cinema, Victoria, London ('Britain's Oldest Cinema') 1956*, https://www.youtube.com/watch?v=Dz-SyFRdrWo&t=4s, 14 October 2011.

221 'wilful hanky-panky', *Independent*, 31 August 1994.

221 'I'm eighty-three', and all quotes from Howard Schuman from author interview, 19 July 2023.

226 'to enormous lengths to disguise', *Sight & Sound*, vol. 16, no. 5, May 2006.

226 'When it transpires that Lola', *Daily Express*, 27 August 1999.

18 Velvet Goldmine

228 'They ordered pepperoni pizza . . .', and all quotes from Wash Westmoreland from author interviews, 21 November 2023 and 21 February 2024.

231 'The narrative was not there', BBC Radio 2, https://www.youtube.com/watch?v=Pg3do3VZEn0&t=1564s, 29 June 2022.

19 Theorem

All on-set quotes throughout chapter from 21 April 2023.

235 'They were shooting in Brixton', from author interview with Peter Strickland, 5 December 2023.

236 'The real Foreign Legion wanted to stop us', *New Statesman*, 20 April 2018.

239 'send me your most decadent actors', https://www.bfi.org.uk/interviews/meetings-remarkable-men-terence-stamp-interview, 30 April 2013.

239 'Pasolini told me', *Guardian*, 12 March 2015.

239 'Tell him to play' and 'It didn't take me long to realise', https://thehollywoodinterview.blogspot.com/2013/09/terence-stamp-hollywood-interview.html, September 2013.

239 'He was just somebody', https://www.maramarietta.com/the-arts/cinema/t-v/teorema/, 10 July 2007.

245 'There never is', and all quotes from Bruce LaBruce from author interview, 28 April 2023.

245 'Pornography is boring!' https://vestoj.com/a-conversation-with-kenneth-anger/, accessed 11 October 2024.

247 'that dour, quasi-Stalinist organisation', *Sight & Sound*, vol. 5, no. 3, March 1995.

20 Chocolate Babies

249 'flung out of space', Patricia Highsmith, *The Price of Salt* (New York: Bantam Books, 1953).

249 'Building a garden', Derek Jarman, *Modern Nature: The Journals of Derek Jarman, 1989–1990* (London: Vintage, 2018).

251 'He'd made this little 8mm film', *Sunday Times*, 28 December 2008.

252 'Many times, they got agitated', author interview with Sanjay Sharma, 4 July 2023.

253 'How will there be progress?' and 'The response was', from Beti Ellerson, '*Dakan*: Visualizing Homosexualities in Africa – *Dakan*: An Interview with Filmmaker Mohamed Camara', in *African Masculinities*, eds L. Ouzgane and R. Morrell (New York: Palgrave Macmillan, 2005).

253 'You can be sure that your career is over', https://www.bfi.org.uk/features/dakan-mohamed-camara, 7 March 2022.

254 'Will queers of colour', *Village Voice*, 24 March 1992, reprinted in B. Ruby Rich, *New Queer Cinema: Director's Cut* (Durham, NC: Duke University Press, 2013).

254 'there were more inflatables of colour', ibid.

254 'were always walking around', *Interview*, 31 August 2021.

254 'I'm 6'4"', and all quotes from Stephen Winter from author interview, 4 February 2023.

256 'It was well known among Black filmmakers', *Interview*, 31 August 2021.

261 'paedophile chic', *Premiere* (UK), November 1995.

21 Portrait of Jason

265 'The whole thing is like watching him', Winter, author interview.

265 'I was very curious', *Afterimage*, December 1983.

267 'There were very few at the time', Schulman, author interview.

22 Blue Jean

270 'Each letter of LGBT+', Schulman, author interview.

271 'excitement of the idea', *Sight & Sound*, December 2015.

271 'not a narrative about' and 'There's all this surprise', *New York Times*, 13 February 2020.

273 'As a "positive" portrait of homosexuality', Rio cinema programme, March 1988.

273 'I grew up during Section 28', and all quotes from Georgia Oakley from author interview, 25 July 2023.

276 'Why does every homosexual film or book', https://tylekurner38.medium.com/nowhere-to-run-william-friedkins-cruising-4ce8c7dd669d, 23 November 2022.

23 All of Us Strangers

280 'Even trying to raise that', and all quotes from Andrew Haigh from author interview, 13 February 2024.

24 Beauty

291 'I thought the shot of him putting the dress on', John Boorman, Walter Donohue and Fraser MacDonald (eds), *Projections 12* (London: Faber & Faber, 2002).

293 'When you make a film', *Independent*, 15 August 2003.

25 Appropriate Behaviour

294 'Why would you?' and all quotes from Desiree Akhavan from author interview, 18 September 2023.

26 End of the Century

302 'Hi Ryan', from voice messages to the author from Ramon Pujol between 24 September 2023 and 27 February 2024.

303 'There should be something a bit off', *Guardian*, 20 February 2020.

303 'What happened with that T-shirt?' and all quotes from Ramon Pujol from author interview, 29 February 2024.

307 'Destination means death to me', David Wojnarowicz, *Close to the Knives: A Memoir of Disintegration* (New York: Knopf Doubleday, 1991).

311 'an apparition of this kind', Genet, *The Thief's Journal*.

311 'a very complicated subject', *Lana Wachowski Receives the HRC Visibility Award*, https://www.youtube.com/watch?v=crHHycz7T_c&t=819s, 20 October 2012.

311 'I'm not on my way anywhere', Maggie Nelson, *The Argonauts* (London: Melville House UK, 2016).

SELECT BIBLIOGRAPHY

Books

Anger, Kenneth, *Hollywood Babylon* (New York: Dell Publishing, 1975)

Ashby, Sam (ed.), *Little Joe* (London: SPBH Editions, 2024)

Barthes, Roland, *Camera Obscura* (London: Jonathan Cape, 1982)

Bogarde, Dirk, *An Orderly Man* (London: Chatto & Windus, 1983)

Cagle, R. L., Scorpio Rising: *A Queer Film Classic* (Vancouver: Arsenal Pulp Press, 2019)

Coote, Stephen (ed.), *The Penguin Book of Homosexual Verse* (London: Penguin, 1983)

Cowley, Patrick, *Mechanical Fantasy Box: The Homoerotic Journal of Patrick Cowley* (San Francisco: Dark Entries Editions, 2019)

Delany, Samuel R., *Times Square Red, Times Square Blue* (New York: New York University Press, 1999)

Dyer, Richard, *The Culture of Queers* (London: Routledge, 2002)

Frankel, Glenn, *Shooting* Midnight Cowboy: *Art, Sex, Loneliness, Liberation, and the Making of an American Classic* (New York: Farrar, Straus and Giroux, 2021)

Gardner, Caden Mark and Maclay, Willow Catelyn, *Corpses, Fools and Monsters: The History and Future of Transness in Cinema* (London: Repeater Books, 2024)

Genet, Jean, *The Thief's Journal* (London: Faber & Faber, 1949)

Giles, Jane, *Criminal Desires: Jean Genet and Cinema* (London: Creation Books, 2002)

Green-Sims, Lindsey B., *Queer African Cinemas* (Durham, NC: Duke University Press, 2022)

Griffin, Mark, *All That Heaven Allows: A Biography of Rock Hudson* (New York: HarperCollins, 2018)

Hammer, Barbara, *Hammer! Making Movies Out of Sex and Life* (New York: The Feminist Press at CUNY, 2010)

Hanson, Ellis (ed.), *Out Takes* (Durham, NC: Duke University Press, 1999)

Hester, Diarmuid, *Nothing Ever Just Disappears* (London: Penguin, 2023)

Houlbrook, Matt, *Queer London: Perils and Pleasures in the Sexual Metropolis 1918–1957* (Chicago: University of Chicago Press, 2005)

Ivory, James with Cameron, Peter (ed.), *Solid Ivory* (New York: Farrar, Straus and Giroux, 2021)

Jackson, Kevin, *Withnail & I: BFI Modern Classics* (London: British Film Institute, 2004)

Jarman, Derek, *Blue* (New York: David Zwirner Books, 2023)

Jones, William E., *Halsted Plays Himself*, expanded edn (Los Angeles: Semiotext(e), 2022)

Jones, William E., *Tearoom* (Los Angeles: 2nd Cannons Publications, 2008)

Krämer, Peter, Needham, Gary, Tzioumakis, Yannis and Balio, Tino (eds), *United Artists* (Oxfordshire: Routledge, 2020)

Lambert, Gavin, *Mainly About Lindsay Anderson: A Memoir* (London: Faber & Faber, 2000)

Landis, Bill, *The Unauthorised Biography of Kenneth Anger* (New York: Harper Collins, 1995)

McDonald, Boyd, *Cruising the Movies* (Los Angeles: Semiotext(e), 2005)

McGilligan, Patrick, *George Cukor: A Double Life* (New York: St Martin's Press, 1991)

McGillivray, David, *Little Did You Know: The Confessions of David McGillivray* (London: FAB Press, 2019)

Olson, Jenni, *The Queer Movie Poster Book* (San Francisco: Chronicle Books, 2004)

Page, Elliot, *Pageboy* (London: Doubleday, 2023)

Payne, Robert, *L'Homme blessé: Queer Film Classics* (Montreal and Kingston: McGill-Queen's University Press, 2022)

Poole, Wakefield, *Dirty Poole: A Sensual Memoir* (New Jersey: Lethe Press Inc., 2011)

Rich, B. Ruby, *New Queer Cinema: Director's Cut* (Durham, NC: Duke University Press, 2013)

Russo, Vito, *The Celluloid Closet: Homosexuality in the Movies*, revd edn (New York: Harper Collins, 1987)

Sanderson, Terry, *Mediawatch* (London: Cassell, 1995)

Sweet, Matthew, *Shepperton Babylon* (London: Faber & Faber, 2005)

Thomson, David, *Sleeping with Strangers: How the Movies Shaped Desire* (New York: Knopf, 2019)

Tyler, Parker, *Screening the Sexes* (New York: Holt, Rinehart and Winston, 1972)

Welborn, Yvonne and Juhasz, Alexandra (eds), *Sisters in the Life: A History of Out African American Lesbian Media-Making* (Durham, NC: Duke University Press, 2018)

White, Edmund, *City Boy* (London: Bloomsbury, 2009)

White, Edmund, *Genet* (London: Chatto & Windus, 1993)

Podcasts

Elizabeth Purchell and Tyler Thomas, *Ask Any Buddy*, https://www.ask-any-buddy.com/podcast (2020–)

Karina Longworth, *You Must Remember This*, https://www.youmustremember-thispodcast.com (2014–)

INDEX